Endorsements

"Candid, comprehensive and pragmatic, Dave Rizzardo's book, *Lean –
Let's Get It Right!* is a must-have reference for any Lean practitioner, novice,
and expert alike. Dave cleverly transforms his wealth of Lean knowledge,
his passion for lifelong learning, and years of 'boots-on-the-ground'
expertise into a realistic and practical guide to effective continuous
improvement and cultural transformation. His unique and upbeat
approach to using 'lessons learned' to help achieve success will surely
benefit any organization or individual in any aspect of their Lean journey."
                    – Rebecca R. Jackson, LBC, Maryland State Government

"Finally, there is a book on Lean that balances theory, application,
and culture. Dave Rizzardo has laid out the keys to successful Lean
implementation and sustainability by simplifying the elements of Lean
for every reader, ranging from those just starting their learning journey
to experienced Lean leaders. Dave's charismatic approach to presenting
his topics are easy to follow and should be re-read from time to time
to ensure you are remaining focused on the big picture view that Lean
must be adopted as part of the culture and not to be seen as a project
with a beginning and end. This book is a must-read for any individual
and/or team desiring a continuous improvement future to remain
competitive in the ever changing world where we all need to thrive."
                    – Doug Cooper, Director of Supply Chain, Tilley Company

"David Rizzardo knows what he is talking about. This book documents
David's considerable knowledge and experiences in simple terms that
will keep your organization from making the same mistakes so many
other companies have made."
                    – Todd K. Davis, President, New Tack Consultants

Lean – Let's Get It Right!

Lean – Let's Get It Right!

How to Build a Culture of Continuous Improvement

By David Rizzardo

Routledge
Taylor & Francis Group

A PRODUCTIVITY PRESS BOOK

First edition published in 2020
by Routledge/Productivity Press
52 Vanderbilt Avenue, 11th Floor New York, NY 10017

2 Park Square, Milton Park, Abingdon, Oxon OX14 4RN, UK
© 2020 by David Rizzardo

Routledge/Productivity Press is an imprint of Taylor & Francis Group, an Informa business

No claim to original U.S. Government works

Printed on acid-free paper

International Standard Book Number-13: 978-0-367-42991-1 (Hardback)
International Standard Book Number-13: 978-0-367-33507-6 (Paperback)
International Standard Book Number-13: 978-1-003-00055-6 (eBook)

Library of Congress Cataloging-in-Publication Data
Names: Rizzardo, David, author.
Title: Lean—let's get it right! : how to build a culture of continuous improvement / David Rizzardo.
Description: New York, NY : Routledge, 2020. | Includes bibliographical references and index.
Identifiers: LCCN 2019044458 (print) | LCCN 2019044459 (ebook) |
ISBN 9780367335076 (paperback) | ISBN 9780367429911 (hardback) |
ISBN 9781003000556 (ebook)
Subjects: LCSH: Lean manufacturing. | Continuous improvement process. |
Organizational change. | Organizational effectiveness. | Industrial management.
Classification: LCC TS155 .R569 2020 (print) | LCC TS155 (ebook) |
DDC 658–dc23
LC record available at https://lccn.loc.gov/2019044458
LC ebook record available at https://lccn.loc.gov/2019044459

Visit the Taylor & Francis Web site at
www.taylorandfrancis.com

Contents

Action Items

7   Making it Happen

Figures

Acknowledgments

I need to begin this section with an apology to those of you, though deserving, who are not specifically mentioned here. I could fill a whole separate "acknowledgments book" to recognize all who've contributed to this endeavor. The book of acknowledgments would include names spanning experiences from when I was a young manufacturing engineer at AMP, Inc. to the folks I've recently worked with directly or in Lean peer group meetings. You've taught me and inspired me to learn more. Thank you!

There are a few who I will acknowledge here. I'll start with my family, whose love is my foundation. Not only do they add the value to my life, but their encouragement and questioning of *"How's the book coming?"* was more helpful than they realize.

There are a couple folks without whom this book would never have happened. The first is Todd Davis. His initial support for the book, content input, and chapter reviews enabled the project to move forward. It would have remained a collection of jumbled notes in my laptop without Todd's encouragement and assistance.

The other individual is Charlie Protzman, who has authored a number of excellent Lean books and is referenced multiple times in this book. Charlie provided expert guidance, which gave structure and flow to the book, and a Lean book should definitely *flow*! Charlie reviewed, and then re-reviewed, a number of chapters. These are just a few of his contributions. Again, this book would not exist if it weren't for Charlie Protzman.

I am grateful to Doug Cooper, who reviewed an early draft, even in spite of my suggestion to delay until the next, more readable, draft was complete. Doug has also contributed to the book's body of knowledge through our numerous Lean discussions/debates.

Steve Jozwiak, Jesse Hood, Joe Douthard, Sherry Jordan, and Chris Bunai all provided extremely helpful early feedback on the draft manuscript. The contributions of all of these Lean thinkers extend well beyond manuscript reviews. Stan Fickus and Thomas Dahbura are a couple Lean leaders who challenged me over the years and made me reflect and continually learn.

Thanks to Jeff Fuchs, not only for what he has taught me, but for bringing me into an organization which introduced me to so many exceptional individuals and provided a forum for ongoing Lean thinking and collaboration.

Joe Bero, Rich Joines, Greg Campbell, and Bec Jackson are a few other Lean scholars who contributed either through manuscript reviews, Lean engagements, discussions, debates, or all of the above. Of course, thank you to the Taylor & Francis publishing team for making this book a reality. I am extremely appreciative of their support, patience, and guidance.

I'd like to thank one other individual, though he's no longer of this earthly world. He has set a standard for living which I will never come close to attaining, but will continue striving towards. Thanks, Dad!

About the Author

Dave Rizzardo's personal mission can be simply stated as, "*just trying to make the world a Leaner place.*" His passion for Lean predates the time when Lean became synonymous with business excellence. After obtaining his mechanical engineering degree from the Pennsylvania State University, he worked in industry for 17 years in various positions, focusing on quality/ productivity improvement and the application of Lean principles. In 1999 Dave joined the University of Maryland's industry outreach program. As Lean Services Manager, his area of concentration was the development of Lean training and implementation services. In 2012 he was co-developer of the Lean Peer Group service and has been facilitating multiple groups since that time. The focus of these groups is to help organizations develop a Lean culture of continuous improvement. In 2014 Dave joined the Maryland World Class Consortia (MWCC), where he has served as Associate Director and Lean Peer Group service provider. He also founded Lean Peer Groups & Consulting LLC. Dave continues facilitating the Lean Peer Groups and working directly with organizations in helping them on their Lean journeys of excellence. Dave can be reached at daver@Leanconsult.org.

Introduction

Let's start by me explaining why I felt the need to write this book. Lean has proven to significantly enhance the competitiveness and profitability of companies throughout the world, and some have been transformed into organizations that are characterized as "world class." Lean transforms the workplace into one of participation, challenge, fulfillment, and even fun. These companies naturally become the employers of choice. However, far too many companies have fallen short in developing this Lean, continuous improvement culture that is essential for long-term sustainable excellence. Results from research studies and anecdotal evidence all generally agree that a majority of Lean transformations fail to meet expectations and achieve anticipated results. Since the definition of "failure" varies, the actual percentage can be debated. However, most would agree that Lean has a failure rate of 70 percent or more. The question is why? Why is Lean so difficult that so many companies fail to meet their objectives?

This book will explore the reasons for these failures, and will provide insight into how to avoid the stumbling blocks that plague many Lean transformations. Whether you are a leader immersed in your first attempt at Lean, or an experienced leader or Lean practitioner who has already hit your share of bumps along the Lean journey, this book will confirm where your journey is going well, and more importantly will help identify where you may need to re-evaluate your Lean strategy.

It is not my intent to create a deflated atmosphere of past failure as we begin our journey together; but we should have an awareness of the daunting challenge ahead of us. Sure, some aspects of Lean may actually be simple, but don't ever assume that *simple* is necessarily equivalent to *easy*. If we do accept the challenge and have the commitment and courage to move forward towards our goal of developing a Lean culture within our organizations, the payoffs are transformational in every sense of the word, for both the company and employees. This is the dual reason for writing this book, to provide information for both company *and* employee renewal.

In Chapter 1 we'll develop a working definition of Lean and provide clarity of our Lean objective prior to delving any deeper into the details. Without this initial step of clarifying our challenge, we would risk creating even more Lean confusion by readers unknowingly traveling in different directions and paths.

Then in Chapter 2 we'll make sure that we learn from history and experience. We'll look at our past missteps, blind spots, or what I refer to as *Lean failure mechanisms*, which have derailed many Lean efforts. My top six are reviewed. Of course, your top six based on your own experience and observations may be different than what is proposed. However, I am extremely confident that if you address the failure mechanisms outlined in Chapter 2, and basically flip them 180 degrees from failure modes into Lean success factors, you will establish a solid foundation from which your Lean transformation can be built upon and grow.

Keep in mind that with Lean, as with many things in life, one size does not fit all. We simply cannot just copy the standard Lean recipe, apply it to any situation, and watch as the continuous improvement culture begins to grow and create a competitive advantage for our organizations. We can only wish it were that simple and straightforward. Though this is obviously not the case, there are some universal principles of Lean which apply regardless of type of organization, whether manufacturer, distributor, healthcare, service, or non-profit. Specific Lean implementation steps, timing, and methods may vary, but the principles are universal. The principles provide direction and guide you in developing the most effective roadmap for your own unique situation.

These principles, which are reviewed in Chapter 3, must form the backbone of a Lean strategy. Ignore or violate them, or simply don't believe in their validity, and enduring Lean success is not possible. These principles should be treated as the organization's Lean Constitution, the framework and foundation that everything else is built upon. In Chapter 3 you'll also see how some of the failure mechanisms can result from a direct violation of one or more of these principles. Chapter 4 reviews a few of the key systems, practices, and tools/techniques of Lean. Key performance indicators (KPIs) will be a significant topic in this chapter.

Chapter 5 will address the role changes essential for Lean success. Lean affects everyone's "job." Chapter 6 will focus on what can be considered the psychology of change, where topics such as influence, motivation, and resistance to change will be covered. Employee engagement is a key topic throughout these two chapters and is a common thread throughout this whole book. Lean not only requires an involved and engaged workforce, but I believe that the prevailing paradigm of "work" itself must be altered through redefinition of the roles and responsibilities of every single employee.

This book was written to help you develop a Lean culture to not only transform your company and gain a competitive advantage, but simultaneously to help you change the lives of your employees for the better. In fact, the improvement in company performance can be considered a result or outcome of the workforce transformation that enables everyone to contribute, be challenged, fulfilled, and even have some fun during the workday, where most of us spend at least half of our waking hours.

Chapter 7 provides some application and transformation roadmap guidelines. A repeated message throughout the book is that each organization must experiment and develop their own transformation roadmap, but some guidelines and suggestions will be provided to aid in this effort. Chapter 8 provides a few summary and concluding thoughts.

My objective is to not only provide information to help you along your Lean journey, but more generally, my intention is to make you *think* … to make you think and reflect upon where you are now, and what actions and experiments should be done next. My other goal is for you to want to learn more, to search many of the references which I provide throughout the book, to become a Lean scholar. Learning should be continuous, and I hope this book is a facilitator to that end.

You'll notice that action items are scattered throughout the book. If you don't like the action items I proposed, then, better yet, create your own. This bias for action is critical as we travel along our Lean journeys, so I suggest we follow this practice during our exploration throughout this book. I agree wholeheartedly with the words of Winston Churchill, *"I never worry about action, but only about inaction."*[1] So, let's get started on this journey, which will hopefully provide some insights to help you on your personal and organizational Lean journey of excellence.

Note

1. Churchill, Winston. "Quote about Action by Winston Churchill on Quotations Book." QuotationsBook.com. Accessed January 8, 2019. http://quotationsbook.com/quote/486/.

Chapter 1

What is Lean?

Let's begin our journey by defining the challenge before us. The challenge can be described as a gap, from where we are now to where we want to be. Closing this gap is the problem that we are trying to solve, and understanding *where we want to be* is essential. All problem-solving processes start with defining and clarifying the problem, whether the process being followed is PDCA or PDSA (Plan-Do-Check/Study-Act), DMAIC (Define-Measure-Analyze-Improve-Control), or any other model grounded in the scientific method. So to address this initial problem-solving step, let's begin by answering the basic question, "What is Lean?" Without an adequate answer to this question, we may be working with a vague concept that we desire to achieve, but is not defined sufficiently to enable us to develop an effective plan for moving forward. Due to lack of clarity, we won't even be sure that we're launching our journey in the right direction. This obviously would not be a good starting point. Or, just as ineffective, we might begin our journey with different ideas as to our objective. Let's have a uniform understanding of where we want to go.

It seems like a simple question – "What is Lean?" – but there really isn't a short, Webster-like, definition of Lean that effectively captures the magnitude of what it really means to be Lean or to have a Lean culture. Our objective at this point is to create a clear enough vision and direction for us to move towards as we delve deeper throughout this book. Research on the internet will produce at least a dozen different variants of the definition of Lean – some of which will point you in the right direction, others which might sidetrack you for a while. Most of the inadequate definitions aren't necessarily wrong or totally misaligned with Lean, but rather they are insufficient, incomplete. They don't tell enough of the story to be effective.

Eliminating Waste

One of the most popular definitions of Lean is *eliminating waste*. As for a short, compact, powerful definition, this is pretty good. I've used it often myself. We'll definitely revisit this topic of *waste* in subsequent chapters. Eliminating waste is one of the principles we'll review which form the framework that our Lean culture is built upon. Adding a few more words to this short definition gives us more insight as to the target of our waste-busting activities, *eliminating waste from company processes*. However, it's difficult to gain a vision of our objective even with this expanded definition, and at the start of our journey, we need more clarity.

Lean Tools

Another common definition of Lean is that it is a *set of analysis and improvement tools*. We definitely need tools to identify and eliminate waste, but a tool-based definition of Lean is not only incomplete, but it can actually lead us down an ill-advised path. Too many companies have passionately used as many of the tools in the Lean toolbox as they could find, but then have been disappointed when progress has been made only in a few isolated areas, or has plateaued or regressed over time.

Let's think about the tools approach for a moment and compare it with an example from outside the factory: the building of a house. Does the house builder start the day by saying, *"Let's see how many of my tools I can use today!"* or *"Today is hammer day! Let's use the hammer everywhere! Let's do it team; it's hammer time!"* Of course, this is absolutely ridiculous. The objective is not to use the hammer, a tool, but rather it is to build the house by utilizing the appropriate tools.

However, isn't this absurd scenario exactly what many organizations have done with Lean, by laser focusing on the use of the tools, when Lean success has been defined by how many Lean tools were utilized? Assessments based primarily on tool usage have been used to measure Lean status and progress. *"We've employed more Lean tools this year, so we're doing better!"* Well actually, that may be true, but maybe not. Back to the house analogy, it depends on how you've used that hammer and circular saw. Posting value stream maps, implementing 5S, and putting up communication boards everywhere, all gain us points. These are, in fact, a few of the tools or techniques which you will notice in most robust Lean cultures. But, in some organizations, for some reason, after a few months, maybe it will take a year or two, Lean seems to be something we used to do back when, not now, and we are left wondering what could have possibly happened to our Lean "program." *(It's okay to nod your head in agreement. Believe me; you're not alone in traveling down the Lean tools path.)*

Sure, we need the right tools to identify problems and eliminate waste. We don't want to try to build our house with a sharp stick and a rock as our tools. Lean tools are powerful, are critical components of our Lean strategy, and deserve mention in our definition of Lean. But as a stand-alone description, they're insufficient and can actually drive us down an ineffective pathway. Our Lean vision is still too cloudy for moving forward with only the understanding that we want to eliminate waste from company processes, and we need effective analysis and improvement tools to accomplish this.

Culture Change

There's one word which has already been used in previous text, and will be one of the most repeated words throughout this book, which we must include in our Lean definition … *culture*. We are striving to develop a *Lean culture*. The word *culture* implies that we want to embed something into our organization's DNA. Lean is not a specific improvement project, initiative, or program, but an integral part of what we do around here. This phrase, "the way we do things around here," can serve as a definition of what we mean when using the word *culture*. Lean must become woven into the very fabric of our organizations, part of our culture. We go beyond just *doing* Lean to *being* Lean.

Continuous Improvement

So at this point in building our baseline Lean definition, we know we want to create a *culture*, and we know something about the activities which will occur within this culture – waste reduction efforts which utilize the appropriate Lean tools. However, there is a key descriptor of the desired culture which is still missing … *continuous improvement*. We are trying to embed a *culture of continuous improvement*. These two words, continuous improvement, change everything. Much of the remainder of this book is devoted to what must change to develop this culture and for it to take hold within an organization. The adage, *"If it's not broke, don't fix it,"* is no longer an acceptable mantra. Rather, *"If it's not broke, let's take it apart and put it back together even better,"* is a more appropriate Lean mindset.

Institutional Obsession with Improvement

To expand our understanding of the desired Lean culture, consider the following statement in reference to Toyota's competitiveness from an article titled, *No Satisfaction at Toyota:*[1] *"It is rooted in an institutional obsession with improvement that Toyota manages to instill in each one of its workers, a pervasive lack of complacency with whatever was accomplished yesterday."*

I believe the four-word phrase *"institutional obsession with improvement"* does a great job of capturing the essence of a Lean culture. An *obsession* with improvement is quite different than the culture of status quo which exists in many organizations. Remember, *"If it's not broke, don't fix it."* If you're holding on to this obsolete mindset, watch your competition pass you by due to their *obsession* with experimenting and moving forward by engaging everyone, every single day.

Adding Customer Value

Value and *customer* are implicit in the definition of waste, but I believe that no definition of Lean would be adequate without their inclusion. Having them hidden behind some of the other words just isn't enough exposure. Another word which should be added to our definition is *strategy* to emphasize the fact that developing a Lean culture requires a plan of action specific to your organization. It's not going to happen by simply wishing it to be; we need an effective plan and strategy of continuous improvement to embed Lean into "the way we do things around here." One note of warning is to make sure that the Lean strategy and the overall business strategy are integrated together.

Let's try to put our Lean definition pieces together to see if we've created a working definition that is satisfactory in describing our Lean objective. Our Lean baseline definition would look something like this:

Lean is a *strategy* designed to embed a *culture of continuous improvement* where *everyone* strives to *eliminate waste* in company *processes* by utilizing the *appropriate tools* to add ever-increasing *value* for the *customer.*

Of course, even our proposed definition is incomplete, and we can continue to add key words and phrases such as philosophy, mindset, or experimentation in an attempt to complete it further and expand an already long-winded statement; however, I do believe that it provides an adequate vision and direction for us to move forward. The remainder of this book, especially Chapter 3 – which focuses on the Lean principles – can be considered a continuation of the clarification and expansion of the answer to the basic question which we began with: "What is Lean?"

Transformation

We've focused on establishing a baseline definition of Lean. Admittedly, we've defined a daunting objective. It's hard to imagine that any sort of cultural transformation will be easy to accomplish. No one promised that our journey was going to be an easy one. It will be challenging, fulfilling, and transformational for your company and employees, but *easy* ... unfortunately not.

In the next chapter we'll take a look at some of the areas where we have stumbled in the past so as to learn from our past mistakes and blind spots that have knocked us off our Lean course of excellence. If we address these, our likelihood of success increases exponentially; we can flip or transform these failure mechanisms into success factors. If we fail to address them, our Lean progress will likely be described as "spotty" at best, where isolated islands of excellence may exist, but Lean never becomes part of our company's DNA where *everyone is engaged* in *improving processes* ... everywhere, every single day.

Action Item – *Lean Definition Review*

At your next Lean steering committee meeting reflect upon your Lean efforts to date and discuss if a faulty definition of Lean may have led you towards an objective that is misaligned with the baseline definition proposed in this chapter. Or, possibly your team members have not had a uniform understanding of the objective or direction. Maybe some had envisioned Lean to be a program or initiative for the next so many years which they somehow have to "fit in" around their *regular jobs* rather than a cultural transformation which never ends, and which redefines their *regular* jobs. Chapter 5 is devoted to this redefinition of roles and responsibilities. If your team is striving towards different objectives due to bypassing the critical first step of the problem-solving process, long-term success is impossible.

Note: If you are not familiar with a "Lean steering committee" and its purpose and responsibilities, refer to Chapter 5.

Note

1. Fishman, Charles. "No Satisfaction at Toyota." Fast Company. December 2006/January 2007. Accessed January 3, 2019. www.fastcompany.com/58345/no-satisfaction-toyota.

Chapter 2

Learning from the Past

Where We Have NOT Gone Wrong

Why are we still at the point where the development of a Lean culture is the exception rather than the rule? Shouldn't we be much better than that by now? I will start this discussion of past history by stating what we have *not* done wrong. This goes back to a point in Chapter 1 regarding our infatuation with the tools of Lean. With rare exception, a failure in meeting our Lean potential has nothing to do with a failure to implement the tools properly or using the wrong tools, or using the right tools incorrectly. These may be reasons for wobbling or minor stumbling along the Lean journey causing some short-term delays, but these setbacks should be expected as we experiment and figure out the details of applying Lean to our particular organization and circumstances. This is a natural and vital part of the learning process. In any endeavor, we definitely need the right tools to get the job done. We'll review a few Lean tools in Chapter 4 and their place within the continuous improvement strategy. However, this is not where we should focus when searching for the root causes of significant roadblocks which are stifling us from moving forward on our Lean journey.

Lean Failure Mechanisms

Six key stumbling blocks, or what I refer to as *failure mechanisms*, of Lean will be reviewed. They are referred to as failure mechanisms since any one of them can destroy attempts at developing a robust continuous improvement culture. Following are the six failure mechanisms which are the subject of this chapter:

■ Wrong or Incomplete Definition of Lean
■ Leaders Aren't Leading
■ Front-Line Leadership is Unprepared
■ Everyone's "Job" Doesn't Change
■ Lean "Training" Isn't Effective
■ Demotivation is Tolerated

These are my top six, but others can be added to the list. For example, violating any one of the principles of Lean which are reviewed in the next chapter will also destroy, or at least significantly derail, Lean plans. You'll notice how some of the six failure mechanisms can be traced back to a violation of one or more of the principles. The failure mechanism discussions in this chapter are brief overviews, since supporting information and detail is provided throughout the subsequent chapters.

I focus on these failure mechanisms due to their destructive power, and their prevalence even in companies many would consider *Lean-mature*. The failure mechanisms may be hidden and not recognized, so a better descriptor might be *blind spot*. In other cases they are recognized, but we don't have the courage to do anything about it. It does take courage to be an effective Lean leader to confront the numerous challenges that a cultural transformation entails, especially since it usually requires leaders to take a long, serious look in the mirror, which is related to the topic of our second failure mechanism. However, to get started with number one of my top six, we need to return to the topic of Chapter 1.

Failure Mechanism #1 – Wrong or Incomplete Definition of Lean

Chapter 1 was devoted to developing a working definition and basic understanding of Lean, so I suggest that you go back and read this chapter if you decided to jump ahead and begin your journey at Chapter 2. The following is a short story that depicts one misguided definition of Lean which can cause damage.

A Short Story of Misguided Thinking

The internal Lean coordinator, we'll call him L.G. for Lean Guy, at Company X just took his seat at the leadership team staff meeting, and he's feeling pretty good about how things have been going. Though they've only been on their Lean journey for about six months, he felt that they were finally starting to gain momentum. Admittedly, there has been a fair amount of resistance that he and some of the managers have run up against, and he can foresee some challenges down the road, but things are starting to happen. The kaizen events have accelerated a number of improvements, and the floor supervisors, now called team leaders, have begun working with their teams in making changes in their own areas. They've even started doing some of the Lean training that only L.G. used to do.

These changes are especially impressive considering the fact that Company X has a history of not changing anything until the customer repeatedly screams about an issue. The company president has lived by the motto, *if it's not broke, don't fix it, and even if it is broke, delay fixing it for as long as possible; maybe it will still work well enough without spending any money on it.* L.G. knew that this was definitely not a winning mindset for today's competitive business climate. In fact, Company X has recently lost some significant business to the new competitor down the street. This does have the president very concerned. Regardless of the president's past actions, or more accurately, inactions, L.G. viewed his apparent support of Lean as a step in the right direction. Maybe he was starting to see the light, and now that some positive Lean progress was obvious, the light should be shining even brighter.

So the leadership meeting begins, and the company president calls the meeting to order. L.G. and a few of the managers who have been leading the early Lean activities just can't wait for their chance to report on the progress. When the president started speaking, they sensed their opportunity was about to happen. The president said, *"Ladies and gentlemen, the first thing that I would like to address is the status of our Lean program."* L.G. straightens up and is about to speak up, but then the president continues to say,

> *… unfortunately, this program has not provided the return on investment which we had anticipated. We began this program to dig us out of the financial mess we are in mainly due to that pesky new competitor down the street, and the results after six months*

have not met expectations. We can't wait forever to see the returns from Lean. Sure, our inventory levels have dropped, which has freed up some cash, and we've gotten some positive feedback from our customers for improved quality and better on-time deliveries, but the documented cost savings are unimpressive, especially when considering all the time and money invested in training the employees. And those kaizen events always take key people off of the production floor and disrupt the schedule. How in the world our on-time delivery has gone up during the past couple months when we're messing with production like that, I'll never know. Dumb luck I guess. But all I do know is that our CFO, Jim BeanCounter, doesn't see an acceptable ROI, and neither do I … and we thought this was going to provide the quick financial windfall we needed. I think it's time to pull the plug on this failed program! Now, does anyone have any questions?

Well, where can L.G. start? He couldn't speak. After he got over the shock, it was clear to him that he needs to spruce up his résumé since the president sure has a different definition of Lean than he does. There's obviously no future for a Lean guy at this place.

The Financial Impact

Sad story, isn't it? Why do we sometimes treat cultural change the same as if we are purchasing a new piece of equipment? In our story, the president gave a hint to how he defined Lean by his use of the term "program." Programs have a finite timeframe, an end point, but Lean doesn't. His definition was laser-focused on *return on investment* and based on Lean providing some quick, and significant, short-term financial results. Are there ever impressive short-term financial results with Lean? Absolutely, it all depends on the situation and your definition of short-term. Reduced inventory levels of 60 percent or more can be very impressive from a cash flow perspective, and reduced scrap and rework levels will also get attention at places with high material costs. The freed labor, space, and equipment capacity can be equally impressive in the *short term* – although there's a chance that this may not be acknowledged until the freed capacity is actually converted into new sales.

The eventual financial benefits which result from a Lean transformation are astronomical. What's the price tag of company existence? However, defining Lean as a short-term cost savings program which must meet a particular ROI similar to the purchase of a new widget bending machine is obviously too narrow and not aligned with our broader definition and baseline understanding proposed in Chapter 1, and thus will not lead to the cultural change that we are striving for.

> If you don't know where you are going, you might wind up someplace else.[1]
>
> *– Yogi Berra*

The above short story depicts only one example of Failure Mechanism #1 and the damage that can occur when Lean is not properly defined and understood. Make sure there is agreement on the direction and vision prior to attempting to move towards it … otherwise, *you might wind up someplace else*. The Lean principles reviewed in the next chapter will add more clarity to the proper definition of Lean. The principles should be considered the founding constitution that all else is built upon. But now let's move on to our remaining five failure mechanisms and see what else we can learn from our past missteps.

Note: The financial, ROI discussion in this section is much deeper and broader than what we will cover in this book. I strongly recommend the reader refer to Jerry Solomon's book, *Who's Counting? A Lean Accounting Business Novel,*[2] and *Accounting for World Class Operations*[3] written with Rosemary Fullerton. Both are winners of the Shingo Prize for Manufacturing Excellence.

Failure Mechanism #2 – Leaders Aren't Leading

The next place to look for a root cause of our Lean struggles is at leadership. Even though I don't present a hierarchy of importance regarding the six failure mechanisms, a strong case can be made that this is the overriding failure mechanism and all others are a result of *leaders aren't leading*. This failure mechanism is not focused on any specific leadership mistake or faulty decision, but rather it has to do with *who* is actually leading the Lean strategy.

Leaders and the Lean Team

Lean requires leadership capability to effectively traverse through the difficulties of a transformation. Lean leadership cannot be considered *someone else's* responsibility. As long as company leaders try to delegate Lean leadership responsibility to a functional department or a specific person, Lean will be viewed as "their job," the role of the Lean Department, and Lean will never take hold throughout the whole organization. What if someone walked into your facility and asked a random employee, *"Who is responsible for leading Lean in your company?"* Would the employee's answer be, *"That would be the manager of our Lean department; he is really a Lean zealot. Lean is his baby! You'll love him!"* If so, you will have uncovered some opportunities in the area of Lean leadership.

Sure, in the early stages of Lean, the Lean coordinator or manager may be the only internal person who is knowledgeable about Lean and has the responsibility of teaching and facilitating the initial Lean activities. Eventually the Lean coordinator must transform their role into one of support, coaching, and mentoring. The Lean coordinator may be the Lean subject matter expert, but no one should view them as the person responsible for leading Lean. The role of the Lean department is covered in detail in Chapter 5. Company leaders must lead the Lean charge.

Didn't we learn a related lesson many decades ago during the quality revolution of the 1980s? A similar scenario as described above applies. Who is responsible for quality around here? Once again, if you are directed to a quality function or a staff position, I guarantee you that a quality culture does not exist. *"It's the quality department's responsibility to assure quality!"* … wrong answer. Everyone has a role and responsibilities in creating a quality product, and company leaders must lead the way for this culture to develop. This can't be relegated to a single functional support department, and neither can leadership of a Lean transformation.

Leaders Must Lead!

Lean affects everything in your organization. Lean is too all-encompassing to be a functional responsibility. Leaders occasionally try to justify delegating this role in the name of empowerment, or a desire to not micromanage the change, but both of these reasons are usually cop-outs and an abdication of their own critical responsibility. Anti-Lean micromanaging behavior should never be confused with essential Lean-aligned behaviors. Once again, with Lean, leaders must lead. More details forthcoming in Chapter 5.

Failure Mechanism #3 – Front-Line Leadership is Unprepared

The third Lean failure mechanism is really an extension of Failure Mechanism #2 since it deals with a particular leadership level, the front-line leader. However, it definitely deserves its own designation as a failure mechanism. This is the leadership level that the vast majority of the workforce typically reports to, but often is the least prepared for their role in a Lean organization. But it is not their fault! Lean changes the leader role, and we've often failed to even inform them of their new role and responsibilities, let alone involve them in the redefinition of their job. And if we did provide some form of training, it has typically been of minimal value in setting them up for success.

The TWI Lesson

The importance of this leadership level was realized in the early stages of World War II. Because the ability to produce goods was key to the war effort, the U.S. government created a program to identify how to produce better and faster despite the problems presented by the war. Training within industry (TWI) was formed in 1940 to support the war effort and had such great results that it is considered by some to be the foundation on which Lean is based.[4] The originators of TWI considered several options as to where to focus their training. Their decision? … the front-line supervisors. Their reasoning was that supervisors had the most influence on production and productivity since they were in direct contact with the people making the product. That logic is as applicable today as it was in 1940.

"Supervisor" – What's in a Name?

Personnel in the front-line leader role often hold this title of supervisor. The title itself indicates our lack of understanding regarding the Lean leadership needs of our organizations. The Merriam-Webster Dictionary defines *supervise* as "to be in charge of (someone or something): to watch and direct (someone or something)."[5] By definition, a supervisor's role is to *watch* and *direct*. Does this capture the essence of what we want our Lean leaders to be doing? Though watching or observation is a critical component of a Lean culture, and there are times when directing is appropriate, this definition of supervisor doesn't quite exude the idea of employee engagement or the supervisor as teacher, coach, team builder, and developer of people. To me at least, *watch and direct* doesn't produce this image. If the very definition of the role is out of phase with the results we are looking to achieve, should we be surprised when the actual results are not what we intended? Furthermore, should we be shocked when the person in this position is ill prepared for a new role as teacher and coach?

Note: The reason for continued use of the title supervisor in this book is due to reader familiarity to assure understanding; however, feel free to take your pen and strike through this word and replace with a more appropriate title such as "team leader" or "group leader" every time you run across it … unless, of course, this is a library book! Then, please keep your pen down.

Leader Alignment – Front Line to CEO

It is critical, but not sufficient, that the CEO passionately presents the Lean strategy and direction of the organization and paints a compelling picture of how everyone will be intimately involved in the transformation; however, if Lean leadership does not exist at the front line, in the trenches, a Lean transformation will suddenly come to a grinding halt. And if decisions and actions at the floor level are actually in contradiction to the CEO's Lean message, the deadly cultural poison which I refer to as *organizational hypocrisy* will begin to spread, which leads to workforce distrust and will destroy any hope of developing the desired workplace environment. I believe that the role of the front-line leader is the most significant position redefinition within a Lean environment. Trying to obtain "buy-in" or passive "support" from your supervisors isn't enough; leadership is required and it is imperative that we make sure that this level is the most prepared for Lean leadership, not the least.

Within a Lean organizational structure, the front-line worker may officially report to a management position titled "group leader"; however, a more localized, work area or cell, non-management "team leader" also often has an employee support and people development role. Though these two positions have some different responsibilities, for the purposes of our discussions throughout this book, we'll blur these two positions together. If any distinction is made, it will be to contrast this *"closer to the front line" leader* with *executive or C-Suite* leadership positions. (However, in a Lean organization, all leader levels can often be spotted at the front line.)

Jeffrey Liker and David Meier's *The Toyota Way Fieldbook: A Practical Guide for Implementing Toyota's 4Ps* provides specific details of the team leader versus group leader roles at Toyota.[6]

Failure Mechanism #4 – Everyone's "Job" Doesn't Change

Improvement is Part of the Job

It's time that we accept a fact of Lean life, that which deals with what we call "the job." The job has changed. It must change – we cannot, and will not, come close to creating the desired culture without the understanding that the "job" now includes an improvement component. By stating that I don't have time for Lean since I have to do my job, makes absolutely no sense in a Lean environment. It would be like stating that I don't have time to make a quality product today; we'll do it when we can find the time to "fit it in." Too often, that is what we are trying to do with Lean, "fit it in" whenever we can find the time. *"Right now, I have to get back to my job!"* You may as well be saying that you don't have time to breathe.

From a structural level, dedicated improvement time, time to review performance, time to discuss issues, time to analyze and perform improvement experiments, must be built into the workday – once again, *built* into the design of the workday, not the "when we can fit it in" approach, which never works. *(I can see you nodding your head at this last statement. That's okay; we've all tried the "fit it in" approach.)*

Everyone – No Opting Out

A key word which must be taken literally in "everyone's job must change" is *everyone*. Though this point is implied from some of the previous text, it is too critical to be left to implications. The job change isn't only for the before-mentioned leaders of Failure Mechanisms 2 and 3, or only for those manufacturing types who do the value-adding work. I've heard some company leaders loudly chant the Lean mantra of "everybody doing Lean every day" but then have no problem allowing certain, seemingly untouchable, personnel or whole functions to opt out of the challenge. I guarantee you that this type of organizational hypocrisy will squash any chance of positively changing your culture. It will create an even more distrusting, demotivated, and disengaged workforce. Whether intentional or not, this is being hypocritical, and this will be obvious to everyone.

From the CEO to the janitor to production to sales to the finance group to field support … everyone's job must include improvement. A theme of this book is that Lean is primarily about people improving processes, and engaging the workforce to transform the company and often their own lives for the better. However, this does not mean that everything is up for debate. Lean does have directive components to go along with the many empowering aspects. We don't take a poll as to whether our companies should develop a Lean/continuous improvement strategy, and we don't allow individuals or functions to state:

> *That makes sense for you guys, but we've been doing all right doing what we do and have been doing for the last 30 years, so thanks but no thanks. We're doing just fine!*

There's no debate. The bus is traveling in the Lean direction. The empowering component of this message is that everyone will have input in determining the route which the bus travels, and even have the opportunity to drive the bus at times. That turns out to be pretty exciting to most folks. Initially, this may be a little scary, but when provided with the necessary support and tools, it is exciting and fulfilling.

Since the job is changing for everyone, it becomes critical that our training and learning methods effectively prepare everyone to be successful in their new Lean roles. This leads us to Failure Mechanism #5, which addresses the effectiveness of our typical training approach … I contend not too effective, and definitely not near enough to develop a true Lean culture of continuous improvement.

Failure Mechanism #5 – Lean "Training" Isn't Effective

With all of the great Lean training programs, certifications, and Lean, Six Sigma, or LeanSigma, or Lean Six Sigma yellow, green, black belt, master black belt, super-duper master black belt *(sorry, I got carried away)* programs, how can Lean training possibly make a top ten, let alone a top six list of Lean failure mechanisms? The standard approach to training provides some extremely valuable information and skill development; however, it is simply not sufficient. It is not effective in changing behaviors and developing new habits. And that is the current need, not only skills, but behavioral modification due to the new Lean roles and responsibilities that an effective Lean strategy demands.

Changing Behaviors

The first four failure mechanisms all involve some drastic behavioral changes. But our usual Lean training approach is along the same lines as our approach to training on the new ERP system, or a new machine, or a new company health plan. Throw everyone into a room for a while, inundate them with information, and send them on their way. Then we brag about the percentage of the workforce trained on Lean as if that automatically guarantees our success. This batch type of training not only sounds un-Lean, but it doesn't have the habit-forming staying power needed to enable people to learn and grow into their new roles.

Developing the "Want To"

Rather than *isn't effective,* maybe it would be more accurate to state that the current training approach is just *too simplistic.* With behavioral change, there is not only the challenge of developing new habits that stick, but there's an additional motivational component which must be considered that complicates the training challenge even further. Simply presenting the new roles and skills in a training program usually doesn't result in the active engagement of the workforce. We not only must provide the "what to do" which our training typically provides quite well, but we also need to somehow instill the "want to do it" for everyone to thrive in their new Lean roles. Developing the *want to* in people is a primary topic of Chapter 6.

Teaching for Improvement

Another complicating factor of Lean training is that we are not just training on the standard work, the current best method of doing something. We are also teaching and coaching on how to *improve* the standard work. This goes beyond simply learning a series of process steps. We are teaching *improvement processes.* We're growing problem-solving capability. This is not developed during a one-hour or even a one-day session.

So how can we modify our training approach to be more effective? As on the factory floor, we need to transition from a batch approach towards more of a continuous flow approach. The Lean principle of *continuous flow* applies not only to material flows, but to other aspects of our Lean journey, such as our Lean training and learning approach. Our training must be ongoing. Developing problem-solving capability requires experience, repeated PDCA cycles, and ongoing coaching. This is why Lean leaders must take on the role of teachers and coaches rather than traditional supervisors and managers. This leadership issue flips back to Failure Mechanisms 2 and 3 and the Lean responsibilities of company leaders. Training is no longer the sole property of the training department or human resources.

Holistic Learning Approach

Besides continuous teaching and learning, it is critical that everyone is influenced and motivated to be actively engaged in their redefined jobs. Typical training sessions and workshops are needed, but they're not nearly enough. A more expansive, or holistic, approach is required which combines these traditional training methods with motivational considerations and ongoing coaching. This will develop new Lean habits and continually grow employees into better problem-solvers and idea-generators, plus they'll love their jobs! Without this broader learning and development perspective to what we normally refer to as "Lean training," employees will never be successful in their new Lean roles.

Once we accept the point of Failure Mechanism #4, that everybody's job must change, we then obviously must develop an effective approach to training and learning for everyone to be successful. However, if we allow demotivation to exist in the workplace, all of the above is irrelevant and a waste of time, since no one is really listening. And there are usually definable reasons why this is so … which brings us to Failure Mechanism #6.

Failure Mechanism #6 – Demotivation is Tolerated

Why people just don't seem to be motivated to change is a common angst of many leaders, regardless of the change. This is not a concern solely with Lean transformational change, the topic of our journey. I contend that the issue is not necessarily motivation, but rather the culprit is *demotivation*. With Lean, we need to break down problems, and this issue is no different. We should break it down into the components of motivation and demotivation. Frederick Herzberg taught us this many years ago with his Motivation–Hygiene Theory studies.

Motivation versus Demotivation

One key finding of Herzberg's work was that factors involved in producing job satisfaction (and motivation) are separate and distinct from the factors that lead to job dissatisfaction. "The opposite of job satisfaction is not job dissatisfaction but, rather, *no* job satisfaction; and, similarly, the opposite of job dissatisfaction is not job satisfaction, but *no* job dissatisfaction."[7] Basically what I interpret this tongue-twister to mean is that though some overlap exists, there are things which do a real good job of motivating us, and then there are totally separate things which do a real good job of demotivating us. We need to take Herzberg's lead, and delve into each component as separate, albeit, related entities. We'll take a deep dive in Chapter 6.

Demotivators Trump All!

The reason "demotivation" made it into the top six failure mechanisms is because, if demotivators are present and thriving within our organizations, no amount of counterbalancing motivators will enable the Lean culture to grow. That's a tough pill to swallow. We may be doing a whole lot of things right, but a few, maybe even only a single demotivator, can squash our plans. Demotivators trump all. They destroy trust. They block the communication pipeline and people quit listening and paying attention. A drastic demotivator example involves company safety policies. If it is perceived that employee safety is not a top priority of company leaders, that people are viewed as easily replaceable resources, no amount of motivational tools and techniques will turn the workforce into an engaged, Lean, continuous improvement machine.

There are many demotivators which most would deem much less severe as compared with poor safety practices, but the effect can be the same. Lack of basic respect, or not being listened to, or policies perceived to be unfair, or inadequate compensation, any of these can have the same damaging affect. Few will be open to the benefits of working in a motivating and engaging environment if demotivators are in the neighborhood. Unfortunately, the converse is not true. Piling motivators on top of demotivators is just a waste of time. Demotivators trump all!

Hard on the "Soft" Issues

People, not only policies, practices, and procedures, have the power to demotivate. Unfortunately, *everyone* has this culture-damaging capability. This is not a power owned by any one company faction. In the title of this failure mechanism, we use the word *tolerated, "demotivation is tolerated."* This word was chosen to emphasize this people aspect of demotivation, that we often tolerate or ignore this bad behavior. I bet you know of some folks who are quite skilled at wielding their demotivating sword. This is why company leaders need to be tough or hard on these soft issues, because it's these so-called *soft*, people issues that ultimately will determine whether you obtain the *hard* bottom-line results. This type of non-Lean behavior cannot be tolerated or ignored.

This sometimes forces tough decisions to be made by company leaders. Take this scenario: Joe has been with the company for many years and when Sally Supervisor retired he was promoted to supervisor, not only due to his tenure, but he was the best machine technician in the department. Joe was the obvious choice … wasn't he? Or, is there a chance we may have lost a good machine technician and gained a poor supervisor? Joe really loves making all the decisions and being the boss. He contends that he is not here to make friends:

> *Just shut up and do what I tell you to do! I've finally made it to a position where I can call the shots and make sure these knuckleheads do their job, the way I want it done. Empowerment, what's that, some new sort of energy drink?*

Well, on second thought, maybe Joe wasn't the best supervisor choice when trying to build a Lean culture. He has effectively created a demotivating environment through his overbearing and disrespectful behavior. Lack of respect, along with any lack of fairness or equity, is the fuel of demotivation.

Joe's department may have performed adequately in the status quo world of yesteryear, but in today's hyper-competitive business environment, compliance to the status quo is insufficient. Joe needs to be trained, coached, and mentored to understand his new Lean role to enable him to be successful. After adequate training, coaching, and mentoring, if Joe basically refuses to transform into the role of a Lean leader, what do you do? The best situation is that Joe realizes that a Lean leadership position is just not suited to him, and he enthusiastically agrees to return to his front-line position of operating a CNC machine where he had excelled; however, if his disrespectful behavior continues upon returning to the technician role, this cannot be tolerated either. Or possibly Joe decides to pursue employment elsewhere since he's starting to get the impression that a Lean environment is not aligned with his personal goals and desired behaviors. One way or another, Joe cannot hold a leadership position, nor hold *any* position, within the company if he refuses to cease his demotivating behavior.

This last failure mechanism, which introduces the damaging effects of demotivation, would be #1 if this was a prioritized list, or at least it would be a dead heat with #2, *Leaders Aren't Leading*. Since, if enough demotivators exist, you may as well be preaching Lean to the wall. The workforce attention is focused only on the demotivators that are making their time at work a painful, unfulfilling, unenjoyable experience, and that's a characteristic of a very un-Lean workplace, obviously just the opposite of what we are trying to accomplish.

Chapter Summary

As previously noted, the failure mechanisms reviewed in this chapter are not all-inclusive, but these top six have thwarted the development of a Lean culture in a number of organizations. We began this chapter by referring back to Chapter 1 to assure that we have a uniform understanding of "what is Lean." Then we emphasized that company leaders must lead the Lean effort. This is not a responsibility to be delegated to a functional department. Failure Mechanism #3 expanded on the leadership issue by focusing on the front-line leaders, or supervisors, as they are typically titled. This critical leadership level is usually the least prepared for taking on their new role. Failure Mechanism #4 reminds us that everybody's job must change, not only the leaders of #2 and #3, but *everyone*, in every corner of the organization. We then questioned the effectiveness of our current methods of training and preparing everybody for their new roles, and the final failure mechanism, *demotivation is tolerated*, must be addressed to have any chance to develop the desired culture. If not attended to, no one will be listening to the Lean message and any employee involvement will likely be described as *going through the motions*.

Our ultimate goal is not simply to evade the failure mechanisms, to sidestep a landmine, but rather, by effectively addressing them, we totally reverse and transform them from *failure* mechanisms into *positive* success factors, a complete 180-degree turn. They are then converted into solid foundational elements of our Lean strategy which will put us well on our way to ongoing improvement and sustainable success.

Action Item – *Lean Failure Mechanisms*

Schedule a Lean steering committee meeting and discuss whether any of the six failure mechanisms are preventing you from making significant progress in developing a Lean culture. If so, put a plan together to address the major issues, or you may want to jump to a later section of this book for more details on a particular topic. Your Lean strategy will never gain traction if you leave these issues unattended. Turn them from culture-killing negative roadblocks into positive culture-supporting elements of your Lean system. The subsequent chapters will provide further information to enable more effective action planning as you move forward.

Notes

1. "Yogi Berra Quotes." BrainyQuote. Accessed January 3, 2019. www. brainyquote.com/quotes/yogi_berra_391900.
2. Solomon, Jerrold M. *Who's Counting? A Real-life Account of People Changing Themselves and Their Company to Achieve Competitive Advantage.* Fort Wayne, IN: WCM Ass., 2003.
3. Solomon, Jerrold M., and Rosemary Fullerton. *Accounting for World Class Operations: A Practical Guide for Providing Relevant Information in Support of the Lean Enterprise.* Fort Wayne, IN: WCM, 2007.
4. Dinero, Donald A. *Training within Industry: The Foundation of Lean.* New York, NY: Productivity Press, 2005.
5. "Supervise." Merriam-Webster. Accessed January 3, 2019. www.merriam-webster.com/dictionary/supervise.
6. Liker, Jeffrey K., and David Meier. *The Toyota Way Fieldbook: A Practical Guide for Implementing Toyota's 4Ps.* New York, NY: McGraw-Hill, 2006. pp. 219–241
7. Herzberg, Frederick. "One More Time: How Do You Motivate Employees?" *Harvard Business Review.* August 25, 2015. Accessed January 3, 2019. https://hbr.org/2003/01/one-more-time-how-do-you-motivate-employees.

Chapter 3

The Lean Culture Foundation

The Lean Principles

Abide by the Principles

In this chapter we will review the following ten principles of Lean. Some we'll delve into deeply, but others will only be addressed at an overview level since supporting details are provided in subsequent chapters.

1. Add Value for the Customer
2. Eliminate Waste
3. People Principle #1 – Everyone
4. People Principle #2 – Respect for People
5. People Principle #3 – Teamwork
6. Process Principle #1 – Focus on the Process
7. Process Principle #2 – Optimize the Value Stream
8. Process Principle #3 – Continuous One-Piece Flow
9. Improvement Principle #1 – Scientific Thinking (PDCA)
10. Improvement Principle #2 – Continuous Improvement

Before we proceed, let's understand exactly what we mean by the word *principle*. A principle is defined as *a basic truth or theory: an idea that forms the basis of something*.[1] I believe that the ten principles, which overlap and integrate with each other, are the foundation of Lean, the *basic truths* which cannot be violated if we desire a Lean culture. Many of the Lean failure mechanisms reviewed in the previous chapter can be traced back to a misalignment with one or more of these principles.

#1 Add Value for the Customer

This first principle is the overarching principle. If your Lean strategy is not laser-focused on adding ever-increasing value for your customers, there is no need to review any of the subsequent principles; whatever culture you are forming will never resemble anything close to Lean. In his groundbreaking book, *Lean Thinking*, Jim Womack's first step of Lean is to *specify value*, and he makes it very clear who defines value. "Value can only be defined by the ultimate customer."[2] Notice the word *only* in Womack's statement. He did not state that the customer has the most input in defining value, or that we should always make sure to consider the customer's perspective heavily when we are defining value ... once again, *only* the ultimate customer can define value. If confused as to where to begin or where to refocus your Lean efforts, look at the customer. What are the customers' expectations on quality and delivery? What are your customers complaining about? What real value is the process providing to the customer?

When analyzing your processes, a great way of determining if an activity is really adding value for the customer is to ask whether your customer really wants to pay for that activity – "wants to," not "have to," pay for an activity is the criteria for this litmus test. A great way to envision this is to think about what Bruce Hamilton states in his classic *Toast Kaizen* video, where he says, *"We can't put on the bottom of the invoice this product was stored many times so we are charging you extra for it."*[3] Consider if we had to list on the invoice every single activity that the customer is paying for, most of which they would rather not be paying for since the activities add absolutely no value to what they desire. Think of all the excess motion and transportation, the waiting, the excess inventory, the scrap; this all adds time and cost but absolutely no value at all for the ultimate customer, who defines product or service value (refer to Figure 3.1 for an itemized invoice from WASTE, Inc.). Bottom line, if you keep making the customer pay for all of your waste, eventually he'll find a different supplier who won't!

At this point, we've been talking about the external customer, the paying customer who receives the product or service which your organization provides. However there are also *internal* customers, and the many internal supplier/customer connections eventually lead to the delivery of the product or service to the final external customer. Everyone in an organization has a customer. This is someone who receives your output, whatever it is that you produce, whether this is a component, sub-assembly, schedule, product design, financial statement, quotation request, or some type of information.

TO: Customer X	**ITEMIZED INVOICE**	FROM: WASTE, Inc.

"Moving Material Around" Labor Cost (Note: We have a very big facility.)	$39.24
Storage Cost (Note: We have lots of inventory! Space costs money!)	$75.26
"Waiting for Materials" Labor Cost (Note: Can't do anything without material!)	$34.89
"Tool Searching" Labor Cost (Note: Can't do the job without tools!)	$17.29
Inspection Labor Cost – 10 times (Note: Quality is #1 with us!)	$77.54
Sorting Labor Cost (Note: We'll make sure you don't get the bad parts!)	$85.26
Rework Labor Cost (Note: We eventually get it right for you! We promise!)	$62.30
Machine Changeover Cost - Standard (Note: 4 hours, usually takes longer!)	$42.26
- Additional (Note: 4 hour "Tweaking Cost")	$42.26
Product Assembly and Packaging Cost (Note: This is pretty quick!)	75 cents
Material Defects Cost (Note: We scrap it, so you don't have to!)	$29.59
Expedite Cost (We go the extra mile to make sure we're not too late!)	$82.33

Note: Your prompt payment would be appreciated. Most of our cash is tied up in our inventory, so we could use the money ASAP!!!!

Figure 3.1   Itemized Invoice from Waste, Inc.

The internal customer also has expectations based on the value which you are providing to them. One of the strengths of the value stream mapping tool is that it facilitates discussion and improvement of these internal supplier/customer connections which occur *between* the actual processing activities where the value is being added. These linkage points are a great breeding ground for wastes to grow and cause delays throughout the value stream.

Very early in my career, as a young manufacturing engineer, part of our Lean (before we called it Lean) training was to interview our internal customers as to their expectations. That simple exercise really drove home the point that we all have a customer, even if we're not the individual on the loading dock who is actually shipping the product directly to the external paying customer. A lack of internal customer awareness will result in broken links in the value chain that leads to the external customer. If you feel that you are immune to this concept, that your job really doesn't apply to this *everyone has a customer* idea, all I can say is that if you are not a component within the supplier/customer chain that leads to product or service delivery to the final customer, which ultimately results in payment, shouldn't the business need for the existence of your position be seriously questioned? Think about it!

#2 Eliminate Waste

Can all waste ever be eliminated? Unlikely … never seen it, never heard of it. This is why Lean is a never-ending journey. The question is, are we "out-improving" our competition in moving towards that ideal condition of no waste for the benefit of the customer? … And also for the benefit of our associates and society?

Taiichi Ohno originally classified waste into seven different categories. Most waste lists of today have added one additional waste to the original seven proposed by Ohno. Some sources have even added more categories; however, the original seven, plus one, provide a solid set and an effective Lean lens to look through as we observe our processes.

> **D**efects
> **O**verproduction
> **W**aiting
> **N**on-Value-adding (Extra) Processing
> **T**ransportation
> **I**nventory
> **M**otion
> **E**mployees Underutilized

When the wastes are listed as above, the first letters of each waste combine to form the word DOWNTIME. This is simply to make it easier to remember the wastes; no prioritization is intended. Also, it reminds us that unscheduled downtime results when wastes flourish in our processes.

The eight wastes should not be viewed as independent non-value-added activities, but rather as interrelated, where one waste naturally leads to the occurrence of one or more of the other wastes. This can be flipped into a positive, since if we eliminate a waste in a process, we likely will have eliminated or reduced other associated wastes. For example, if we address the root causes of defects and incorporate effective countermeasures, we also reduce the need to *overproduce* to replace the defects, thus less *inventory* is created. And we require less rework, which is non-value-adding *extra processing*, and less *transporting* of the excess inventory, which could lead to even more *defects* due to damage.

I believe the worst waste is the *employees underutilized* waste, which is the waste of unutilized talent, creativity, skills, and growth potential of every single employee; a significant portion of this book is devoted to addressing this people waste. From Ohno's original seven wastes, many consider *overproduction* as the worst waste of all, since its existence can cause most of the other wastes to occur. However, once we get past the *employees underutilized* waste, there really is little benefit in ranking or prioritizing the waste categories. Prioritization will be unique to each process and value stream being analyzed based on the needs of the final customer and internal customers. However, since it does carry the other wastes on its back, you should always be on the lookout for *overproduction*.

Many Lean references separate non-value-adding activities into two distinct categories. The first category being *non-value-adding activities* that add no customer value, serve no useful or necessary purpose in the process, and therefore are the true wastes that should be eliminated from the process. The other category is non-value-adding *but necessary activities* that don't add value for the customer, but the process still requires that this activity must be completed for some reason and therefore cannot be eliminated.

The problem with this type of non-value segregation is that once we put items into the "but necessary" category, we have a tendency to ignore them or possibly address them much later than we should have. Waste is waste! If it doesn't add value for the customer, consider it waste. We must attack our processes and eliminate the non-value where we can and continuously strive for improvement in what we can't totally eliminate at this time. Don't spend your time playing the game of "which non-value-adding bucket does this activity go into, necessary or not necessary?" It's a *wasteful* game to play!

A reference I previously cited that provides an excellent and humorous overview of the wastes is *Toast Kaizen* by the Greater Boston Manufacturing Partnership starring Bruce Hamilton. I consider this a classic introduction to Lean which should be part of every company's Lean learning plan.[4] Everyone must be fitted with their Lean goggles that focus on and detect the wastes in all company processes, and once seen, can be eliminated or reduced.

People Principles

There are a few *people principles* of Lean that, if we fail to acknowledge as fundamental truths, a Lean culture will not develop. These principles combine to form a perspective or mindset of how we view people, their abilities, their potential, and what their roles should and can be within a

Lean organization. If company leaders do not accept these basic people principles of Lean, I believe that long-term success and the development of a Lean culture is impossible … not difficult or challenging, but literally impossible!

Let's begin by making sure we are all at the same starting line – our point of reference. If not all at the same line, and heading in the same direction, obviously we will be traveling on totally different journeys. In Douglas McGregor's management classic, *The Human Side of Enterprise*,[5] he presents two models or assumptions of human nature and behavior, Theory X and Theory Y. McGregor contends that all decisions made by management are based on our assumptions about human behavior. The Theory X model represents a negative view of human nature that assumes individuals generally dislike work, are irresponsible, and require close supervision to do their jobs. The Theory Y model denotes a more positive view of human nature and assumes individuals are generally inherently industrious, creative, and able to assume responsibility and exercise self-control in their jobs.

Viewing anything as fitting solely into one of two distinct categories is often too simplistic of an analysis; however, depending on where our assumptions gravitate towards, Theory X or Y, our decision-making will be greatly influenced by this mindset. To develop an employee-driven culture of continuous improvement, it is absolutely essential to sincerely have a positive mindset regarding human nature. We must reside on the Theory Y side of the X/Y human nature fence.

In Chapter 6, where we will dive deeply into the topic of motivation and engagement, the assumptions about people are based on this Theory Y foundation. Your own fundamental belief in people will determine whether we are all at the same starting line and moving in the same direction. As McGregor proposed, all decisions made by management are based on our assumptions about human behavior. So we will now proceed on our journey, with a Theory Y mindset regarding human nature as our starting point, and begin by investigating some *people principles* of a Lean culture.

People Principle #1 – Everyone

This principle reflects back to Failure Mechanism #3, *Everyone's Job Doesn't Change*. Even prior to *Lean* being coined by Womack, Jones, and Roos in *The Machine That Changed the World*,[6] this principle was widely known and referred to as "total employee involvement," or TEI. So this is definitely not a new idea or one which was created after many years of Lean experience and learning; however, finding companies who exemplify the TEI ideal is unfortunately still a rare sighting. The words *involvement* and *engagement* are often used in the literature surrounding this topic. Engagement is a more appropriate word than involvement to describe our Lean goal and the essence of this principle. Engagement is not synonymous with involvement. Someone can be passively involved in a project or task, basically going through the motions, but you *cannot* be passively engaged.

Engagement implies an emotional attachment to the effort. It is linked to intrinsic motivation, discussed later. So this principle of "everyone" is founded on a deeper personal level than simply involvement in the process. Why the need for this distinction? It's because the task of truly engaging the workforce is a decidedly more daunting leadership challenge than just tossing your employees into teams and claiming total involvement. Engagement is more of a challenge, but it's what we need!

This principle cannot occur unless company leaders truly believe in the creativity and potential of every employee, and have a belief that within the right motivating environment, people will passionately *want* to participate in this journey, and not only contribute their hands and arms, but their minds and hearts as well ... to be engaged!

Can We Measure Engagement?

We often ignore measuring these "soft" issues due to the difficulty in developing an appropriate metric; however, the need for some form of engagement measurement is no different than the need to measure other critical aspects of your business, such as quality or on-time delivery. One option to consider is bringing someone in to perform an engagement survey, or do some research and create your own in-house version. How about getting serious about counting the number of employee ideas, number implemented, and what area of the organization they are coming from?

Another option is to hold one-on-one or small group discussions to get a quick pulse on the current state of employee engagement. Regardless of the information-gathering method, it is critical that you share and act on what you hear. Otherwise, don't do it! Not acting on what you hear would be disrespectful to the people providing the input. Respect is the topic of our next Lean principle. More to come on metrics and measurement later in this book; however, right now, get the conversation started. It is too important to delay!

Action Item – *Employee Engagement Measurement*

Add "employee engagement measurement" to the agenda of your next Lean steering committee meeting. Employee engagement is too important to assume or take for granted. As with anything else you desire to improve, you measure and monitor it.

People Principle #2 – Respect for People

Toyota created an internal document titled *Toyota Way 2001* to enable Toyota employees throughout the world to gain a uniform understanding of the guiding principles and philosophy of Toyota.[7] There are two main pillars which the principles fall within: one being *continuous improvement* and the other *respect for people*. The selection of *respect for people* as one of the two primary pillars indicates Toyota's people-centered approach that we all should emulate. Without this pillar as part of our own Lean strategies, the other pillar, continuous improvement, will suffer. In fact, it won't happen!

So why *respect for people*, which some may consider another one of those soft trivial issues? We will revisit this topic when we review motivation and demotivation in a subsequent chapter. But at this point, your answer to a simple question will provide sufficient justification for this principle. Make it personal. Are you motivated to apply your personal creativity, initiative, and heart to any effort if you are not provided the basic respect that all human beings deserve? Is it even possible to be motivated when you are treated as a *resource*, or *capital*, rather than an intelligent and creative person with a capability and desire to contribute and learn? (Refer back to Failure Mechanism #6 – Demotivation is Tolerated.) Of course not, so why shouldn't respect for all people be an unarguable, non-negotiable principle of Lean, and why should we tolerate any violation of this principle within our organizations?

This principle entails so much more than simply being nice to each other. In a Lean environment, it refers to respecting every person's intelligence, their ability to contribute, and their *right* to be successful. This is a right. Anything else would be disrespectful. It really shouldn't be difficult to provide a respectful work environment; however, unfortunately, it's also not too difficult for leaders to unintentionally or unknowingly damage an employee's initiative and morale with just a few words, sometimes even a single word, of disrespect. The following story demonstrates this point.

A Simple Act of Employee Disrespect

Earlier today, prior to an appointment, I thought I'd stop at a popular fast food chain and obtain a large cup of coffee to get me going. Immediately, I spotted a young man who worked at this popular fast food chain, who was obviously experiencing the "waste of waiting." He was waiting to mop the floor due to a liquid spill near one of the registers, and he had to wait for a customer to finish their order at the register. He suddenly had an idea, and asked the manager, "Could the other register be opened up so that I would be able to start mopping the floor in front of the other one?" Also, the spill was inconvenient for the customer, who had to crawl in front of it to place an order, and it was actually a slipping hazard, so there were multiple benefits of this employee suggestion.

The manager paused for a couple seconds, and then simply stated, "No." There was no explanation as to why, nor any other response, just "No" in a very clear, short, expressionless manner. Then she turned around and proceeded to do something else. I guess totally ignoring the question would probably have been slightly less respectful to the employee, but not by much. I immediately mentioned to the young employee that this seemed like a fantastic idea to me. It made perfect sense! *(I was not quiet.)* He then commented with that mantra of many a demotivated, non-engaged employee over the years. He simply stated, "I just work here," in a deflated, defeated tone.

The manager must have heard my comments or possibly had a change of heart, since suddenly without saying a word or providing any acknowledgement of the original employee idea, within three to five seconds the other register was miraculously successfully opened up, and I proceeded to place my order. Unfortunately, this after-the-fact action likely did little to alleviate the impact of the manager's previous *simple act of employee disrespect*.

Unless, however, the manager did in fact follow up with the employee and apologize for originally not listening and explaining the why of her initial reluctance to open the other register *(though I doubt there really was an acceptable reason)*, then thank the young employee for not only showing initiative in completing his own work, but also by identifying an issue which was clearly a customer inconvenience and safety issue. Thus, it should have been of major importance and priority. In fact, if there was a simple instant recognition policy in place (e.g., movie/dinner tickets, thank you note, $25, etc.), the young man's act should have qualified.

However, I seriously doubt that any of these positive reinforcement acts took place *(I hope I am wrong)*, but most likely, this young man unfortunately just got pushed further and embedded into the non-engaged employee category by his manager's *simple act of employee disrespect*. Please remember that the first and most important step in creating a motivating environment and motivated employees is to **quit demotivating your employees**.

I should go back to that popular fast food chain and offer some free one-on-one coaching with that manager. However, unfortunately, I believe that after stating my generous offer of assistance, this manager would pause for a couple seconds, and then simply state, "No." There would be no explanation as to why, nor any other response, just "No" in a very clear, short, expressionless manner. Then she would turn around and proceed to do something else.

The manager in this story obviously did not exhibit the leadership behavior required to develop a Lean culture of continuous improvement. She didn't need to say much. A single, stern "No" was effective in *disengaging* an employee, just the opposite of our objective in a Lean environment. Her behavior was a clear violation of the *respect for people* principle.

People Principle #3 – Teamwork

Teamwork is required! Of course, there are many instances when individual assignments are completed in the absence of a team setting, and individual accountability is a critical prerequisite for building an effective team; however, if the importance of working as a cohesive team, within departments, across departments, and even across multiple-facility locations, is not a guiding principle of a Lean strategy, waste will not only fail to be addressed, but additional wastes will develop. The before-mentioned Toyota 2001 document highlighted the importance of teamwork by listing it as one of the principles within the *respect for people* pillar.[8] Teamwork could easily fall into the overstated buzzword category of business. No one has ever argued against the cry for more teamwork in the workplace. Each work area group must work together as a team, not a collection of individual performers, to assure that they effectively meet their goals. And teamwork is even more crucial when we look beyond one's own work area team.

The value stream which transforms a product from customer order through production processing to shipment and delivery has a number of linkages and hand-offs. If the employees at these hand-off points operate as isolated islands, or silos as we typically refer to them, rather than as an integrated team, stoppages or delays will occur, not to mention the non-value-adding finger-pointing which often follows. This principle aligns with the concept of the internal customer as previously discussed within the customer principle, and supports the value stream optimization principle, which will be covered shortly.

How Do We Make It Happen?

So, what is the key to infusing teamwork into our organizations? For one thing, the work area leadership role must not only include developing an effective work area team, but strengthening internal customer/supplier connections must also be a priority. This latter component is sometimes referred to as *boundary manager* responsibilities. Also, the measurement system or key performance indicators, KPIs, must support and encourage teamwork within and across work area boundaries. We'll dive deeper into KPIs in Chapter 4.

The multi-personnel and cross-functional nature of the product fulfillment process, almost by definition, demands that teamwork be listed as one of the Lean principles. Managers and supervisors at all levels must become *team leaders*, and strive to enhance teamwork at the local level and at the value stream level as well. Lean, and business in general, is a team sport, so employ, grow, promote, and support team players, and provide the structure and systems that support the team approach.

Process Principles

Process Principle #1 – Focus on the Process

We add value for our customers through a series of processes. In a manufacturing organization we have the value-adding product-producing manufacturing process as well as a web of support processes. Therefore we should target improvements at our company processes to enable us to add ever-increasing value to our customers. The development of standardized processes is a fundamental principle of Lean; however, in a Lean environment, keep in mind that the current standard is only current until we make an improvement, then the improvement becomes the standard. Unfortunately, we've often been trying to hit multiple moving targets because of a lack of process standardization.

The Non-Lean Approach – "Whatever It Takes" Method

To help us understand this *focus on the process* principle, let's look at the often utilized *non-Lean* approach to obtaining any desired result or outcome. This can be referred to as the *"do whatever it takes, just get it done!"* method. We even have a common cliché to fall back on to justify our actions, *the ends justify the means.* Our sole focus is on the outcome, the ends. The process, or means, used to obtain the outcome has our secondary attention, if at all, and is allowed to vary considerably. Do whatever it takes NOW to get the job done! A standard, consistently applied process is not a goal in this approach.

Though we will always need folks who can jump through hoops when needed or to slay the dragon or put out the fire *(choose your favorite analogy)* to get the product out the door today, holding on to this short-term mindset as our established processing method will only produce exactly that ... short-term results, and inconsistently. Before we delve into the more effective Lean approach of building a standard robust process from which to improve upon, let's look closer at the common *whatever it takes* method by meeting a character known simply as H.J. We'll look at the ramifications of utilizing his mode of processing. Though H.J. is a fictional character, I am quite sure many of you will be able to relate to him, maybe personally.

Hoop Jumper Extraordinaire

Let me introduce you to H.J., who works for Any-Company, Inc. I'm not sure what H.J.'s real name is; everyone just calls him H.J., for hoop jumper, since he has the unique ability to jump through the necessary hoops to do whatever it takes to *get it done.* When chaos is all around Any-Company, Inc., and it looks like they'll miss a customer delivery, or fall short of reaching a desired target, H.J. swoops in to save the day ... well, most of the time. The positives from his actions, when successful, are obvious; the order was shipped on time or a goal or target was met, outcome achieved!

The other benefit of this H.J. approach is that no effort is expended in the hard work of establishing a standard process and then providing the necessary training to help assure that everyone follows the process, not to mention the time required to get folks involved so as to engender buy-in and support for the developed standard process. Plus, no process monitoring required! The H.J. method sure seems to be efficient, it is no wonder so many of our organizations follow this approach. Processing methods can vary from person to person and shift to shift; it doesn't matter. A single standard process is not what assures the outcome, H.J. does! Any one of the processes which may be utilized at the time, whether Jim's, Mary's, first shift's, second's, whichever, seem to work reasonably well most days, but that's good enough since H.J., or his small team of dragon-slaying cohorts, gets us across the finish line … usually. Now let's look at some negatives of the *just do whatever it takes* approach.

I've already been alluding to one of the negatives: H.J. will miss a hoop now and then; no one is perfect. Therefore, unfortunately, a customer may occasionally not get their parts on time or at the expected quality level. Maybe the H.J. approach was sufficient 40 years ago, but in today's hyper-competitive business environment, a missed delivery now and then is not desirable, to say the least. Another concern is that since everyone is relying on H.J. to step up and deliver the goods when needed, no one else is engaged and able to pick up the slack when H.J. is having an off day, or when H.J. is taking a well-deserved vacation.

The irony is that guys like H.J. often view this dependence on him as job security; however, in reality, for H.J. and the rest of Any-Company, Inc., this situation creates a *lessening* of employment security. The unreliability, and thus risk, of having a process which depends upon a single individual, or maybe a small group of elite hoop jumpers, is irresponsible company leadership. The problem is not with H.J. at all, for he is one of the most creative and enthusiastic folks within the company. He is excelling within the current work environment and culture, and he is a deserving recipient of many of the motivational benefits which we'll discuss later. Rather, there needs to be a fundamental change in the process of work, and that is a leadership responsibility and challenge. Every company needs guys and gals like H.J., but their enthusiasm and creativity need to be channeled in a different direction.

There's another major drawback of the H.J. approach. We must always remember that the "job" in a Lean workplace does not only entail getting today's product out the door, but also includes *improvement*, solving problems every single day, everywhere. What is the baseline for improvement in H.J.'s approach? There is no baseline. Since the process is allowed to vary, we have no standard process to improve from, or even a single process in which to focus the collective brainpower of the workforce. In addition, how do we know when we are deviating from the process? If a quality error occurs, we can't even ask the simple question, "Was the process being followed?" since there isn't a documented standard process which we all follow. Everybody does their own thing, their own way.

So as we can see, along with violating the *everyone* principle of Lean, where engagement of the whole workforce is needed, not just H.J. or a few of his friends who perform Herculean efforts on a daily basis, the *do whatever it takes* approach obviously carries with it a number of issues which are misaligned with Lean.

"Well, It Depends" Processes – How to Standardize

Sometimes, even though the critical need for standardized processes is clearly recognized and applied in many situations, we may believe that a particular process, or a portion of it, is inherently incapable of being standardized. We accept the fragility of the process as a given condition. *"Sorry, standardization is just not possible here! Definitely applies over there and for sure, for that other product, but unfortunately not in this case!"* Or, I'm told, *"It's just the nature of the beast. We just have to accept that!"* There are other clear indicators of when people have accepted a process as incapable of standardization, believing that any attempts would be futile. *"It depends,"* as in response to the question of what are the steps of the process, or how long it takes to perform a particular step. *"Well, it depends."* It may depend on who the operator is, or what lot of material is being used, or what phase the moon is in, or a host of other variables. Another indicator is when you're told that there is *an amount of feel, touch, or technique* required to complete the activity, or maybe even a little *art*, possibly bordering on *magic*.

I do not question or challenge the fact that some processes are inherently more technique-dependent than others. Hey, that's real life, but what is not in alignment with Lean is an acceptance that the process is unchangeable and incapable of progression towards a standardized state, that the process variation and resulting quality and delivery casualties are simply a way of life … *the nature of the beast*. It is exactly these fragile processes which require our full attention and concerted workforce brainpower to transform them into processes which can be consistently produced and standardized and improved. Redirecting the passion and initiative of your H.J.s to this effort is a more effective use of their skills and creativity.

A good starting point may be to observe, consider videoing, the operator with the "technique" which works best. Break down the technique into definable steps. Engage them in being the expert trainer to enable others to replicate the technique. Possibly the *technique* or *art* of the process can be eliminated through simple operator aids such as fixtures or locating pins which enable the operator to repeatedly position the part, rather than "eyeball" manual positioning. Automating or semi-automating a portion of the process may remove the *art*. For example, manually dispensing an adhesive onto a product could require some technique in order to dispense the proper amount. A semi-automatic adhesive dispenser could be utilized to only meter out the amount needed. Do something, anything, to get moving, but whatever you do, don't ever use the process itself as an excuse to violate any of the key principles of Lean – in this case, the need for standardized processes. One by one, start attacking the obstacles to enable movement, even if only miniscule incremental progress, towards the target standard condition.

Our Objective – Robust Standard Processes

Lean requires the development of a robust standard process to obtain the desired outcomes and to serve as the baseline for subsequent improvement. I've utilized the word *robust* as a descriptor for the Lean approach to achieving the desired outcomes; but what exactly do we mean by a robust process? A few synonyms for robust are stout, tough, or rugged, but one particular definition, which is borrowed from the software engineering world, most closely describes what we are searching for in a robust process. *Robust – resistant or impervious to failure regardless of user input or unexpected conditions.* Just think of a process which is so resistant to failure, that regardless of our attempts to screw it up *(us humans have a tendency to unintentionally do this now and then)*, and regardless of unexpected stuff that just happens, the process is so solid that it remains unaffected and on track. In the production of your product, regardless of whether a physical product or an information product, just think of some of the benefits of creating a robust process which is impervious to failure.

For one thing, we'll gain predictability via consistency, what does that do for us? With a robust process, we can confidently predict the outcome. We don't rely on guys or gals like H.J. to ride in on their white horse to save the day to hopefully deliver the desired outcome. The process itself gives us the confidence that this specific process will produce a specific outcome within a specific time period. Customers like this predictability also; they can believe what you tell them! Also, when there is any deviation from the process, it now becomes possible to identify the deviation and respond to it. Process deviations may involve issues such as quality, processing sequence, or timing variances. By identifying and addressing these deviations, we can quickly get back on track and move closer to our target condition. Or, from a more optimistic viewpoint, if the process deviation is a positive variant, maybe it should become part of the new standard!

Action Item – *Fixing Fragile Processes*

Identify any fragile processes where the answer to any processing question is *"Well, it depends!"* The question could be, *"How long does this step of the process take?"* or *"What is the sequence of steps?"* This is a clear signal of variability and a lack of a standard process. Create a plan to incrementally reduce process variability to move towards a stable and standardized process. Talk with and engage the experts, those actually doing the work, and work with them to identify one obstacle at a time that is preventing you from reaching your desired target condition. Begin experimenting and learning by cycling through PDCA cycles.

Paradox #1 – The Improvement/Standardize Paradox

Admittedly, at first glance, there does seem to exist a contradiction within this principle … *to continually improve, and thus change the process, we must focus on developing a standard process. Standardize* and *change* don't easily sit on the same side of the fence in our minds. We often think of standardization as a *casting in stone*. Once we have a process we desire, we want to lock it in, to make sure it never gets changed, and put policies in place so that everyone follows the process … forever. Well, that is partially correct; we do want to lock it in, but *only* until the next improvement/ change to the process. To improve effectively, it is critical that we build from a foundation of standardization. This process principle is so vital since, even if we are wildly successful in getting the workforce excited and engaged in the Lean process of continuous improvement, we're still doomed to failure if this principle is violated.

Think about Anyplace-Company, Inc. where H.J. is employed. What if the whole workforce somehow got 100 percent behind the Lean strategy and understood the need to improve their processes, but the critical need to develop a *standard* process was still a missing ingredient of the plan. Remember, the current condition at Anyplace-Company is that it has various processes in place in order to accomplish the exact same task. Joe might run the machine at a slightly different speed than Mary, or second shift has a slightly different method of setting up the equipment and running it, since I'm told, *"first shift doesn't know what the heck they are doing half the time!"* These are just a couple of the myriad of process variants.

So let's assume there are at least a dozen process variations in place for the exact same job. When the workforce starts making process improvements, we can easily imagine how these dozen processes can turn into two dozen or more since everyone will be excited about incorporating their particular ideas. And as Joe is improving his flavor of the process, he becomes even more adamant that his process is the right one. *"It was good before, and now I've made it even better!"* Multiply this by the number of other work teams at Anyplace-Company, and you get the picture – extreme chaos. Another unintended consequence is the inevitable disharmony within the workforce. *"This Lean stuff has everyone on edge. I just hope a fight doesn't break out; the only thing keeping second shift from attacking first shift is that second shift continues to squabble amongst themselves."* This is not quite the Lean culture we had hoped for when we started on our Lean journey, all because we failed to acknowledge and heed the process principle which demands that we focus the creativity and skills of the workforce on the *current standard process*.

The "Process" of Creating Standard Processes

One point which is worth injecting here and is pertinent throughout our Lean journey regards the change process itself. When transitioning from an environment which is lacking in standard work discipline to a Lean environment and mindset where the establishment of standardized work processes is a foundational element, don't expect immediate agreement as to the determination of the standard process. Many folks are passionate about the process which *they* have been utilizing over the years. This passion is an extremely positive, even essential, human element during our journey; however, when you have a team of passionate associates, many with over 20 years of experience on the job, who all walk into the room believing that the method which they have personally used for X number of years is the only "correct" way of doing it, coming to a consensus is a facilitation challenge, to say the least.

The key is to keep the focus on establishing the best standard process, based on the desired target condition, regardless of whether it may be Jim's, Mary's or John's current mode of operation. Idea evaluation is based on customer-centric metrics such as quality and delivery. Oftentimes the standard process ends up being some combination of Jim's, Mary's, and John's original process. Again, it's all about the process and what your customer wants from the process.

Conduct experiments to learn and help determine the most effective method; gather the facts. There is more to come on experimentation when discussing the next Lean principle category, *improvement principles*. The key takeaway now is to understand that many of the changes and challenges required as part of the overall Lean transformation require hard work, patience, perseverance, and even courage, and the transition to the development of standard processes is no exception. *No one ever said that this stuff was easy! Simple? Well sometimes, but even something simple can often be extremely difficult!*

Paradox #2 – The Creativity Paradox

The previous references to workforce creativity bring up another paradox that we need to come to grips with: *that workforce creativity thrives in an environment of standard work processes.* An occasional rebuttal to the concept of standard work is, *"What are you trying to do, turn us into robots?"* Just as our minds initially have trouble reconciling *standardization* with *improvement*, we struggle with *standardization* being aligned with *creativity*. However, if we look closely at our everyday activities outside of the workplace, we'll find that we utilize standard processing all the time, even with respect to our hobbies, whether fixing up old cars, gardening, painting, cooking or whatever, and this doesn't take away from our enjoyment of the task.

Since Lean is about continuous process improvement, we have the opportunity to unleash our creativity on improvement of the process ... forever. Also, since we are all focused on improving the same current standard process, which provides us a baseline to build from, we obtain the synergistic effects of the engaged team. So, a standard processing mindset and approach in no way restricts or limits employee creativity one iota. In fact, just the opposite is true; standard processes provide the focus to unleash our brainpower and skills, along with unifying the team in striving towards our target condition. And when we reach the target condition, what do we do? We create the next target condition to works towards. The creative cycle never ends.

Hidden Benefit of Standardization

There's always a hidden benefit which results from engaging the workforce in establishing a standard process. You inevitably end up improving the process. This will automatically occur to some degree, since it is reasonable to assume that at least a few of the process variations that currently exist are not very effective, so by removing those from the work equation, things get better. However, this hidden benefit goes much deeper than this quick improvement hit.

Even if our intention is to simply agree on what the standard should be so that we all can follow it, we can't help ourselves but to start thinking and questioning a few things. We naturally, maybe instinctively, question as to whether there is a better way. *"Why did we ever start doing that? That isn't really needed, is it? How does that help us meet our objectives? That doesn't make sense!"* And when properly led and facilitated, the team starts seeing the process as not only what it currently is, but what it can or should be in the future. This begins a critical restructuring of the mindset of how we look at a process, and the understanding of our roles within a Lean organization. If we can initiate this improvement mindset change, almost by accident, via the development of standard processes, just think of the possibilities when we really try!

Lesson from Another Place

Sometimes to gain the most insight into an issue, we not only need to look outside of our particular industry, but rather totally outside of industry or the business environment, so let's take a sharp turn on our Lean ride to a place outside of the business world and into the sports arena, specifically basketball. During the 1960s and part of the 1970s, John Wooden was the head basketball coach of the UCLA Bruins, and during a 12-year span, from the 1963–64 season to the 1974–75 season, his teams won ten NCAA Division I Championships. If ten championships in 12 years isn't impressive enough, in four of those years, his teams didn't lose a single game … talk about consistency! You are probably thinking, *"Impressive yes, but what could this possibly have to do with the Lean principle of focusing on the process."*

UCLA's success actually had everything to do with having a process focus. The desired outcome for the season, of course, was winning the NCAA Championship, and the shorter-term desired outcome was winning each particular game. The following is a statement from Coach Wooden from *Wooden on Leadership*, which he wrote with Steve Jamison.

> Thus, in all my years of coaching I rarely, if ever, even uttered the word *win*, talked about "beating" an opponent, or exhorted a team to be number one, including those picked by experts to win national championships.[10]

How can arguably the greatest college basketball coach in history seldom, maybe never, utter the word *win* in an effort to motivate his team? It's because Coach Wooden knew the power of having a process focus. By laser-focusing on the process, you therefore have the best chance of obtaining the desired outcomes. (And for the record, Wooden's success on the basketball court dwarfs in comparison with how he prepared his players for success in their lives after basketball.)

Did Coach Wooden not care about the outcome? Of course he cared deeply about the outcome. Just as in industry, it would be ridiculous to state that we need to only focus on the process and not even concern ourselves as to whether we gain the outcome. Try telling your customer that you really aren't too concerned about delivering their product on time, that your only concern is the process. The understanding and clear definition of the desired outcome is absolutely critical, but only by focusing our efforts on continuously improving the process do we obtain the outcomes of quality, delivery, and cost for our customers and create a fulfilling and worthwhile work environment for our associates. The key point is *how* we obtain the desired outcomes, and John Wooden – and successful leaders in all walks of life – understands the principle of *focus on the process*. Once again, let me make it clear: they know exactly the outcomes and results which they are striving for; otherwise, they wouldn't be able to effectively focus the team on the process. I've probably overemphasized this last point since I've heard it said that Lean is less concerned about the outcome, and more concerned on the process. I feel that this is a major misinterpretation of the *focus on the process* principle. Again, of course we want the outcome, but how we obtain it makes all the difference in the world. Now what if we don't reach the desired outcome? We then learn from the experience and reflect and adjust the process as needed.

This cycle of process focus and improvement, then evaluation of actual results or outcomes, and then subsequent learning and adjustment, is the never-ending process of PDCA, which is one of the foundational elements of our next Lean principle category, the *improvement principles*. However, before we get there, we have a couple more *process principles* to cover.

In this section we've looked at the two processing extremes, very little if any standard processing on the one end, and at the opposite extreme, the Lean approach of utilizing standard processes as a foundational component of the Lean strategy. (Refer to Figure 3.2 for a standard processing scale.)

Action Item – *Process Standardization*

Get the Lean steering committee together, and reflect upon and discuss where your company lies between these two extremes. As needed, develop plans to engage the workforce in the development of this core Lean cultural element, the establishment of standard processes from which to improve.

Process Principle #2 – Optimize the Value Stream

The value stream: all actions, both value-adding and non-value-adding, required to bring a product or product family through the main flows of design, information, and physical transformation. This principle of value stream optimization requires us to look beyond our own individual place within the value stream to assure that our improvement activities optimize the whole system and we aren't just moving the waste to another location within the system due to working in a vacuum.

The Ninth Waste – False Improvement Waste

I often add a ninth waste to the standard eight previously listed: *making a "local" or departmental "improvement," but where the waste has simply been moved to a different location in the value stream.* Sure, this activity can be placed within the category of non-value-adding processing, or extra

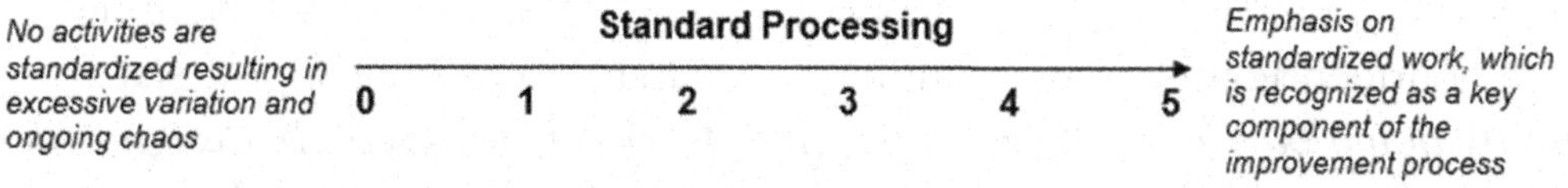

No activities are standardized resulting in excessive variation and ongoing chaos

Standard Processing

0   1   2   3   4   5

Emphasis on standardized work, which is recognized as a key component of the improvement process

Figure 3.2 Standard Processing Scale

processing as sometimes labeled, but I believe it deserves its own billing since we are actually disguising a waste under the veil of improvement. What can be more non-Lean than doing that? Simple example: purchasing has made a siloed "improvement" by changing to a different supplier who can provide the parts at a less expensive price. But now, production must fight every day with the quality issues from the parts produced by the new supplier! *(I know, impossible, could never possibly happen at your organization.)* It's only from the perspective of the functional silo of purchasing that this is deemed an improvement. Our objective is to tear down this silo mindset so that everyone can focus on optimizing the whole system, the value stream.

The value stream optimization principle presents one of the many challenges of Lean. It's necessary to focus on the minute details of each individual process to root out and eradicate waste, while at the same time maintain a broader system or value stream perspective. Focusing on only one OR the other is insufficient, both a detail AND broad viewpoint is needed. A value stream perspective requires *horizontal (systems) thinking* where we focus across or through the vertical functional areas of the organization. These functional areas often act as independent silos whose primary goal seems to be building increasingly higher silos rather than looking horizontally to their suppliers and customers.

Tearing Down the Silos

Optimizing the value stream may actually require an obliteration of these separated functional fiefdoms in order to directly connect the value-adding steps of the value stream. Where this is possible, we move closer to the ideal of continuous flow, our next Lean principle. The value stream focus also alters leadership roles and responsibilities, especially at the front-line leadership level. Much more to come on this topic.

In *Lean Thinking*, Jim Womack's next step after *specify value* is to *identify the value stream*.[11] Though the terminology of the value stream may have been popularized by Womack and later by Mike Rother and John Shook in their book on value stream mapping, *Learning to See*,[12] this really isn't a new concept to the business world. Point #9 of Dr. Deming's "The Fourteen Points," which outline his management philosophy, states *"Break down barriers between departments. People in research, design, sales, and production must work as a team, to foresee problems of production and in use that may be encountered with the product or service."*[13] Deming even created a flow diagram which depicts the basic structure and system integration of our modern-day value stream map.

So what's been our problem? What has kept us from effectively optimizing the value stream? The fact is that traditionally our organizations are perfectly structured to encourage a functional, silo mentality. Personnel reporting arrangements and even the facility layout often support a functional design, and our measurement systems and defined roles and responsibilities aren't aligned well with the value stream optimization principle. We'll delve into these root causes in the subsequent sections of this chapter and in Chapter 5 on key roles and responsibilities.

Process Principle #3 – Continuous One-Piece Flow

This principle states that the ideal process and value stream can be envisioned as continuous one-piece flow, where the product or service flows from value-adding step to value-adding step with no stoppages, scrap, or backflows. This principle aligns with the *eliminate waste* principle since a process would naturally advance towards the continuous flow ideal as waste is removed from the process. There are a number of reasons why the product or service currently stalls, waits, and collects, prior to being processed by the next downstream value-adding step of the process.

The Batching Problem

One major cause of delay is batch processing. Whenever we transfer products in batches rather than one piece, lead times are increased since product sits and waits for further processing until the whole batch is completed. The resulting overproduction creates excess inventory, which requires more transportation and space. Because of the time lag between when an item is processed to when it is processed at the subsequent step, uncovering the root causes of any quality issues becomes more difficult, adding more non-value-adding investigation time and rework, and likely more scrap. And, of course, preparing and moving all of these batches around requires labor, thus productivity decreases.

With all of these downsides of batch processing, why do we do it? Why do we sometimes insist that it makes more sense to process items in nice bundles before initiating subsequent processing? For one, the human desire to batch is such a deeply ingrained and prevalent mindset that it seems to be a component of our DNA. Besides this apparently instinctive desire to batch, there are other more definable conditions to recognize and address. For example, the physical layout itself can force batching. If sequential value-adding steps are 200 feet away from each other rather than two feet, it is doubtful we'll transfer a single item at a time; we'll likely collect a skid's worth or more prior to transport. Until the physical layout is modified, a significant transition to one-piece flow by reducing the transfer batch size will not occur.

Long changeover times on equipment will also force batching. Due to a long changeover process, we run a large batch of product prior to changing over to run the next product; otherwise, we'd run out of capacity if we attempted one piece, or even small-lot production, with our lengthy changeovers. We'd spend all of our time changing over the equipment! This type of batching not only drives up inventory and extends lead times, but our flexibility in adjusting to changing customer demands is severely restricted. For an interesting and thorough review of batching versus one-piece flow, I suggest Charles Protzman's book, written with Joe McNamara and Dan Protzman, *One-Piece Flow vs. Batching: A Guide to Understanding How Continuous Flow Maximizes Productivity and Customer Value.*[14]

I know some of you are thinking, *"This may make sense for some processes, but not ours. Heck, we have 16 cavity injection molds, and it would be ridiculous to have 16 separate single cavity molds running in 16 separate presses!"* You know what, you are exactly right! That would be ridiculous based on the capability and technology of your current equipment. Each situation is unique and must be analyzed to determine your current condition and what your next target condition should be as you strive towards the ideal of continuous flow.

In this injection molding example, your 16-cavity mold dictates the number of units produced per cycle; however, can you reduce your *transfer batch*? How many cycles do you run prior to product arriving at the next value-adding step, such as a downstream assembly operation? Do you fill up a skid, move it to another area where it waits in queue until it finally gets processed further? Or, do the 16 freshly molded parts drop onto a short conveyor which leads directly to an assembly cell where the next value-adding step is completed? You tell me, which scenario is closer to the ideal of continuous flow? (Note: A discussion of the use and misuse of conveyors is outside the scope of this book; however, a key word regarding conveyors in production operations is *short*.)

Equipment and Tooling to Facilitate One-Piece Flow

This injection molding example is based on the assumption of an existing process, but what if you have a new product in the development stage? How does the principle of *continuous one-piece flow* affect your planning and process design? Lean product development is an extensive topic which we won't elaborate on here; however, if we abide by the *optimize the value stream* principle and develop the process and product design based on the principle of *continuous flow*, we may develop alternatives which are quite different than the current 16-cavity mold standard. For example, two eight-cavity molds may balance better with the downstream assembly steps, so more of a *continuous flow* can be maintained. And possibly, the quality issues may be significantly reduced with this option due to the reduced variability across cavities, thus decreasing the stoppages and delays of addressing the defects.

Assembly operations can have a similar process design decision to make. Do we purchase the super-duper 24-station automatic assembly machine, or three smaller eight-station machines? Even though the cost of a single 24-station machine would likely be less than the total cost of the multiple eight-station machines, the evaluation is not simply an initial purchase financial one when you consider the principle of *continuous one-piece flow*. The three eight-station machines can possibly be incorporated into three separate production lines which would move each production line closer to our ideal of one-piece flow processing. There are other advantages of the multiple-machine approach, but we'll limit our focus here on aligning with the principle of *continuous one-piece flow*.

These are only a couple examples where the principle of *continuous one-piece flow* and the previously reviewed *optimize the value stream* affect equipment and tooling design decisions involving support functions such as engineering and machine design. This highlights the point of the *everyone* principle, where, regardless of position within the organization, all personnel must be engaged and thinking Lean!

The "One-Piece" Ideal

The principle of continuous one-piece flow applies to any processing environment. Having the product flow continuously from value-adding step to value-adding step results in the shortest lead time, highest quality, and lowest possible cost; however, the current process capabilities and even technological constraints definitely affect not only your current condition, but also what your next target condition should be. You may even have to spend some time defining your "one piece" that you are attempting to continuously flow. The key point is that you should never allow the concept or idea of *one-piece* provide an excuse of, *"That just doesn't work here. We don't make pieces!"*

The previous injection molding example is actually inspired by an experience I had while working for a company whose value stream included injection molding, assembly, and packaging operations. These operations were previously physically separated into departments prior to consolidation into a multiple workcell arrangement. After the team implemented the first few workcells, a manager said to me, *"Dave, you aren't doing Lean with these cells since you don't have one-piece flow. You have a 16-cavity mold and you still have small batches between molding and assembly, and then again, between assembly and packaging within the cell."* His motivation for stating this was clearly his desire to justify his status quo mindset of, *"I told you Lean doesn't apply here!"* Well, at that time, I chose not to educate him on the true definition of Lean/continuous improvement and simply stated that, based on his definition of Lean, I guess he was absolutely correct. I suggested that we take a look at what the team actually accomplished and are continuing to improve upon while we stand here engaged in this wasteful conversation *(The "wasteful conversation" statement was not actually said, but I should have said it!)*, regardless of your belief that this is not defined as Lean.

Compared with the previous functional, departmental, batch-processing environment, the team's new cellular design had reduced both the lead time and work-in-process inventory by over 50 percent; rejects have been reduced by 14 percent. The flow distance has been reduced from 280 feet to 34 feet, thus improving productivity due to the reduced excess transportation and motion. The number of transactions has been reduced by at least 67 percent, and due to the reduced overall lead time, we will begin offering customers a shorter delivery lead time for some products, which is expected to result in an increase in sales.

So my final statement to the individual who was wedded to the status quo was:

> *Regardless of what you choose to label what we are doing, we have clearly moved closer to the ideal of continuous flow, which has enabled all of the before-mentioned benefits plus more, and*

the engaged team continues to improve the developed design even further. So all in all, I think this is a pretty good thing, even if you don't want to call this thing Lean!

He never brought up the topic again; in fact, he soon left the company. My assumption was that he realized that his mindset would prevent him from ever becoming a Lean leader in this organization. This is an outcome which does occur at times when you are committed to developing a Lean culture of continuous improvement within your organization.

Action Item – *Observe the Flow, or Lack Thereof*

Observe your product flow and look for areas where the product piles up and where you process the product in batches and move products from value-adding step to value-adding step in large batches. Start digging into the root causes of this batch type of processing. Rather than quickly concluding that any move towards one-piece flow just can't be more effective since our process really is different, set up some experiments to learn and to determine if an alternative approach would be beneficial. You may be surprised; in fact, I am sure of it!

Improvement Principles

We will now look at a couple improvement principles of Lean. We conduct our experiments by following a logical and robust step-by-step process. Improvement in a Lean environment is not a free-for-all where everyone is doing their own thing and making changes in an unorganized, unintegrated, and totally random manner. Rather, there is a defined process as to how processes are improved. This is where we will begin, by looking at the Lean principle of *scientific thinking*.

Improvement Principle #1 – Scientific Thinking (PDCA)

Numerous sources will cite the scientific method or scientific thinking as a key Lean principle or a foundation concept of Lean, but what is this really referring to? So we should think like scientists? Does it just mean to be curious and inquisitive, the way we'd imagine a scientist would be? These are indeed admirable qualities which we all should possess; however, when we refer to *scientific thinking* with respect to Lean, we are referring to a scientific *process*, a process which may be repeated hundreds of times in a single day at a Lean organization.

Rather than reviewing the long history of scientific thinking which many believe originated with Aristotle, let's quickly get a working explanation of the processing steps of what is commonly referred to as the *scientific method*. Let's do this within the context of our desire to make an improvement to a process or system. The exact number of steps of the *scientific method* may vary slightly in the literature; however, they all encompass the following basic processing steps:

1. It all starts with observation. This immediately fits well within our Lean mindset, since we know we must go to the *gemba*, the real place, the place where value is being created, to observe directly and learn.
2. The next step is to propose a hypothesis. We propose that if we do X, we expect Y to occur. For our purposes, we can consider this to be a prediction; what do we expect to happen once we initiate some action or change?
3. We then want to design an experiment to test our hypothesis. *Experiment* is the correct terminology, even in a manufacturing environment. If we are going to make any change to a process, it's usually not advisable to make changes based purely on assumption.
4. We then obviously must conduct the experiment.
5. Then we evaluate and analyze the results of the experiment. Is the original hypothesis accepted or rejected? What did we learn?
6. If necessary, propose and test a new hypothesis. And as always, we recommend that the process is directly observed by going back to the *gemba*.

Many of you may already see parallels to a problem-solving process that you are familiar with, the PDCA (Plan-Do-Check-Act) cycle, which is also known as the Shewhart or Deming cycle. Deming preferred *study* rather than *check*, and thus PDSA. Those who have a Six Sigma background may cite the DMAIC process. These and other variants of the process are all built upon the basic steps of the scientific method. (Refer to Figure 3.3 for the problem-solving and improvement process.) We'll standardize on the PDCA process for purposes of our discussion here and throughout this book.

In Figure 3.3, notice that the "**C**heck" step of PDCA states to verify the results *and* the process. Remember, the *focus on the process* principle

P	**Define**	1. Clarify the Problem
	Measure	2. Break Down the Problem
		3. Set the Target Condition
	Analyze	4. Conduct Root Cause Analysis
		5. Develop Countermeasures
D	Improve	6. Implement Countermeasures
C	**Control**	7. Monitor both the Results and Processes
A		8. Standardize (Continue Experiments)

Figure 3.3   Problem-Solving and Improvement Process

demands that we create a robust process to obtain the desired result. The *means* do matter with Lean, not just the *ends*.

The WHY of PDCA

So what does the PDCA process do for us? Why is it so important? As already indicated, not having a robust standard improvement process would directly conflict with the *focus on the process* principle. Without a standard process for our improvement efforts, the results will vary significantly in effectiveness. In some cases we likely wouldn't be addressing root causes and subsequently will only be treating the symptoms of the problem; thus, any countermeasures put in place will not provide the desired results, at least not for very long. In other cases, we'll bypass the standardization required and any countermeasures will also not survive the test of time.

The PDCA process assures that we are thorough and rigorous in our improvement and problem-solving efforts. You can think of it as a type of checklist to assure you don't hastily try something in a random trial and error basis, where the disappointing outcome is that no learning has occurred, only confusion. Keep in mind that the outcome of the PDCA process may only be exactly that … learning. Often you need to structure your experiments not to test a proposed solution, but rather to deepen the understanding of the problem or situation. This will subsequently help you develop effective countermeasures. As you know, some problems are tough to crack. Move towards the target condition via multiple PDCA cycles to gain knowledge, learning your way to improvement. This brings us to our final Lean principle, which requires that we move towards the ideal of *continuous improvement*, where we'll expand on this discussion of repeated PDCA cycles.

Improvement Principle #2 – Continuous Improvement

This principle addresses the *frequency* of improvement activities. Do we only work on improvement every once in a while, or only when initiated by a major customer issue, or when we can manage to find the time in our busy schedules? What we need is a proactive and ongoing attack on eliminating waste from all company processes to add ever-increasing value for our customers. We must develop systems to enable and support these activities and everyone's job must be redesigned to include an *improvement* component. We must transform from an environment of primarily episodic improvement events or projects to a work environment where the "job" entails both performing and *improving* the work on a daily basis.

Some of you may be thinking,

> *Daily improvement makes sense for the incremental, kaizen, types of changes, but some of our problems are very difficult; it takes some time to figure out how to solve some of these issues. Improvement like this will naturally be more occasional rather than anything close to continuous, wouldn't it?*

My answer would be "Yes" from an improvement *solution* perspective. Some challenging problems do take an extended length of time to solve. Challenges come in all sizes, simple to extremely complex. But let's change our perspective slightly and take a look at the *process* of making the improvements rather than simply looking at the frequency of the solutions.

WARNING: If you work in a manufacturing organization, this next statement will initially seem ridiculous, but read the section and give it some time to sink in prior to outright rejection. (Remember, in all things Lean, we must keep an open mind!)

Manufacturing Needs to be More Like R&D!

What really is the research and development (R&D) process? Isn't it a series of PDCA learning cycles? Value is being added when learning has occurred that moves the researcher towards the desired research target.

A goal of "Lean R&D" can be considered an increase in frequency, speed, and the amount of learning gained via these continuous PDCA cycles. The desired research discovery or solution may be multiple years, maybe even decades away, but by developing an experiment to gain further insight, the researcher takes one step closer to the ultimate objective. Then, after being enlightened by the knowledge gained from the experiment, the researcher does it all over again, and then again, and then again. You get the point. The process of improvement is continuous. The *improvement* may actually be a countermeasure to provide the solution to the problem, or it may be an experiment to gain knowledge. In either case, we are improving towards our objective.

This has parallels to how Mike Rother describes Toyota's improvement process in his book *Toyota Kata*:

> The desire to turn rapid PDCA cycles has an influence on the nature of the steps that we take toward a target condition. The idea is to not wait until you have a perfect solution, but to take the step now, with whatever you have, so we can see further. A provisional step now is preferable to a perfect step later, and investing in prototypes and experiments up front, which may seem like extra expense, often reduces overall cost in the long run.[15]

As Rother states, don't wait until you have a perfect solution! Individuals and teams often stall in their improvement efforts due to their search for this "perfect" solution. Sometimes the path to an effective solution is too foggy to currently see, regardless of the amount of brainpower on hand, and the best thing you can do is to try something that will move you incrementally forward into the current unknown. The team attitude needs to change from, *"Woe are we; this problem is just too complicated; there could be a hundred causes to this problem,"* to a more experimental mindset of, *"Let's simplify this problem by learning more; what experiment can we perform to increase our understanding? What can we try and what do we expect to occur?"* Besides preventing the stalling of forward progress, consider some additional benefits of this scientific and experimental approach.

Experimentation and People

"Sure, let's give it a try and see if your hypothesis is confirmed!" An experimental work environment significantly changes our reactions concerning a proposed improvement action. Most people are more willing to agree to an *experiment* even if it may not be one's own recommended next step. Hearing the team leader state, *"Since a majority of the team is leaning in this direction, let's try it and see what we can learn, even if the expected outcome may not be obtained,"* is a lot easier to swallow than, *"A majority of us are very confident that this is going to solve our problem so this is what we are going to do."* As teams are addressing obstacles, it becomes easier to gain consensus when the improvement process involves a series of PDCA experimental cycles.

"Failure" Redefined

In a later chapter we will address resistance to change and the role that *fear* plays. One of the fears which we can probably all relate to is the *fear of failure*. However, in an experimental environment, failure has less of a debilitating connotation since it really has little or no meaning. Through our series of experiments, we can expect many of our hypotheses to be refuted. The experiment really hasn't *failed* since the knowledge gained has provided insights to help us move forward more effectively. In fact, if someone states, *"See, I told you it wouldn't work!"* my response would be, *"I expected that the prediction of the outcome may prove incorrect. Now let's discuss what we have learned so that we can continue to move forward."* Just think of the creativity and team synergy that can be unleashed in an open environment where *fear of failure* is not even an applicable concept!

So is there such a thing as a *failed experiment* in a Lean environment? If the PDCA process was not rigorously being followed and experiments were in reality just totally random "trial and error" attempts where very little learning has taken place, I'd think *failure* might be an applicable tag. Even if you do somehow stumble upon a solution via this random non-scientific approach, I would still have a difficult time calling this a *successful* experiment since you've lost the cause-effect relationship. The word *experiment* is probably not even appropriate.

In summary of our last Lean principle, which states that our improvement activities should be continuous in nature rather than episodic, even with issues which obviously don't have daily, short-term solutions, some of which may even have similarities to the types of long-term challenges being addressed in our R&D labs, the principle of *continuous improvement* still applies since the daily *learning* is the improvement. The improvement *process* requires frequent and rapid PDCA cycles to move us closer to our objective. So whether making incremental or breakthrough improvements to our processes, and whether our challenges are simple or complex, we must develop effective systems to support this need for continuous improvement.

Lean Principles Summary

In this chapter we've reviewed ten principles of Lean, two of which can be considered baseline or fundamental principles, *add value for the customer* and *eliminate waste*. We then followed with three *People Principles*, three *Process Principles*, and two *Improvement Principles*. These ten principles are not simply a random set of characteristics or features of Lean, but are a set of fundamental beliefs which provide the foundation for the Lean culture. Everything is built upon these *basic truths* of Lean. All company leaders must commit to these principles. One of the root causes of *Failure Mechanism #1 – Wrong or Incomplete Definition of Lean*, reviewed in Chapter 2, is based on a lack of understanding, agreement, or commitment to these Lean guiding principles. Violations or misalignment to any of the principles must be highlighted and addressed. Just as a house will crumble with a weak foundation, the Lean culture will crumble without commitment to the foundation of Lean principles.

Notes

1. "Principle." Merriam-Webster. Accessed January 3, 2019. www.merriam-webster.com/dictionary/principle.
2. Womack, James P., and Daniel T. Jones. "Introduction." In *Lean Thinking: Banish Waste and Create Wealth in Your Corporation*, 16. New York, NY: Simon & Schuster, 1996.
3. *Toast Kaizen*. USA: Greater Boston Manufacturing Partnership, 2008. DVD.
4. Ibid.
5. McGregor, Douglas. *The Human Side of Enterprise*. New York, NY: McGraw-Hill, 1960.
6. Womack, James P., Daniel T. Jones, and Daniel Roos. *The Machine That Changed the World*. New York, NY: HarperCollins Publishers, 1991.

7. Liker, Jeffrey K., and Michael Hoseus. "The DNA of Toyota Lies in Its Culture." In *Toyota Culture: The Heart and Soul of the Toyota Way*, 12–16. New York, NY: McGraw-Hill, 2008.

8. Ibid.

9. "Robust." Women's Rights Dictionary Definition | Women's Rights Defined. Accessed January 4, 2019. www.yourdictionary.com/robust.

10. Wooden, John R., and Steve Jamison. "Introduction." In *Wooden on Leadership*, 8. New York, NY: McGraw-Hill, 2005.

11. Womack, James P., and Daniel T. Jones. "The Value Stream." In *Lean Thinking: Banish Waste and Create Wealth in Your Corporation*, 37–49. New York, NY: Simon & Schuster, 1996.

12. Rother, Mike, and John Shook. *Learning to See Value-stream Mapping to Create Value and Eliminate Muda*. Cambridge, MA: Lean Enterprise Institute, 1999.

13. Deming, W. Edwards. "There is no such Thing as Instant Pudding (Deming's 14 Points for Management)." In *The Essential Deming: Leadership Principles from the Father of Quality*, compiled by Joyce Orsini, PhD, 134–6. New York, NY: McGraw-Hill, 2013.

14. Protzman, Charles, Joe McNamara, and Dan Protzman. *One-Piece Flow vs. Batching: A Guide to Understanding How Continuous Flow Maximizes Productivity and Customer Value*. Boca Raton, FL: CRC Press, 2016.

15. Rother, Mike. "Problem-solving and Adapting: Moving Toward a Target Condition." In *Toyota Kata Managing People for Improvement, Adaptiveness and Superior Results*, 129–74. New York, NY: McGraw-Hill, 2010.

Chapter 4

Key Support Systems, Tools, and Practices

Key Support Systems and a Focus on KPIs

There are a number of support systems which are critical components of an effective Lean strategy. The use of the word *support* is to indicate that these systems and related policies are in place to *assist* the primary value-adding flow and *enable* the value-adding personnel of the organization to be more effective in their roles. For example, in a manufacturing organization, the primary flow of value-adding production processes is integrated with support systems such as maintenance, purchasing, accounting, measurement, information technology systems, and people-related systems such as hiring, onboarding, performance evaluation, promotion, compensation, recognition, and training. Regardless of the specific system, a key word is *alignment* … alignment with your strategy and vision, and designed to optimize the value stream in which they are an integral part. Any misalignment would be a violation of the *optimize the value stream* principle. For example, if the hiring process produces new managers who are not effective team leaders, both within their work function and across to their internal customer/supplier teammates, this would not only be a violation of the *optimize the value stream* principle, but the *teamwork* principle as well.

It's not only that an inadequate support system won't be capable of encouraging and enabling the right Lean behaviors, but when there's misalignment, workforce trust in the Lean strategy will erode due to the conflicting messages. Without this trust, a Lean culture will crumble! How can this erosion of trust occur? Just as in our personal lives, if I announce to you that I will do something for you, but then proceed to do just the opposite, it's kind of tough for you to trust me. That's really what we are doing if we have systems which are misaligned with the Lean principles which we espouse. This is textbook *organizational hypocrisy*. We proclaim that we'll be traveling in a certain direction for the benefit of all, yet allow a system or policy to be in place which clearly is sending us on a different route in a completely different direction. For example, we value teamwork, but if we promote the prima donna who is the worst team player in the organization to a leadership role, we're hypocrites. There's no way to explain away this misaligned behavior and decision; the promotion system needs to be fixed. In this section we'll take a closer look at one particular vital system which must *enable* Lean, not disable it: our KPI measurement system.

Key Performance Indicators (KPIs)

You have to keep score. This may be common sense, but many companies have woefully inadequate scoring systems or no scoring system at all. It's like driving your vehicle with a blank dashboard. Some organizations have KPI systems which actually drive the wrong behavior. The analogy for this would be like sinking a foul shot in basketball but the scoreboard takes away a point rather than adding to your score. Doesn't make much sense, but that's basically what can happen with a conflicted KPI system. I don't believe anyone consciously sets out to create a KPI which is in conflict with their Lean strategy, but in practice, this can occur unless we carefully design and monitor the system to assure alignment.

KPI System Purpose

A good starting point is for us to be clear on the basic purpose of the KPI system. This clarity of understanding is a significant factor in determining whether your measurement system will be effective or not. The image of a compass is sometimes utilized to depict the KPI purpose as a direction-setting and monitoring mechanism. It shows us the way. Are we on the right path and moving in the right direction? Do we need to make any course adjustments due to unexpected obstacles? Have we improved our location over time as anticipated? Our KPIs provide vital feedback which enables us to make informed decisions regarding our planned actions.

The KPI system and its display format should be capable of providing immediate answers to the following two questions. In the next section, these two baseline questions will be expanded into additional questions:

- Are we on schedule today?
- Are we improving over time?

The first question addresses our ability to meet today's commitments. The second question can be considered a longer-term inquiry since, if we do not continually improve our processes, *tomorrow* we likely won't even have the opportunity to ask the first question; the competition will have passed us by. Our KPI system should effectively address both of these questions.

A KPI dashboard may appear to be a static display of various numbers, charts, and graphs; however, it must provide feedback for action. It should be anything but static. If so, it is basically worthless. The KPI board will be relegated to *organizational wallpaper.* (We'll elaborate on creating effective visual KPI boards in the next section.) Organizational wallpaper may be nice to look at, but does absolutely nothing to help you move towards your next target condition and meet your objectives. I notice plenty of it in many companies, but wallpaper is not a Lean tool or technique. Our visual systems must be "action systems." Key performance indicators provide critical feedback information. The word *key* kind of implies this.

Effective KPI Components

An effective KPI system can be broken down into the following three key success components:

1. We must have the right KPI. It must provide information which, if accurate and utilized properly, will move us in our intended direction. It must drive the right behavior.
2. We need confidence that the KPI information is accurate so that this information can be used to make effective decisions regarding actions. Inaccurate input equals faulty conclusions resulting in ineffective decisions.
3. We have to properly utilize the information which the system is providing. Even if it's the right KPI and the information provided is clear and accurate, if we don't understand how to use it properly, we'll still make poor decisions.

The Right KPI

I don't mean to disappoint, but unfortunately, there are no magic KPIs that will assure Lean supremacy for all those who prominently display them in the workplace. However, there are some common people and customer-centric categories that all KPIs should fall within. Let's briefly look at each one individually, which are listed in order of priority.

People

It should not be surprising that the first metric category is *people* since the engagement and growth of every member of the organization is fundamental to our Lean journey. Refer back to the people principles reviewed earlier. This category could include a variety of people-related issues such as safety, morale, cross-training status, or employee growth plans.

Quality

In today's competitive environment, providing quality products and services to customers should be considered the admission ticket for being in business. Besides the competitive ramifications of not providing the paying customer what they had expected *(They just might go ahead and find someone else who can!)*, quality issues and the resultant rework all contribute to performance issues in the final two KPI categories.

Delivery and Cost

Delivery is negatively affected by the delays which result from quality problems, and cost is negatively affected not only by the cost of the scrapped product, but often there is a hidden factory filled with personnel who inspect, sort, scrap, return, and coordinate a multitude of wasteful activities which are consequences of quality issues.

Customers of course want their products or services provided on time. I doubt this is a new revelation to any of you. By focusing on reducing value stream lead times, it is possible to provide deliveries in a significantly shorter customer lead time than the competition. Think about the potential sales and market share ramifications if the industry standard is 4–6-week delivery to the customer after receipt of order, but you are able to reliably provide product within three days? You don't only beat the industry standard; you establish the industry standard and own more of the market. Is Lean a sales and growth strategy? You bet it is!

Cost is primarily a result of the performance of the previous three categories. For example, a company currently mired in quality issues most likely is also mired in ever rising costs, and dedicating the workforce to sorting, rework, or scrap activities will do nothing to help any type of productivity index. Processing waste adds time and cost. A continual effort in eliminating waste from our processes will naturally improve the cost picture.

As you can see, there is nothing magical or enlightening about these four categories. They have existed for many years, even prior to our use of the word *Lean* coined by Womack and Jones.[1] An argument can possibly be made that the focus on people metrics is new; however, an *underutilized* concept or principle rather than anything *new* would be more accurate. And customers have always wanted a *quality* product delivered *on time* at a competitive price appropriate for the value being provided.

KPIs versus Metrics

So how is it even possible to have the wrong KPI in place if there are a clear set of categories to work with? One issue arises due to the lack of understanding between key performance indicators versus other secondary or supporting metrics or indicators. All KPIs are metrics, but not all metrics deserve to be elevated to the status of key performance indicator. A secondary indicator is also monitored and decisions made based on status, but if erroneously considered a KPI, can actually drive the wrong behavior. These secondary metrics should always be evaluated based on their effect on the KPIs which depict performance and progress to goals. The KPIs serve as our compass. They show us the way and keep us on track. Let's try to provide some clarity with an actual example.

Machine Utilization – Metric or KPI?

Consider the indicator *machine utilization*. We most definitely need to have a pulse on our machine utilization for capacity reasons. Critical decisions on capital equipment purchases or where to focus improvement activities are influenced by information that our machine utilization data is providing, so what could possibly be the negative aspect of a utilization indicator? Following is a personal example of an experience in which machine utilization was incorrectly being used as a key performance indicator.

I was called into a company to assist them in reducing changeover times. I spent some time talking to the area supervisor, who showed me the machine utilization charts prominently posted on the wall. Since our focus was to be on changeovers, I asked questions about his current changeover times and batch sizes and how scheduling is coordinated with the downstream internal customer, whether visual kanban or other replenishment mechanism. I won't elaborate on his specific answers; however, his response was provided in a cursory, not rude, but obviously in a distracted manner. What was distracting him? It was his machine utilization KPI.

Reducing setup times or batch sizes was not on his KPI radar screen at all. Coordinating with downstream internal customers did not have any performance ramifications in his mind. He batched as many orders as possible and ran his machines as long as possible to minimize the number of changeovers per day. This standard practice surely helped him keep his utilization numbers up, regardless of the mounds of inventory and the resultant long customer lead times which this policy generated, not to mention the cost and quality consequences. And since those mounds of inventory were produced for future orders based on a forecast, I am confident that some of it ended up being the wrong inventory which eventually moved into the *obsolete* or *expired* category. There's one thing I know about forecasts; they are always wrong. *(Feel free to disagree with me, but you will be the first.)* There is actually one other thing that I know about forecasts. By shortening the planning horizon, the forecast accuracy improves. Naturally if your crystal ball doesn't have to look as far into the future, it gets a little less cloudy. With Lean, as we continually shorten our order fulfillment lead times by eliminating waste, we can move closer to maybe being able to throw that crystal ball in the trash. Anyway, back to my story.

The supervisor's performance was measured on keeping those machines running, plain and simple. *"If we have no current orders, just run something. We'll eventually need it. If the machines aren't running, they aren't making any money, right?"* Though this may sound somewhat logical, this performance metric was clearly driving the wrong behavior and violated many principles of Lean. For one, this approach did not optimize the value stream; the *local* optimization, as defined by high machine utilization, only added waste to the overall value stream … excess inventory, overproduction, and transportation to name a few. I left that company suggesting that until they address their performance scoreboard, they're going to have a rough time getting any traction with changeover reduction efforts. Some of the key players won't even be listening to you since *machine utilization* will have their undivided attention. In addition, the mixed signals from having a KPI which is driving you in a direction which conflicts with your Lean strategy will inevitably increase concerns of credibility and trust, probably even competence.

Now let's imagine how this experience may have played out, with the same machine utilization chart, but if it was being used as a secondary indicator only, not a key performance indicator.

"Well Mr. Supervisor, what's this machine utilization chart over here on your wall?" "That's an indicator to help us keep a pulse on our capacity. It's not something that we spend a lot of time with on a daily basis like some of our other indicators like quality, changeover time, and other downtime tracking. However, when we do see this utilization number start approaching around 80 percent, we dig into it a little deeper. We try to determine if we are seeing a demand spike, or if there is a specific machine that we need to focus some improvement efforts on. Actually, if the latter is the case, there is a good chance we are already working on it, but this utilization awareness may heighten the priority."

"Or maybe due to the sales forecasts, even though we know these forecasts are always wrong (we take that into consideration), this utilization indicator may be telling us that we actually do need to look at putting some money into the capital budget for next year for a new machine. However, unless there is a significant demand increase, we take pride in finding creative ways to free up additional capacity with what we have. However, with one opportunity in particular, changeover times, I just know we have a lot of things we could do to shorten this up if we really focused on it. We've done a few things and are tracking it, but we haven't really rigorously attacked it. That is why I asked whether there was someone who could help us get rolling with this. I guess that is why you are here."

Now that would have been a much better conversation which would have led to something positive. The indicator, machine utilization, existed in both situations, both the real and imagined; however, in the imagined scenario, machine utilization was a secondary indicator which provided needed information, but not a KPI which was driving behavior on a day-to-day, even hour-to-hour, basis. Does the final customer really care that your machine utilization number increased from 60 percent to 65 percent last month? It can be argued that he does care indirectly, since, if you are over capacity, it will cause delays and affect deliveries. There definitely is a linkage back to the customer. This metric does provide needed information; otherwise, it should be eliminated. However, unfortunately, many a warehouse has been built to store millions of dollars of unneeded product for the sake of increasing the machine utilization number since it was treated as a measure of performance. Needless to say, this is not the behavior we are looking for. Who benefits in this situation? Definitely not the customer, neither internal nor external customers. The only beneficiary may be the person who justified the need for additional equipment. *"See, I told you we needed that new machine! Look at the numbers, we're running it all the time; maybe we should get another! I'll start working up another capital appropriations request. It should be easy due to this great machine utilization data which we have!"*

This section on secondary indicators versus key performance indicators really goes back to our discussion on the purpose of the metric. Is it something we must track to enable us to make effective decisions, both short and long term, which will drive behavior aligned with our Lean and business strategy? If so, you are at least starting with an appropriate key performance indicator. Sure, there are other indicators which provide valuable information to us; however, key performance indicators are a special class of indicator since they show us the way. The words *key* and *performance* should signal to us their importance. It would be great if having the "right" metric were enough, but it's not. Let's now look at our second key KPI success component: is the information that is being provided accurate?

Metric Accuracy

This may seem like another no-brainer. Of course the data must be accurate; however, in practice, just because a need is obvious doesn't necessarily guarantee that it actually occurs. Someone or something must collect this information, and whether human or mechanical, the collection mechanism may be prone to error. Let's use an example of a quality performance metric, internal scrap. Is our scrap number based on an estimate made from a cursory look into the scrap bin, or do we have standard practices which accurately account for not only the amount of scrap, but also provides information such as the specific category of scrap which will aid us in our improvement efforts? This could be specifics on the type of scrap, e.g., missing flange, broken flange, wrong color base, bent whatchamacallit, etc. In the *cursory look* process, if asked for this detailed information, you'd get various opinions and educated guesses; however, when using this information to make decisions and commit resources, data-based decision-making is needed. A quote attributed to Dr. Deming is appropriate here: "In God we trust, all others bring data."[2]

Though we have used an example of a physical product, the same data collection weakness can be evident with information "products" in administrative processing. How rigorously do we collect data on errors such as missing or wrong information, or rework activities where we backtrack to try to obtain the information we need? Do you accurately know your *first time yield* of office processes?

Another example where data is collected which can be of questionable accuracy is machine downtime reporting. How accurate do you think the data is when the supervisor fills out the downtime data just prior to the end of the shift? *"Ok, let's see, we spent about 45 minutes on changing over rolls today, another 20 minutes caused by widget jams, and I know we had a rough day getting that print head lined up, let's say 2 hours."* To get an initial rough estimate, this sort of data is better than nothing. Though, especially once we get into the incremental continuous improvement stage, after most of the low-hanging waste has been cleared, the data derived from this "end of shift" method is worthless due to its variability and questionable accuracy.

A usual quick response to the above is to automate all data collection; take out the human intervention. There are some automatic or semi-automatic data collection units which are available and should be considered to determine if they are appropriate for your situation. On the other hand, often a simple manual paper or whiteboard type of tracking mechanism is the best route as long as the manual inputting is not too cumbersome. A common transition is to start with primarily manual tracking methods to test the metric and its value. By manually inputting data, you gain a deeper understanding and ownership of the process, as opposed to a machine automatically spitting out some numbers and charts. Then once the KPI and its usefulness are established, more automated methods can be investigated to relieve some of the manual burden. There are no hard and fast rules here as for what is appropriate. It's one of those case-by-case situations. In the next section we'll discuss some visual methods such as KPI boards. Even these methods which may appear to be manual-based are often supported by some information technology data-gathering. A hybrid approach often makes sense; however, don't ever underestimate the power of simple, manual, highly visual methods. In spite of the technology available today, in most cases, visual/manual measurement methods are still the most effective.

Who Owns the KPI Information?

Data accuracy also has a lot to do with ownership. Who owns the KPI information? Who utilizes it? Who really cares? A work area KPI system, usually displayed on a visual KPI or communication board, must be owned by the workers in the work area. Too often if you ask one of the value-adding workers why they are recording the data, and who uses it, you'll get a shrug. Or, only slightly better, they point to a manager who stops by occasionally to take a look. The "right" answer would have been:

> *Us, we use the data for a couple reasons. Some of the information helps us determine if we are on or off track for the day, and if off track, we make sure to record what happened on the "issues board" so we can work together to come up with a plan to eliminate it from happening again. Also, the information alerts our team leader to pull in other resources if needed to get caught up. Some of the other information helps us determine how much of an impact our improvement activities are having. We like to see a nice gradual upward line on our trend charts. Some of the other information on the board, such as those charts over there with the multiple bars of different heights, helps us break down some of the issues to see where we should focus our improvement time. Maybe you aren't familiar with those charts; they're called Pareto charts, named for Vilfredo Pareto,[3] the 80/20 guy. Anyway, basically, the KPIs and supporting data help us stay on track along with continuously improving what we do around here. Also, when we need help, it's real easy to show the managers what is happening and where and why we need some help.*

Now in which scenario do you think the collected KPI data will be more accurate: the situation where the data is being collected simply because the worker is told to do it, that someone else needs it for some unknown reason? Or, the situation where the worker and teammates use the KPI information, where it's part of their job?

> *I collect it. I use it. I own it. If there is an accuracy problem due to what I am doing or if the automatic data collection system is spitting out information that doesn't make sense, I'll get it fixed or*

alert someone who will fix it. Otherwise, our team would be making faulty decisions based on the faulty data, and it's going to be tough to meet our objectives in that case!

If you have a KPI which is providing confusing information, and you're wondering if the data is an accurate depiction of what is actually happening in the process, ask a few key questions. *Was the standard data collection process followed?* A good follow-up question would be, *who uses the data?* Followed by, *is this the same person who collects the KPI data?*

Once we are confident that we have the right KPIs, and the collected data is accurate, it's still all a waste of time and resources if we don't understand how to use the KPIs to help us make effective decisions. Even good information can be used improperly, or, just as bad, not be used at all.

Metric Usage

One misuse of KPI information is where there is an overemphasis on reaching an industry benchmark or universally accepted milestone which is deemed "world class" or "Lean-mature" or some other lofty rank of greatness. I am not implying that the pursuit of recognized exemplary levels of excellence is not worthwhile. In fact, I whole-heartedly strongly encourage it! Any target which is beyond our current state and aligned with our ideal vision should definitely be pursued, plus publicly or industry-recognized achievements can be highly motivating for the workforce. It's an issue of *emphasis* and disproportionate focus which may drive the un-Lean behavior and result in unintended consequences.

OEE

Let's look at one KPI which some companies utilize where metric usage could actually drive non-Lean behavior: the measurement of overall equipment effectiveness (OEE). The OEE metric comprises three separate components: availability, performance efficiency, and quality. Each component is calculated as a percentage. The OEE number is a product of these three components. OEE is most often used as a KPI for capital equipment type of processing. The details of the OEE calculation will not be elaborated on here – many other great sources are available. What I'd like to focus on is the often stated world-class OEE standard of 85 percent. This is the product of 90 percent availability, 95 percent performance efficiency, and 99 percent quality. What could be wrong with having this world-class standard of 85 percent as our target?

Consider if a particular process is currently at a significantly lower OEE number, such as 30 percent. An excessive focus on the 85 percent standard as a winning score can be demoralizing and demotivating to the team. *"We're not even close! Management has no idea what is going on if we're expected to get to 85 percent by the end of the year! Another poor performance review is surely on the horizon no matter how hard I work!"* Remember Failure Mechanism #6 from Chapter 2, *Demotivation is Tolerated?* Regarding this KPI conversation, we may not only tolerate demotivation, but we may have unintentionally designed demotivation into our systems. The temptation would be to search for some high-impact, likely costly, changes, while ignoring the incremental changes which typically yield a more effective long-term result; and ironically, it's often these *small* improvements which lead the way to the larger high-impact advances.

An overemphasis on an outcome target can also lead to an overemphasis on adjusting and manipulating the calculation details. By instituting a few minor changes to one of the measurement components of OEE, we might be able to increase the number in our favor. I am not suggesting that this is a purposeful devious act attempted by an unscrupulous band of Lean zealots. Rather, it's a natural reaction to ensure fairness of the scorecard. A strong case can be made that this OEE altering is quite appropriate from a Lean perspective. *"Our company is different! We don't build automobiles, and adjustments or customization to meet our particular situation is the Lean thing to do, isn't it? In fact, our Lean sensei has stated that we need to apply the Lean principles and tools to our unique challenges and processing environment. We have to make it work for us. That's all we're doing, right?"* In reality, the so-called "Lean thing to do" would be to focus our limited time and resources on improving the process to be able to add more value for our customers. Sure, the OEE formula should be reviewed to assure that it is appropriate for your particular monitoring and improvement needs; however, this review and resultant calculation tweaks will be quite different depending on whether *process improvement* is your primary purpose, or whether *obtaining the highest number* is the overriding purpose. This distinction may seem subtle, but often it's these subtle perspective differences which affect our behaviors and decision-making, and thus will determine whether our system is driving Lean behaviors or taking us down a wasteful path.

Consider if you have the opposite situation. A particular process may already be at or near the 85 percent OEE world-class level, or possibly even beyond this benchmark. Does that mean that you are done? *"We're already at a world-class level, no use expending any more resources on improving that process!"* In reality, further improvement may yield significant results. Of course there is always prioritization as to where we should focus our resources. For example, if we have a bottleneck piece of equipment that is limiting our ability to produce and thus sell more product, guess where we should focus our time and resources? The decision is not based on any specific OEE status.

Comparing Apples with Oranges

The above scenario had to do with an unhealthy overemphasis on external targets or milestones. Another way in which good KPI data is misused and abused has to do with comparisons within an organization. Internally, we definitely need to share and learn from each other. Many companies don't do this nearly enough; however, when we compare the KPI performance of different machines, work areas, or even facilities within the same organization, we must recognize that usually we are comparing apples with oranges. Even two "identical" machines in the same facility will often use different components and run a different product mix. They may look identical, but when we consider the details, one is an apple and the other is an orange. So if we set up an overly competitive environment where recognition and maybe even bonuses are determined by KPI ranking of different work areas or multiple facilities in larger organizations, it can have negative unintended consequences. Often, a fair amount of non-value-adding time is spent on justifying why my number is not as high as yours, basically explaining why my apple is not equivalent to your orange. There's no value in this exercise.

This is another one of those subtle issues. Yes, we need to share performance information and learn from each other's successes and slips, and yes, there's nothing wrong with a little healthy internal competition. Peer influence is powerful, and the topic of a later chapter, but only effective when in the context of the *optimize the value stream* principle. Remember, we're all on the same team. What is the perspective or mindset? Are we helping each other and learning and growing together in pursuit of organization goals, or are we competing for some carrot, whether company recognition or a bigger bonus? Consider the details of your processes, and if you agree with my apples and oranges analogy, be careful how you compare this mixed bag of fruit. Develop support systems, such as your

KPI system, which encourage the workforce to work together as opposed to competing against each other. Always beware of unintended consequences which drive the wrong behavior. If this occurs, learn from it, and conduct the next experiment … continuous PDCA!

What's a SMART Metric?

The acronym SMART is often used to emphasize some key characteristics of an effective metric. We've touched on a number of these aspects already, but a quick review of SMART metrics will highlight a few additional points to consider. The "**S**" can have multiple meanings, including *simple, specific,* and *sensitive. Simple* can refer to metric understanding, or it can relate to the data collection process. It must be simple enough to be understood by all who need to utilize the metric, and if the data collection method is too cumbersome, not simple, data accuracy can become an issue. *Specific* metrics are applicable, or specific, to the work area where they are being posted. Any metric which is not controllable by the people within their work area is useless for their process monitoring and improvement purposes. *Specific* can also refer to the dangers of aggregate metrics. Due to the multiple inputs, the aggregated information is not specific enough, or at a sufficient detail level, to draw definitive conclusions on the process performance. *Sensitive* is an important aspect regarding a metric's ability to detect a change in the process. A change may occur due to unexpected processing abnormalities, or we may initiate a change as part of our improvement activities. Without a sufficient level of sensitivity, we wouldn't be able to verify our hypothesis of the PDCA process. If we plan to make a change and hypothesize that X will happen as a result, we need a metric to verify whether X did or did not actually occur. Sensitivity can be thought of as metric precision. Is the metric precise enough to detect change? Think of the prior "estimate the scrap by looking in the barrel" example. This data collection method would clearly be inadequate and imprecise in detecting the effects of an incremental improvement to the process.

"**M**" can represent *measureable.* Metrics, by definition, are measurable. *Manageable* is also appropriate. This refers to the number of metrics that the workplace can effectively utilize. Though there are no standard rules as to the proper number of metrics, in order to remain focused, few is usually better than many. What are the few vital metrics which provide the process intelligence that you need? Too many and the process picture gets cluttered due to the excessive amount of information you are trying to digest. This can be considered *information overload*, a little too much of a good thing.

"**A**" is for *actionable*. As previously noted, your KPIs must be anything but static. They provide the information needed for decision-making and action today and tomorrow. *Accurate* is another good A word, one which we've already elaborated on as one of the three key success components of an effective KPI system. *Attainable* is appropriate for goal-setting. If success is measured by reaching a clearly unattainable goal, frustration is likely the result rather than direction-setting and focus. Someone may argue that our Lean ideal vision of no waste and one-piece continuous flow is based on an unattainable goal, but there is a clear difference between direction-setting goals versus the goals associated with the next target condition. Consider how you would feel if you were told that you must reach the "goal" of no waste by the end of the year to obtain your bonus. Needless to say, please don't pre-spend that bonus money. And if your KPIs are not *aligned* with your stated objectives, you've set up the condition for *organizational hypocrisy* to grow.

"**R**" can refer to *reliable* and *relevant*. If a metric is no longer relevant to your strategy and objectives, eliminate it or modify it in some way to bring it back to relevancy. In a Lean environment, all processes and systems, including our measurement systems, require continuous reflection and improvement.

My favorite "**T**" is *timely*. How close can you get to the ideal of real-time information? I wouldn't be comfortable if I looked at my car dashboard and had to wait five minutes before my speedometer informed me of my current speed. Though, in some cases, even if the information can be collected and displayed as it occurs, in real time, a time lag is needed to collect sufficient data to draw accurate conclusions. For example, if you make a process change which you hypothesize will reduce the scrap by 1 percent, *timeliness* in this case could refer to the time required to collect enough data to either verify or refute the scrap reduction hypothesis. Another good "T" is *trending*. If we are continuously trying to improve our processes, naturally a metric which provides performance information over time is essential to know whether we are doing better than before. Often the best way to display time-based information is a simple run chart which quickly informs us whether things have been getting better or worse. Which way is the trend line tilting?

Summary – Effective KPIs and Alignment

In summary, your KPI dashboard must provide the necessary data, be accurate, and be understandable so that you can properly interpret and utilize the provided information. You'll then have an information network which will keep you on track, highlight opportunity areas, and monitor your improvement efforts. It will show you the way! When this is in place, the system will align with your Lean strategy and drive the right Lean behaviors. In this section we've focused on KPIs, but *alignment* is a key word with all other support systems as well. Are your purchasing, IT, and accounting methods supporting your strategy, or hindering progress? Is your personnel evaluation system driving the right behaviors? And are you absolutely sure that your recognition practices are actually recognizing behaviors which are aligned with Lean principles? Misalignment will cause irreparable damage to your quest to build a Lean culture. Most of the damage will come from the *organizational hypocrisy* which becomes evident to the workforce. If the only outcome of a misalignment issue was a performance drop, you would have a decent chance of recovery; however, the mixed signals being sent from the alignment problem becomes a workforce trust issue. This is significantly more difficult to recover from. To engage our employees in our effort to transform the organization, to have them commit their heads and hearts to the cause, not just their arms and hands, trust cannot be just a nicety, it is a requirement.

Action Item – *KPI Alignment Audit*

Conduct an "alignment audit" of your KPI system for alignment with Lean principles and your overall business strategy. Do the KPIs encourage and drive Lean behaviors?

1. Do you have the right KPIs? Do they provide information which, if accurate and utilized properly, will drive behaviors that will move the organization in the direction of your goals and ideal vision? Don't assume this is currently the case; look for any unintended consequences from your current dashboard.
2. Is the KPI information at an accuracy level to enable it to be used for effective decision-making regarding future actions? Inaccurate input equals faulty conclusions, resulting in ineffective decisions.

3. Do you interpret and utilize the KPI information properly? Even if you are confident that you have the right KPIs and the information provided is accurate, if your focus or emphasis is misplaced or you don't have a deep enough understanding of the metrics, faulty decision-making can still take place which will unintentionally knock you off track.

We've concentrated primarily on a single support system, your key performance indicator (KPI) system, and the next section will continue on this KPI focus. However, an equivalent scrutiny should take place regarding all support systems and policies to assure alignment with Lean principles.

Visual KPI or Communication Boards

In this section we'll expand on the previous discussion of KPIs and delve into the physical display of KPIs and related process information. Let's clarify some terminology first. I use the terms KPI board and communication board interchangeably; visual management board or display is also commonly used. Some of the information on these boards is associated with a label of their own, e.g., day by hour board, idea board, kata board; therefore, this information display may actually consist of multiple types of "boards" which make up your process information command center. Some boards may simply display pertinent information, while others are for scheduling and process control. A quick reminder before moving forward: In the previous section, I warned against the wastefulness of having visual KPI boards that are simply *organizational wallpaper.* They may look nice on a tour, but they don't really help you advance towards your destination, so please beware of this trap. Every so often you should check your actions by asking, *"We're not just putting up wallpaper, are we?"*

Let's begin by addressing the purpose and need for *visual* boards. Why the emphasis on visual information? I'll answer this question with another question: If process performance information is hidden and no one can easily, and in a timely manner, access this information to use it, does it have any value? I don't think so. Get information out to where it can be utilized, and utilized when needed. At a glance, the message is clear. No searching is required. We don't have free time for such non-value-adding activities anyway. We understand this simple visual concept quite well in other situations. As I sit here at my desk, I have various pieces of information pasted onto obvious places to assure that it's not hidden and forgotten. I bet your refrigerator has a visual reminder or two conspicuously posted to prod you to do something. Back at the workplace take the advice of Masaaki Imai in his book *Gemba Kaizen*, "All the walls in *gemba* can be turned into tools for visual management."[4]

A great example of a visual information display which I've seen outside of the factory setting would be when I had the pleasure of observing some of the men and women who I consider heroes, those who work in the 911 call centers. This is definitely an information display focused on the short term … extremely short term, since it may literally be a matter of life and death. The method in which the half dozen monitors at each operator station provide immediate information for rapid action is something that all communication boards, regardless of where used, can emulate. Key information is available when needed and visually obvious to the call center hero. No confusing mixed messages and no wasted time searching for information required to address the emergency. Information location and content is standardized and any abnormal situations are highlighted and effectively addressed by a standard process to assure rapid response. Maybe your information display center is not a component of a critical life-saving system, but why not design it as if it were?

Visual Board Components – Key Questions

Now that we have firmly established the obvious, that visual KPI boards should, in fact, be *visual*, let's dig into what exactly should be on a KPI board. Well, of course, our KPIs should be displayed; however, let's get a more specific picture by returning to the two basic KPI questions that were previously mentioned, which should be answered by glancing over at our KPI board or boards:

■ Are we on schedule today?
■ Are we improving over time?

These two questions can be expanded into additional questions which relate to our need to understand our process performance from both a short- and long-term perspective. I'll describe the key components of a visual management board by how the original two questions, along with an additional six questions, are answered in a timely and effective manner by the board. Following are the eight critical process performance questions.

This is not meant to be an all-inclusive list, and a number of follow-up questions will surface based on these eight primary questions. However, if your visual display board can be structured to address each of these questions, you'll have a solid performance information foundation. These are not unique, independent questions; there are many interrelationships. The eight questions are:

1. Are we meeting our schedule today?
2. What is next on the schedule?
3. What problems do we have?
4. What are we doing about these problems?
5. What are some other issues or ideas which are opportunities for improvement?
6. What is the plan and current status?
7. What are our KPIs and targets?
8. Are we improving over time?

The first two questions are focused on whether we are meeting today's customer commitments and production plans. Schedule visibility is essential to assure that sufficient staffing and materials are available, and to enable preparation activities to be completed to minimize delays between product changeovers. The timeliness of production status information is also critical. If we wait until the end of the day to discover that we missed a few shipments today or fell short of our plan, this shortfall naturally rolls over to the next day. If our production monitoring and display process could provide more timely data, such as hourly or even real time, we may have time to recover from any shortages by reallocating resources. Or, at the very least, we can begin developing a recovery plan that will get us back on track before too much damage occurs. A day by hour board is one example of a manual approach. (Refer to Figure 4.1 for a basic template of a day by hour board which includes aspects of some of the subsequent process performance questions.) Automatic production monitoring systems should be considered which provide real-time information as to schedule adherence. If the news is bad, don't delay announcing it. Have a visual system to expose the abnormality so that it can be addressed sooner, rather than later.

Questions 3 and 4 are focused on problems, either deviations from our current standard or obstacles preventing us from reaching our next target condition. What problems are we experiencing, and what are we doing about them? Just as with schedule shortfalls, problems must be exposed.

PRODUCTION STATUS — ASSEMBLY TEAM					
DATE	UNITS PROD.	TARGET PROD.	CUMUL. UNITS	CUMUL. TARGET	COMMENTS AND NOTICES
8:00		30		30	
9:00		30		60	
10:00		30		90	
11:00		30		120	
12:30		30		150	
1:30		30		180	PERFORMANCE CHARTS
2:30		30		210	
3:30		30		240	
OVERTIME					
TOTAL					

Figure 4.1   Day by Hour Board

They need attention. Your visual command center must have a place to record these abnormalities so that effective experimentation (PDCA cycles) can fix the problem, not cover it up. Too many times, in the heat of the battle, if a mechanism isn't in place to record and track the issue, the extremely urgent matter fades away into oblivion once a process *Band-Aid* is attached … until the next time it happens, which starts the non-value-adding cycle all over again. We need to break that cycle of waste by focusing on the process and getting to the root cause. Make these issues/problems/opportunities visible. Notice that Figure 4.1 has a place to record comments and notices. If you have machinery with capabilities such as automatic or semi-automatic downtime cause tracking, make sure you pull this data out of the software and give it life by making it visible. Along with the simple, yet powerful, *5-why analysis*, utilize basic quality tools like Pareto charts and fishbone diagrams to guide you to effective countermeasures and the next experiment. Don't hide them in a file, whether paper or electronic. They are visual tools; make them visible.

Questions 5 and 6 are our idea-generation questions. What other ideas will move us towards our next target condition in the direction of our ideal state of no waste? What are we working on and what is the status? Do we have ideas which need to be escalated to a higher approval level? This goes beyond the reactive improvements of questions 3 and 4 to a more proactive approach to idea-generation. A combined documentation and tracking method could be developed for both the *reactive* and *proactive* issues/ideas. A simple whiteboard approach with the following column categories is often effective:

- Issues
- Ideas
- Action items
- Responsibility
- Status

This component of your visual information display may be an idea board which is part of a formal idea system. Just as with problem-recording, ideas must be written down and visible or else those great ideas, even if discussed, have a tendency to fade away like a puff of smoke.

Questions 7 and 8 are our KPI questions. What are the KPIs, and are we improving towards our targets? Run charts are the standard display method. Is the trend line going in the right direction? If so, it provides confirmation that our improvement efforts are moving us towards our goals. If not, the chart directs us to ask *why* and commands that we get to work digging for causes.

Refer to Figure 4.2 for a depiction of an information board that includes the visuals which we've just discussed along with a couple additions. A cross-training matrix and a PDCA cycle sheet are also depicted. Another addition to consider would be a communication/education board for specific training topics or general information which should be shared.

Why Not in a Computer?

With all of the above types of visual displays, a reasonable question would be, *why not have everything in electronic format, wouldn't this be more efficient?* Doesn't a manually managed visual display board often require non-value-adding activities such as printing out charts and copying manually posted information so that it can be put into an electronic format for

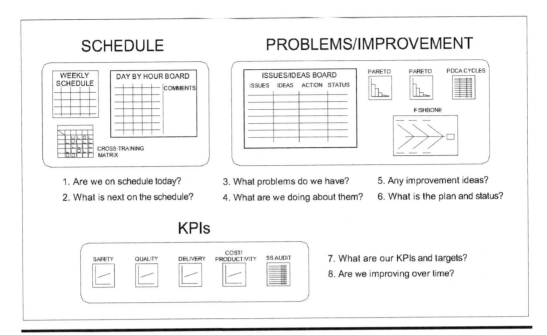

Figure 4.2   Information Board Components

tracking and sharing? This is often true; there can be some duplication of effort, but this is far outweighed by the benefits of having timely information available to the users in the workplace where value is being added, the *gemba. (At times we do need to go one step backwards in order to leap five steps forward on our Lean journey.)* The visual information reminds us what is important, how we are doing, and accelerates our thinking and problem-solving. The area workers use and therefore own the information; it's not hidden on a shared drive which is only accessible to those who have a computer on their desk. The usable visual information helps to unleash the creativity of the workforce.

Menlo Innovations is a software company who utilizes a variety of paper-based information tools. As Richard Sheridan, cofounder and CEO, states in *Joy, Inc.*, "We choose the tools we believe work better for the humans. Sometimes electronic is best, but often it is not, particularly for a team whose members all sit in the same room together."[5] Keep in mind, this is an IT company! If there ever were a company where you would expect to have information locked up and hidden in fancy computer software, this is it! But what do you see? Paper-based systems all over the place!

In some cases, you can have the best of both worlds. For example, large electronic boards showing current production status to plan eliminates hourly manual recording, and large monitors in the workplace can display information such as action items and status. In most cases, though, paper-based visual information is *better for the humans.* I believe that one of the reasons has to do with ownership. Something internally happens to me when I physically move the magnet on the board, or jot down the number, as opposed to having it passively automatically pop up on the screen.

The power of visuals also gets back to primary purpose. If the objective were to simply make information readily available to see, the purely electronic solution has its advantages. Having information at our fingertips, quickly displayed on all of our latest hand-held technology, is great; however, just giving everyone the capability of seeing information is not the primary purpose. We want the information to be discussed, debated, questioned, analyzed, and not just individually, but as a group. Remember, Lean is a team sport!

Granted, it could require a fair amount of wall or board space for all of the suggested visual information. I repeat the words of Masaaki Imai from his book *Gemba Kaizen,* "All the walls in *gemba* can be turned into tools for visual management."[6] The point or goal isn't to cover the walls with charts and graphs, (remember, *organizational wallpaper*), but the goal is to have the information where it can be of most value, provided in a timely manner, to those who can best utilize the information. Based on this criterion, simple visual systems usually prove effective.

Action Item – *Evaluate your Visual Command Center*

Evaluate your KPI and process information system(s) based on the eight questions described in this section. Add any other pertinent questions specific to your situation. Does your current system or systems provide the information to the appropriate people in a timely manner to enable effective decision-making? If not, determine appropriate countermeasures and conduct experiments to develop and test any changes. Consider whether a more visual-based approach as described in this section would be appropriate. Be sure to involve the users of the information in the design of any changes!

Some Lean Tools and Practices

Chapter 1 addressed the topic of Lean tools, where defining Lean as simply a set of analysis and improvement tools is both inaccurate and damaging to your efforts to develop a true Lean culture. This error is a Failure Mechanism #1 issue, *wrong or incomplete definition of Lean*. However, let's be careful not to dismiss the importance of the Lean tools. To continuously eliminate waste from your processes, you do need the right tools, or need to modify or develop a tool that works best for your specific situation. As noted in Chapter 1, we don't want to try to build our Lean house with a sharp stick and a rock as our primary tools of choice. We just need to make sure that the role of the tools is kept in proper perspective. Focus on the problem, and then dig into your toolbox to find the appropriate tool for the job. We should be asking, *"Which tools would help us solve this problem or make this improvement?"* rather than, *"Which Lean tool should we use next?"*

In this section, we'll review only a few of the multitude of Lean tools. This is not meant to be a comprehensive book on the tools of Lean, but rather a highlighting of stumbling blocks along with key success factors to enable a more effective Lean journey and the development of a Lean culture. We'll focus on a select few of the more commonly used, but unfortunately often misused and abused, tools.

Purpose of the Lean Tools

Before jumping into any one specific tool or technique, let's begin by starting with *purpose*. What really is the purpose of all of the tools in the Lean toolbox? It seems ridiculous to develop a single purpose statement which applies to the variety of tools which we have at our disposal; however, from a broad overarching perspective, the purpose of every single one of the Lean tools is to help us improve. Many tools aim to expose abnormalities and problems so we can get better. Some are for planning and analysis to help us move forward, and even others are for reflection to help us improve the process of how we improve processes. The purpose of any Lean tool is not to simply use it, thinking that by using this nice shiny hammer success is guaranteed, nor is the purpose to establish a condition that enables us to more effectively maintain the status quo. It is to *improve*. Let's keep this in mind as we move forward.

VSM

One of the bedrock tools of Lean is value stream mapping (VSM). This tool is directly tied to Process Principle #2 – *Optimize the Value Stream*. Value stream mapping was introduced to us by Rother and Shook in their groundbreaking book, *Learning to See*.[7] Please refer to this excellent reference for the details of this tool. Though flowcharting and various formats of process mapping have been around for many years, the VSM tool does have some unique features which assist teams in surfacing waste and developing improvement plans. Because of these features, VSM is definitely a tool which should be strongly considered for analysis and planning of your value stream improvements.

A value stream map is a visual depiction of material and information flows of a particular value stream. The information flow component and its integration with the primary material flow within the value stream is one of the unique features of VSM. This information component is significant for a couple reasons. First of all, there is often abundant waste embedded within the information processes themselves. Second, poor information integration with the production process will lead to a multitude of wastes. "Why don't we have the material that we need to run this order? It's never here on time! We don't have the proper documentation! I didn't know the schedule was changed! By the time we got the order on the production floor, we were already past due!" These are just a few panicked exclamations resulting from information flow issues which the VSM tool can be of great value by helping to highlight and thus initiate the problem-solving discussion.

Another unique feature of the VSM tool is that by being a visual depiction of the value stream, it cuts across functional, departmental, and work area boundaries and puts a spotlight on the wastes which occur *between* the various processing activities, all of the linkage points which require coordination. Sure, other mapping tools can be used to depict the overall value stream, but these other formats only place emphasis on the processing steps. What happens between the processing steps is generally ignored; a simple connector line on a flowchart doesn't reveal much to the analysis team. On the VSM, the department-to-department integration, or lack thereof, becomes crystal clear when our VSM indicates months of inventory between process step A and process step B. Or if studying and value stream mapping an administrative process where the primary flow is information, often we don't necessarily have a build-up of inventory, but rather an extended delay in the flow. The waste of waiting can be significant.

There are many features of the VSM tool which separate it from other mapping tools, but the focus on the information flow and other connections and linkages, coordination points, are a couple of the unique features which make it an invaluable standard tool in our Lean toolbox. However, unfortunately, the VSM tool may have the distinction of being the most misused and abused tool in the toolbox. It gets back to purpose. The VSM tool is a powerful value stream analysis and planning tool; the purpose or goal is not simply to document the value stream. An attractive, but static, VSM is just another form of *organizational wallpaper.* Sometimes the VSM purpose may be understood, but the thought process seems to be that by simply creating the VSM, waste-busting solutions will magically spew out from the map. Unfortunately, this tool is not quite that powerful; I wish it were. You still have to put in the hard work with your team in analyzing and prioritizing the waste reduction opportunities which the VSM helps to surface.

Other process maps definitely have their place. Often, a value stream analysis should engage the use of other mapping tools to complement the VSM. Especially when you start getting down to a more detailed analysis level, standard flowcharting is often the tool of choice rather than the system-wide VSM. Also, if you and your team do happen to have an extensive amount of experience with other mapping tools, go ahead and see if you can incorporate the features of the VSM tool into the mapping format in which you are intimately familiar. Don't worry, the Lean gods won't strike you down with a lightning bolt … at least I don't think so.

Please refer to Rother and Shook's *Learning to See*[8] to learn about the VSM tool. A couple other excellent references are Tapping and Shuker's *Value Stream Management for the Lean Office*[9] and Keyte and Locher's *The Complete Lean Enterprise: Value Stream Mapping for Administrative and Office Processes.*[10] Use the VSM tool appropriately and modify it as needed to fit your specific analysis and planning needs, and whatever you do, please don't relegate it to *organizational wallpaper.* There is no value in that, though it may look impressive.

5S

The next tool which I'd like to discuss is probably the most well-known and utilized tool in the toolbox, but the one which often fails to sustain itself. In fact, the word *sustain* should reveal the identity of this tool, which is referred to as the 5S system, or just 5S. 5S is a multi-step process of workplace organization and design. The steps are: *sort, set in order, shine, standardize,* and *sustain,* all based on the original Japanese translations. There are a number of slight variants, such as *straighten* rather than *set in order,* and *sweep* rather than *shine,* and many companies have expanded 5S to the 6S system by the addition of *safety.* Though, it can be argued that safety is naturally embedded within the original 5S process and its addition is not necessary. Some have even added a 7th S for employee *satisfaction.*

Why Do We Fail to Sustain?

Why do the wheels often fall off during the *sustain* step? Our newly organized and improved workplace design usually doesn't decline suddenly. Often it's imperceptible erosion over time back to the original disorganized and cluttered condition. One of the reasons can be traced back to *purpose.* If your organization views 5S and workplace organization solely as industrial housekeeping, it probably won't last. This is like going on a housekeeping binge prior to an upcoming party or family gathering at your house, but then once the event is over, the housekeeping seems to lose priority if this activity has not become a standardized habit. It's something we *should* do, but we just can't always find the time. This is no different than what you are trying to do in your workplace. For most, the housekeeping perspective usually doesn't stick.

So what is the purpose of 5S if not just to tidy up a bit for the looming tour by the bigwigs? I've mentioned that 5S is a workplace organization and design process, but why are we doing this? Remember, the tools are for improvement, so we need to think about how 5S can help us improve. The primary purpose of 5S, along with most of the tools, is to highlight abnormalities, or deviations from a standard. Even though *standardize* is one of the 5Ss, standard work and 5S are usually not considered intimately intertwined. The typically defined standard work defines *who* does *what* and *when* (in *what sequence*), *how long* each step should take, to produce *what expected outcome.* However, how about *where*? Shouldn't where items are placed (material, tools, information, machines, carts … everything) be part of our process definition, our standard work? When 5S is considered a component of defining the current process, it takes on a different meaning and priority in the Lean world. Lean practitioners are fanatics about defining *standard work*, a little less so regarding basic *housekeeping* practices. Defining the process and establishing standard work, including *where* items belong, provides a basis to identify any abnormalities; the problems can be exposed. Also, the team has a uniform understanding of the current condition and improvement target. This *standard work* perspective adds the rigor of *discipline* to the housekeeping component of 5S purpose.

Why 6S?

As mentioned above, a sixth S, *safety*, is often added to make it the 6S process. This is done to emphasize safety practices, which of course should always be emphasized and be priority number one. I've always supported this change, but never felt that it was essential since safety should be a component within the original 5Ss. For example, a cluttered workplace is not only inefficient, but can be extremely dangerous due to tripping hazards or even worse. The clutter may hide issues such as frayed electrical wires. I've come upon this condition myself during the *sort* step, which focuses on eliminating unnecessary items from the workplace.

Due to the difficulties of companies defining, sustaining, and improving their workplace design, I've come to alter my perspective on this additional sixth S. I now believe all 5S processes should immediately be modified to add the sixth *safety S*. Why? Because I think everyone will agree that safety is non-negotiable, an automatic priority item regardless of the industry or processing environment. Not providing a safe work environment is the ultimate infraction of the *respect for people* principle. So by tying your workplace design process to safety, then 5S practices may gain a little more priority.

There are many 5S/6S sustainment details which must be put in place, such as integration of workplace organization procedures into the daily work. It must become part of the actual job, every day, and having shift-to-shift handoff policies to prevent backsliding during shift transition is critical. However, the prioritization and emphasis placed on these implementation details, and the rigor in their development, are largely affected by your perspective and 5S purpose definition. Are you simply doing some industrial housekeeping which has a tendency to decline over time, or are you creating standard work and assuring a safe work environment?

Engaging the Workforce

We'll dive deep into workforce engagement in subsequent chapters, but since every single one of us has some type of workplace which needs to be organized, whether on the factory floor, in the office, or at the back of a service truck, we'll use this topic to consider some engagement ideas. With 5S, and Lean transformation in general, we should always try to make it personal to appeal to our emotional nature. If I am a worker on the production floor, what is my emotional connection to the workplace organization? The before-mentioned safety connection is one strong emotional link. But some workplaces may naturally be safe environments with minimal inherent risk, and thus this lever may not build a strong compelling case to get engaged. How about frustration? Doesn't our poor workplace design and organization create frustration to the worker? Here are a few comments from the plant floor:

"Where'd they put the material? Don't they know we need it over here?"

"What happened to our tools? I bet Engineering was over here robbing our stuff again! Dang engineers! I spend more time hunting for tools than I do using the tools!"

"Why isn't the paperwork where it is supposed to be? I always have to track it down. I don't have time for this stuff!"

"Why in the world does third shift always arrange the tools and materials on the workbench this way? Every morning I spend 15 minutes just rearranging everything to how it should be! Bunch of knuckleheads on that shift!"

"Speaking of knuckleheads, sure would be nice if, when I started my shift, there would be some parts left in the bins. I always have to go get some parts before I start the job! And for some reason, sometimes the bins are missing! What's happening? Are those guys on the other shift taking the bins home?"

Or in the office ...

"Where's that form? I know it's here somewhere!"

"You say you left the PO on my desk. I sure can't find it!"

"Why do I have to walk a mile to make one stinkin' copy? I spend more time walking than working!"

"She's not here today, and I sure can't find anything on her pig sty of a desk. What am I supposed to tell the customer?"

Frustration = Waste

Obviously, there's some frustration expressed in the above statements, and there are definitely some *respect for people* violations which need to be addressed immediately if the comments were actually said, not just thought, but I suspect that many readers can relate to at least a few of the above exclamations. When you dig into the root causes, you'll quickly run into workplace organization issues which are causing a number of wastes, such as excess motion, transportation, and underutilization of people. In fact, behind every frustration in the workplace, you'll surely find an associated waste, or two, or a few. So focus on frustration. *"Reducing my frustrations, well that's a strategy which I can get behind! If that's what Lean is all about, count me in!"*

Kanban

Another tool which is not always utilized correctly is kanban. The error which companies make with kanban is that they end the game too soon. Once the system is designed, set up, put in place, and refined during the initial implementation stages, we usually celebrate success and move on to the next challenge, quite satisfied that we can check off the box "implemented kanban system." What more can we possible get out of our kanban system? We've reduced our inventory levels and created a system to control these levels.

One of the beautiful things about a kanban system is that once we get it up and running, it's basically able to run on autopilot. However, it's imperative that we don't succumb to this apparent advantage of kanban and lose focus. The kanban system was designed based on a certain set of design conditions. If these conditions change, such as a significant increase in demand or demand variation, we may have to make an adjustment to the system. If we ignore this fact, we risk an unexpected stockout. The other reason to maintain focus goes back to the *purpose*, which is to surface abnormalities and spur improvement. What really is the ideal theoretical kanban size? Before you claim, *"Need more information!"* think about our Lean vision. If our ideal is one-piece continuous flow, wouldn't our ideal kanban size be zero, i.e., continuous flow? We may never get there, but this is the direction we're heading. Kanban is not simply an inventory control mechanism. It is an improvement mechanism.

Action Item – *Kanban for Improvement*

If you currently have a kanban supermarket that holds 100 parts, what would happen if you changed the system to only allow 90 parts? Conduct a controlled experiment to find out.

This kanban improvement approach goes back to the boat and rocks analogy of inventory which predates our usage of the term *Lean*, where the water level represents the amount of inventory which is in our system, and the boulders beneath the water level represent all the obstacles or reasons why you currently need this amount of inventory. Refer to Figure 4.3 for the boat and rocks of inventory. Sometimes the improvement approach is to dive down beneath the surface of the water to remove a boulder, which then allows you to lower the water level, i.e., inventory level. Or, the water may be too murky, and the only way to uncover the boulders is to reduce the water level and see which boulders appear. Of course, do this in a controlled manner to never put the customer at risk. A statement of, *"I know we missed our delivery Mr. Customer, but we were doing an improvement experiment! Sorry about that,"* usually doesn't alleviate their concern over the missed delivery. In fact, remove the words *"usually doesn't alleviate"* in the last sentence and replace with *NEVER ALLEVIATES.*

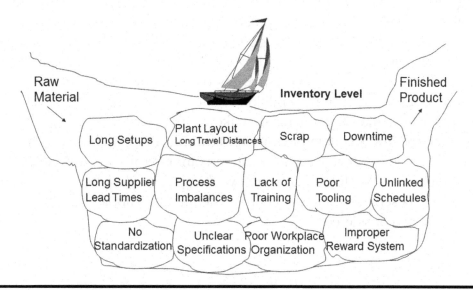

Figure 4.3   The Boat and Rocks of Inventory

Kanban is more than simply a method of effectively controlling inventory. Yes, this is a significant benefit of a kanban system; however, as with the other Lean tools, kanban is a means of continually improving the process.

We've briefly reviewed only three of the numerous Lean tools in our toolbox: value stream mapping, the 5S/6S system, and kanban. There are many other sources of information on the design details of these and other Lean tools. The purpose here in reviewing these particular tools was to highlight some misapplications or misunderstandings of each of these specific tools, but also, the intent was to emphasize that all of our Lean tools are for improvement of company processes to add ever-increasing value for our customers. Application of the tools is not the purpose, but rather utilizing each tool to help us get better and continually learn is where the tool's value lies. Just as when working on a project at home, you need the right tools to get the job done in an efficient and effective manner; but, let's make sure we are, in fact, using the right tool and we understand its purpose so that we can utilize the tool to its fullest potential in pursuit of our Lean goals.

Action Item – *Tool Reflection*

At the next Lean steering committee meeting, reflect upon your use of the Lean tools. Were the tools properly deployed to expose problems and facilitate your improvement efforts? Or, have you been doing it backwards by picking up the hammer/tool and then looking for a problem to solve? The latter is not usually an effective approach. Or, maybe you have a problem which requires a modification of a standard Lean tool to provide the needed capability to help you move forward. Don't feel that your toolbox is limited to the standard set of tools; some specialty or customized gadgets may be required. Assess your current condition regarding tool usage, and develop countermeasures and experiments to make course corrections.

Now let's review a couple of common Lean practices, both of which utilize the previously reviewed information/communication board. Refer back to Figure 4.2. We'll look at *gemba* walks and huddle processes, which we'll review as separate practices, but a system that combines aspects of both should be considered.

The Gemba *Walk*

The word *gemba* is a commonly used term in the Lean nomenclature. It refers to the place where the real work is being done – where the value is being added. In a manufacturing operation, it refers to the plant floor, where the product is being made. We will utilize a typical manufacturing organization to review the *gemba* walk and huddle systems, but these practices are applicable to any type of organization.

The term "*gemba* walk" is often used in a general sense, such as referring to the need for leaders and others to go to the *gemba* to gain understanding. "*Gemba* walk" can also refer to a process of onsite assessment of an operation or value stream, or even a mentoring session which takes place in the *gemba*.

What I'd like to review here is a specific system, the formalized standard practice of regular, typically daily, walks to the *gemba* by representatives of the leadership team and support personnel. As with any Lean practice, you must adapt and design it to fit your particular situation. Try it, improve it, and make it work for you. And if it does not fit your needs, for goodness' sake, don't use it. What we'll cover here are the basic components, advantages, and pitfalls of *gemba* walks and huddle processes, starting with *gemba* walks.

Purpose of the Gemba *Walk*

Before diving in, let's again consider our basic question of *what's the purpose?* Or, *what problem are we trying to solve with this system?* I know I'm being repetitive, but no Lean tool or method should be implemented without clarity on this question of purpose. I believe *gemba* walks address multiple problems and thus serve multiple purposes:

- One purpose is accountability – both from the *gemba* work area team leader, and the leadership team and support personnel who are participating in the *gemba* walk.
- Another purpose is support – support for the people who are doing the value-added work for the organization.
- The *gemba* walk process is also a teaching mechanism to enable higher-level leaders to coach and teach work area leaders in Lean leadership principles and behaviors.
- The *gemba* walk process can also serve as a mechanism to develop future leaders at the work area/*gemba* level.

So what is a *gemba* walk? Following are answers to the basic *who, when,* and *where* questions:

- Who – facility leadership and support personnel
- When – regularly scheduled, typically daily
- Where – each work area at their communication/KPI board for 10–15 minutes at each area
- Who leads – work area leader or associate

A good visual communication board is a key component of this process. This enables a quick review of the production status, problems which are being worked on and if assistance is required, and status of any other improvements. Other communication items can be added, but addressing these elements with the aid of a well-structured communication board will help assure an effective and timely process. The information board questions in Figure 4.2 can also provide guidance when developing the *gemba* walk agenda.

The *gemba* walk process instills accountability for providing timely support to the *gemba* operations. Leaders and support personnel, e.g., maintenance, engineering, IT, maybe even customer service and sales, could, and probably should, be in contact with work area personnel throughout the day, not only during the scheduled *gemba* walk meeting. But the structure and consistency of the daily *gemba* walk facilitates this accountability for helping the people who do the value-adding work of the company. When due dates for assistance from support personnel are missed, what does this trigger? Well, in a non-Lean organization, the non-value-adding blame game or finger-pointing process kicks in. *(This is another place where it is okay to nod your head if you've been there. Most of us have.)* In a Lean organization, these missed assistance dates should be addressed as any missed commitment or due date. First of all, how can we get back on track? Second of all, what is the root cause of the miss? Is it a resource issue, a priority issue, or something else? By addressing issues on a daily basis along with timely action, learning and growth are accelerated. Every day we incrementally get better by addressing any abnormalities or misses. If you've experienced the typical blame game, think about the value of the daily accountability process as described compared with the waste of the common finger-pointing approach.

But there is another subtle teaching and coaching aspect of this process. Consider the situation where one of the managers participating in the *gemba* walk, let's say the engineering manager, doesn't really *buy in*, let alone want to *lead*, this whole Lean thing in his department. He just participates in the *gemba* walk since it is now part of his leader standard work, which he really doesn't quite understand. As the plant manager, or appropriate leader level, questions and coaches the work area team leader, the message becomes very clear to all participants, including the engineering manager, as to what is important, and how we do things around here. The desired behavior is modeled and clarified every single day. Though the teaching and coaching may be directed to the work area team leader, there is a kind of peripheral and social learning aspect to the process which encompasses all participants. Of course, direct one-on-one coaching from leader to engineering manager is also needed. This is one of the topics of the next chapter.

The *gemba* walk process can also serve as a mechanism to develop future leaders at the work area/*gemba* level. Rather than only the team leader representing the work area team, consider incorporating other associates into the process, maybe even a rotating work area leader for the *gemba* walk session. For a small work area team, it may even be feasible to have the whole team participate.

During the *gemba* walk, the leadership and support team travels from work area to work area to review the status and needs of each area. Each stop should only take ten or 15 minutes at most. This is not the time for an extensive discussion or review of all work area issues. If this is needed, a separate time should be scheduled for this purpose.

For some organizations, it is appropriate to have different levels or tiers of *gemba* walks. For example, an upper-level executive walk with staff may be separate from the daily *gemba* walk involving plant or operations management and the support functions which directly support the work areas.

Walk of the Dead

One pitfall to avoid: don't let the *gemba* walk turn into the daily walk of the dead, where the leadership and support team travels from work area to work area in a robotic, zombie-like manner where little of value is accomplished. If you sense this is happening, get back to defining what your purpose is, and adjust the process accordingly. A *walk of the dead* process can become an item of workforce ridicule, which can damage trust and support for the Lean strategy. Its non-value, time-wasting nature will be evident and will directly conflict with what you should be trying to accomplish on your Lean journey. On the other hand, if it is clear, through action, that the primary role of the *gemba* walk is to provide support, this practice will be welcomed and effective in moving you towards your goals. And if you are not sure if the purpose is clear to all individuals involved, ask!

Now let's take a look at another Lean practice, the huddle process or system, which has almost identical purposes as the *gemba* walk process. The huddle process is often a tiered system, but let's start with looking closely at the first-tier huddle which takes place in the *gemba*.

The Huddle Process

For many years, a form of work area huddle has taken place even in non-Lean organizations. What separates the Lean huddle from a non-Lean huddle is the purpose and agenda. The non-Lean approach entails gathering the troops around the work area leader to receive their orders for the day. *"Mary, you work on this machine. George, I want you to finish that order on machine X."* There's also probably some discussion on how the last shift screwed things up so we'll have to work hard to make up for their incompetence. There may be an update as to progress on a particular problem, but during this whole process, the communication is typically only one-way, from the area leader to the troops. This approach is not really wrong or totally misaligned with Lean, rather it is insufficient. (Though, the finger-pointing is definitely anti-Lean and unacceptable.) The Lean version of a work area/team huddle is more standardized, rigorous, and comprehensive as to content. The Lean huddle process extends beyond the sole purpose of current production, and of course does not include the finger-pointing component.

Just as in the *gemba* walk process, the huddle system focuses on production status, problems, and improvements. So there is both a short-term, i.e., current production, and long-term, i.e., improvement, component. Following are the *who*, *when*, and *where* questions of the huddle process; many aspects will look very similar to the previously reviewed *gemba* walk process:

■ Who – the work area team with team leader
■ When – daily (each shift)
■ Where – stand-up meetings at the work area at their communication/KPI board for 10–15 minutes
■ Who leads – work area leader or associate

Refer to Figure 4.4 for additional guidelines for the gemba work area team huddle. As with the *gemba* walk process, the work area huddle is a great method for developing future leaders. Develop a standard huddle agenda to facilitate this development and to prevent the meetings from expanding scope and time.

A common practice is to have multiple tiers of huddle meetings. This multi-level approach is necessary to incorporate the leadership and support function assistance and accountability in providing support for the *gemba* operations. A tiered process would look something like the following:

■ Tier 1 – Work area team members and their team leader
■ Tier 2 – Group leader with the team leaders, and support personnel
■ Tier 3 – Value stream manager with the group leaders, and support personnel and/or staff

Notice the attendance overlap in this system. Team leaders of tier 1 participate in tier 2. Group leaders of tier 2 participate in tier 3. This linkage helps assure timely and accurate information flow. These meetings are typically held sequentially, with the tier 1 meeting being held first at shift start-up, so that issues can be escalated to increasingly higher levels as needed. However, as always, consider what is best for your situation. For example, it may be beneficial to hold tier 1 meetings at multiple times during a shift. Also, having shift overlap is of great value in multi-shift operations. For example, the first-shift team leader attends the second-shift start-up huddle to share pertinent information to the oncoming shift.

To assure visibility and accountability for the *gemba* support activities, a visual task assignment board is often incorporated in the tier 2 or tier 3 meetings. Assignments, responsibilities, and due dates are clearly shown on the board. Refer to Figure 4.5 for the basic structure of a task assignment board. The reaction to the missed date is the same as described in the *gemba* walk process. The root cause of the miss is to be investigated. A red dot or other visual note can be added to the assignment card to indicate the missed due date. The emphasis is on learning, corrective action, and improvement, not the non-value-adding practice of blame placement.

As with the *gemba* walk process, a pitfall to avoid is allowing the huddle sessions to expand beyond the planned scope and timeframe. A standard agenda and approach to huddles and *gemba* walks will help you avoid this pitfall, but when discussing issues and improvement opportunities, the temptation and pull to continue the discussion is very strong. So, developing this meeting discipline may take some time. As with any of the Lean

These guidelines are for the work team, short morning meetings, often referred to as huddles. Other standard facility-wide daily meetings are often also held, but the following pertains specifically to the daily work area morning meetings. Every company must find what works best for their organization, so please view the following with that perspective.

Frequency – Daily (each shift)

When – At shift start-up. However, with a slightly modified agenda, mid-shift and end of shift huddles should be considered as to whether they would add value.

Who Leads Them – Typically, the work area team leader or supervisor; however, with a proper meeting structure in place, rotation of team members into the meeting lead role is a great way to engage and develop leadership skills for all team members.

Where – The huddles should be stand-up (exceptions for health reasons) meetings held at the work area communication board, which will display items such as key performance indicators for the team along with improvement items and status.

Length – 10 minutes but will vary depending on discussion.

Recommended Topics to Cover Daily
- Safety – Issues, and if applicable, resolution status
- Key Performance Indicator Status, and if applicable:
  - New Customer Issues
  - Positive Customer Feedback
- Prior Shift – Any carryover issues
- Current Shift – Any non-standard information needed for the day
- 5S – Reminders of responsibilities, especially if rotated
- Improvement Ideas
  - Review status of open items
  - Open discussion of new ideas or issues – Consider "going around the circle" to encourage and enable each team member to provide input

Topics to Cover as Needed When Information becomes Available
- General Company News – Information such as to pending company visit, cross-functional team opportunities, planned social or charitable events, internal job opportunities, etc.
- Company Performance Information – KPI data not shared or available on a daily basis such as performance trends, changes in customer requirements, hoshin planning information
- New Products, New Customers, or New Employees
- Education – Awareness of products and customer use, or Lean learning topic
- Any Other Company News – Every employee should be considered on "a need to know basis" to assure total transparency

WARNING
Be careful that the morning huddle does not turn into a lengthy problem-solving session. If needed, this should be scheduled for a different time. Of course, the exception to this warning is if standard improvement time routinely follows the daily morning huddle.

Figure 4.4   Guidelines – Work Area/Team Huddles

challenges, learn and experiment your way towards the desired next target condition.

In summary, both *gemba* walks and a tiered huddle system have proven to be effective mechanisms in building and sustaining a Lean culture of continuous improvement, and the power derived from the frequency of these short meetings should not be underestimated. The daily communication, focus, and accountability reveals and addresses issues and opportunities better than the common batch-like communication schemes such as weekly or monthly gatherings or wasteful reports. Weekly or monthly gatherings will still be part of your overall plan, but they should supplement and complement, not replace the daily attention which *gemba* walks and huddles provide. For a company in the early phase of their Lean journey, instituting the tier 1 daily huddle meeting should be considered as a facilitating mechanism, a method to get the Lean ball rolling to gain momentum. This short meeting provides an opportunity for dialogue with the team on production needs, issues, and improvement opportunities, plus these short meetings provide a means to teach and coach to instill the

Assignment Cards

Name	Due Date	1	2	3	4	5	6	7	8	9	10	11	12	13	14
Jim (Team Leader)					▢			▢							
Larry (Engineering)			▢												
Joe (Quality)				▢											
Fred (Maintenance)			▢					▢					▢		
Tom (Manager)					▢										
George (IT)			▢					▢							

Figure 4.5   Task Assignment Board

desired Lean behaviors. To be most effective, both of these practices must be supported by sound visual tools such as the communication board, a task assignment board, and any other visuals needed to provide immediate information for the daily sessions. This highlights the point that the various methods, tools, and practices of Lean should not be viewed as independent entities. It is their interdependence that creates a powerful Lean system which is both powerful in the short term and sustainable for the long term.

Action Item – *Huddle and* Gemba *Walk Review*

During the next Lean steering committee meeting, discuss the usefulness of *gemba* walks and/or tiered huddles for your organization, or whether a hybrid of both systems would add the most value. Begin with purpose then discuss details such as frequency, participation, standard agenda, status of supporting visual systems (e.g., communication board), etc. These activities should become embedded into every leader's "leader standard work." If you currently have a huddle or *gemba* walk process, review its effectiveness in meeting its purpose, and experiment for improvement.

Notes

1. Womack, James P., Daniel T. Jones, and Daniel Roos. *The Machine That Changed the World*. New York, NY: HarperCollins Publishers, 1991.
2. "W. Edwards Deming Quote." A–Z Quotes. Accessed January 4, 2019. www.azquotes.com/quote/353353.
3. "What Is Pareto Chart?" Research Optimus. Accessed March 27, 2019. www.researchoptimus.com/article/what-is-pareto-chart.php.
4. Imai, Masaaki. "Visual Management." In *Gemba Kaizen: A Commonsense, Low-cost Approach to Management*, 95–103. McGraw-Hill, 1997.
5. Sheridan, Richard. "Power of Observation." In *Joy, Inc.: How We Built a Workplace People Love*, 119. New York, NY: Portfolio Penguin, 2015.
6. Imai, Masaaki. "Visual Management." In *Gemba Kaizen: A Commonsense, Low-cost Approach to Management*, 95–103. McGraw-Hill, 1997.
7. Rother, Mike, and John Shook. *Learning to See Value-stream Mapping to Create Value and Eliminate Muda*. Cambridge, MA: Lean Enterprise Institute, 1999.
8. Ibid.
9. Tapping, Don, and Tom Shuker. *Value Stream Management for the Lean Office Eight Steps to Planning, Mapping, and Sustaining Lean Improvements in Administrative Areas*. Boca Raton, FL: CRC Press, 2003.
10. Keyte, Beau, and Drew Locher. *The Complete Lean Enterprise: Value Stream Mapping for Administrative and Office Processes*. New York, NY: Productivity Press, 2004.

Chapter 5

Key Roles and Responsibilities

In this chapter we'll review some of the key roles and responsibilities which are critical to developing and sustaining a Lean culture. We will delve into how Lean affects the roles of leaders along with team members on the front line. We'll also address the Lean responsibilities of two critical teams, the Lean steering committee and the Lean support team, e.g., the Lean Department. We'll begin this portion of our journey by defining the critical role of the Lean steering committee.

The Lean Steering Committee

Who's in the Lean Steering Committee?

In some cases, the existing company leadership team with the addition of the internal Lean facilitator/coordinator serves as the Lean steering committee. The size of this team can vary depending on the size of the organization. I was once part of a small organization where the initial team which acted as the Lean steering committee consisted of only the plant manager, internal Lean facilitator, and human resources manager. John P. Kotter, who has written multiple excellent books on organizational change, lists step two of his *Eight Steps for Successful Large Scale Change* as "build the guiding team," a group powerful enough to guide a big change.[1]

As much as we love the story of the singular hero who somehow moves mountains in spite of the obstacles they seemingly encounter at every turn, to be successful at significant change, a guiding team approach is usually the way to go. A key word in Kotter's description of the guiding team is *big*, as in *big* change. Big change is difficult and requires planning, facilitation, and constant monitoring, and a guiding team with enough clout to remove the inevitable roadblocks that are preventing the organization from escaping the complacency of the status quo.

Another benefit of a team approach relates to People Principle #1 reviewed in Chapter 3, *everyone*. Lean must be an enterprise strategy involving everyone, and having a guiding team of multi-functional leaders will facilitate this enterprise engagement. It would likely become obvious if one of the Lean steering committee members is having difficulty committing to Lean principles and a different way of leading. This would highlight a need for teaching and coaching. As with any problem, it is better to surface issues sooner rather than later. As an organization transforms to more of a value stream type of structure, the guiding team for each specific value stream can take over many of the Lean steering committee responsibilities.

Primary Responsibilities

So what are the primary responsibilities of the Lean steering committee, whose mission is to plan, facilitate, and monitor the Lean strategy? Following is an outline of six key responsibility categories. We'll then elaborate on only a few of the items. Some of the responsibility topics, such as the KPI system, are reviewed in other sections of this book:

1. Lean deployment planning
   - Rollout and expansion planning – training and deployment approach
   - Determine strategic targets for improvement
   - Develop strategy for utilizing freed resources, e.g., labor, equipment, space
2. Establish measurement/KPI system
   - Alignment through all levels
   - Visual in each area
   - Utilized for improvement
3. Develop an improvement status/review process
4. Establish workforce idea-generation processes
5. Provide support
   - Remove roadblocks
   - Provide resources

- Provide time (examples)
  - Daily huddle process
  - Daily/weekly improvement time
  - Kaizen events/projects
6. Assure system and business alignment with Lean (examples)
  - Hiring/onboarding/promotion
  - Personnel performance evaluation
  - Accounting practices
  - IT support systems
  - Organization structure
  - Compensation
  - Purchasing practices

Let's now delve a little deeper into a few of these Lean steering committee responsibilities.

A Closer Look – Lean Deployment Planning

Determine strategic targets for improvement calls for us to alter our perspective when considering our current product portfolio and sales potential. The growth opportunities which Lean can create may transform a low-volume, niche product line to something more substantial. For example, by redesigning a value stream from a functional batch-processing approach, to a cellular one-piece flow design, lead time reductions of 50–90 percent can been achieved. What would a 70 percent reduction in lead time do to your potential sales volume? If the current industry standard is a four-week delivery, and you suddenly show up with a one-week delivery timeframe, what affect would this have? The original low-volume, niche product may suddenly become a major sales contributor. The growth aspect of Lean must be recognized by the Lean steering committee during planning activities.

The Lean steering committee also has a responsibility to be the catalyst for *any* multi-functional improvement opportunities, not only the strategic initiatives just described. Improvements come in all shapes and sizes, from the small daily kaizen activities to improvement projects which cross multiple functions or departments. The urgencies of the day make it a challenge to focus on any improvement opportunity, let alone one which will require the time and commitment of different functions or areas of the organization. Ed Deming said it well: "There are two problems: (i) problems of today; (ii) problems of tomorrow, for the company that hopes to stay in business.... It is easy to stay bound up in the tangled knot of the problems of today."[2]

The Lean steering committee must escape from the *tangled knot of today* and determine which cross-functional opportunities deserve attention, and then commit the necessary resources *today*. These value stream or system improvements will not initiate themselves. They require a proactive approach and a commitment from multiple functions or departments. The Lean steering committee has the members who can make this commitment. Lean mechanisms such as idea systems, *gemba* walks, or huddles can surface these broader issues, but these opportunities disappear unless there is a method to evaluate and commit resources if appropriate. It is a responsibility of the Lean steering committee to make sure this happens.

Lean Deployment Planning – A Formal Process

Lean planning is too important to rely on an ad hoc type of approach. A more formal process is recommended. One rigorous formal Lean planning, prioritizing, and goal-setting process is *Hoshin Kanri*, which goes by various translations, such as *strategic deployment* and *policy deployment*. We won't dig into the details of the Hoshin process here, but in general, the process combines the longer-term perspective of traditional strategic planning with enterprise alignment and review processes. Responsibility item #3, *Develop an Improvement Status/Review Process*, is a component of the Hoshin process.

Regardless of the specifics of your planning process, it is imperative to understand that Lean is not a separate strategic initiative. Lean must be intertwined into the fabric of an organization's business strategy. The core Lean principle of *add value for the customer* should assure this uniform perspective; however, we occasionally get so enamored with the power of Lean that it manages to take on a life of its own. We may inadvertently execute plans and activities which don't necessarily align with the organization's overall business plan. Or even if there is strategic alignment, the prioritization of activities may be misplaced when considered within the context of the business objectives.

There is plenty of waste in any organization, and an abundance of waste-busting activities which can be initiated; however, a formal planning process such as the Hoshin Kanri approach helps assure that the organization is working on things that not only *can* be done, but those important things which *should* and *must* be done. It's the responsibility of the Lean steering committee to assure that the Lean and business strategies are intertwined.

A Closer Look – Assure System and Business Alignment with Lean

Even though a primary purpose of the Lean planning process is to assure enterprise alignment, the Lean steering committee role #6, *Assure System and Business Alignment with Lean*, deserves a few additional words. We've previously used the words *organizational hypocrisy* to describe what occurs when the KPI system, or any system or practice, is not aligned with the principles and goals of a Lean strategy. This can destroy workforce trust and significantly stall Lean progress. Preventing the development and growth of *organizational hypocrisy* is a critical responsibility of the Lean steering committee.

Consider the first item listed under *assure system and business alignment with lean*, hiring/onboarding/promotion, which are actually multiple processes. Think about the hypocrisy of hiring or promoting someone into a leadership position who is disrespectful to their team, who is clearly an anti-Lean autocratic manager. A company leader can preach the Lean message for months or even years, but no one will be listening when anti-Lean *actions* are evident. All systems must be aligned with Lean principles. A key role of the Lean steering committee is to assure this alignment.

The Lean Steering Committee versus the Executive Six Sigma Council

For those of you who may be utilizing a Six Sigma methodology for your continuous improvement strategy, the responsibilities of the Lean steering committee appear almost identical to what is called the executive Six Sigma council. This council has three key roles: strategic leadership, assure progress, and cultural transformation.[3] Sounds like a Lean steering committee to me. Even transformation platforms which may conflict in some areas are in agreement regarding the need for a guiding team.

Lean Steering Committee Meetings

In addition to annual meetings for strategic planning of objectives, goals, activities, and required resources, more frequent improvement review meetings should be held throughout the year. A typical frequency is monthly, but a more frequent meeting cycle may be appropriate for an organization in the early stages of their Lean journey. The primary focus of these meetings is improvement status per plan. When slippages or other problems are identified, the goal is to determine corrective actions and how the Lean steering committee can provide assistance. A forward look to identify potential issues should also be a component of the meeting. Lessons learned, whether from attained goals or from setbacks, are incorporated into future Lean plans and activities.

Along with this review of transformation activities, an educational component can be incorporated into the Lean steering committee meetings. This educational segment, led by the internal Lean facilitator, possibly with the assistance of outside Lean expertise, can be an invaluable Lean leadership development and growth opportunity. A book club approach can also be considered where the steering committee members rotate chapter review assignments. A Lean culture is a continuous learning culture, even for, or maybe especially for, company leaders. The Lean steering committee meetings can be an effective forum for this.

Action Item – *Do You Have a Lean Steering Committee?*

If you do not currently have a Lean steering committee, at your next leadership meeting, discuss whether the mission of this existing team includes the Lean steering committee responsibilities reviewed in this section. If not, consider whether some or all of these responsibilities should be added within the same leadership team and meeting structure, or would a separate Lean steering committee be more effective? If multiple teams are appropriate, the coordination and alignment of these teams is paramount.

Leadership – Key Roles and Responsibilities

Lean redefines the leadership role at all levels, from the front-line supervisor to the CEO. Because of a preconceived notion of what it means to be the *boss*, which was developed over decades where a non-Lean leadership style was embedded into many of our organizations, it is crucial that we properly define the role of a Lean leader. I've divided the leadership discussion into three sections. The first two sections, *Principle-Based Leader Roles* followed by *Supporting Leadership Behaviors and Characteristics*, will delve into the key roles, responsibilities, and traits of a Lean leader. The final section will focus on some specific issues for the leader at the front line. Of course the details of the job and authority are different from an executive leader to a front-line leader. However, the principles of Lean affect and redefine the leader's role regardless of rank, so distinction between leader levels is minimal throughout our discussion.

Principle-Based Leader Roles

We'll begin by looking at a few Lean principles which change, or at the very least emphasize, certain aspects of how we need to lead in a Lean organization. We've already highlighted the need for leaders to actually do the leading in a Lean transformation. Refer back to Failure Mechanism #2 – *Leaders Aren't Leading*. But how do the leaders actually do this leading, and what is it about Lean that directs leaders to lead in this manner? Following are five Lean principles and associated Lean leader roles which we'll review:

- Everyone principle – be a teacher and coach
- Focus on the process principle – be an improver through process
- Optimize the value stream principle – be a system coordinator
- Teamwork principle – be a team-builder
- Scientific thinking principle – be a "fear destroyer"

Everyone Principle – Be a Teacher and Coach

People Principle #1, *Everyone*, demands that Lean is not an activity hoarded by a select few Lean zealots. Each and every employee is a key player in this game. Naturally this requires new workforce skills and the development of new behaviors. This isn't gained by simply attending an offsite five-day training session. Ongoing guidance and support is needed to grasp a deep understanding of Lean principles and to develop new habits aligned with these principles. Therefore, the Lean leadership role must include a strong teaching and coaching component. In Jeffrey Liker's *The Toyota Way: 14 Management Principles From the World's Greatest Manufacturer*, Principle 9 states, "Grow Leaders Who Thoroughly Understand the Work, Live the Philosophy, and Teach It to Others."[4] Notice that Liker didn't insert any sort of qualifier such as this principle only applies to a certain leader category. It applies to all levels, and regardless of team size. If you have a single person reporting to you, you need to be a teacher and coach.

This can be a major role adjustment, especially for the new supervisor who begins their leadership tenure with an outdated perspective of what it means to be a leader. *"Just keep your mouth shut and do what I say and we'll get along just fine!"* Teaching and coaching are not in the forefront of this supervisor's mind. Unfortunately, this anti-Lean mindset is not yet extinct. In order to engage the workforce in the Lean transformation, leaders must be teachers and coaches. But how does a leader teach and coach *problem-solving* skills and build *improvement-thinking* capabilities?

Teaching and Coaching for Improvement

Mike Rother's *Toyota Kata: Managing People for Improvement, Adaptiveness, and Superior Results,*[5] is the go-to source on the coaching process of Toyota leaders. I suggest that you study this invaluable resource. My intent is not to reiterate Rother's work here. I'd like to highlight a few basic teaching/coaching concepts that are more general in nature to provide a starting point for how Lean leaders should approach the teaching/coaching challenge.

The focus or purpose of this discussion is not on how to instruct or train on a specific task. Our target is how to teach and coach for improvement and problem-solving … *for solving any problem.* This is more complicated than simply addressing a particular task or a single problem. Yes, we want to analyze and develop countermeasures for the problem currently in front of us; however, we don't *only* want people to learn how to address this one specific issue. We want people to learn how to attack the thousands of issues which may confront them. Therefore, it is a *problem-solving and improvement process or approach* which we are really teaching. The current problem provides us with an opportunity to teach and learn. The first thing a leader/coach must do is something which may seem painfully unnatural to some.

Don't Give Answers

The leader must resist providing a proposed countermeasure for the problem. *"I've run across this before, here is what you need to do."* This may seem like the "leader" thing to do; impart your wisdom based on years of experience in solving similar problems. However, there are three negative possible outcomes to this approach. One or all three may occur:

1. You may not be correct, or there may be a better option which you did not consider. I know, this may be hard to believe, but since you are not closest to the problem, your countermeasure or idea for the next experiment may not be the most effective.

2. The student has not learned how to think through a problem for themselves.
3. The student does not own the idea. It was the leader's idea, thus they are automatically granted ownership.

Numbers 2 and 3 are the most damaging. Opportunity lost; you have allowed a teaching opportunity to pass you by. But if you are not teaching by imparting your wisdom by providing answers, what do you do?

Ask Questions

You ask questions! Your foundational guidebook for all things Lean is the set of Lean principles, and when addressing problems, the PDCA process is in the forefront. A common PDCA error is proposing solutions prior to truly understanding the problem and root causes. When the leader recognizes this error, they should ask questions to encourage the student to think deeper about the problem to lead to self-discovery. This applies even when a request from the student is clearly not feasible. Here's an example.

The team member, i.e., student, approaches the leader with the following request: *"Hey, we have to get two more widget-bending machines!"* As background, each widget-bending machine costs $2,000,000, and typically has a two-year delivery timeframe. It can be "fast-tracked" to maybe get it in 18 months. Obviously, the purchase of widget-benders is not a feasible solution to address any short-term needs. Rather than the leader rejecting the proposed solution as an infeasible employee request, they realize that this is an opportunity to develop the student into a better problem-solver while at the same time address the problem at hand. Though at this time, the real problem is unknown. Often the teaching which occurs is limited to the leader explaining the budget/timeframe issues of the idea to the employee; however, the teaching and learning opportunity is significantly greater than the student only learning that widget-benders cost a lot of money and that it takes quite a while to get one.

The leader may begin by asking a simple question, such as, *"Why are two new machines needed?"* A response may be, *"We never have enough machine capacity to meet our schedule."* To drill further into the problem, the leader may ask questions to encourage the student to think about other capacity-limiting factors, e.g., unplanned downtime, lack of material, setup times, etc. The leader may have the student gather more data to truly understand the problem and all contributing factors. Or possibly the coach and student may agree to discuss the issue with the whole team and analyze a factor that the data is already pointing towards, for example, extensive setup times which eat away at the machine capacity.

We started with an impractical proposed countermeasure, but then the leader and student travelled on a discovery path that will lead to more effective countermeasures than waiting two years for a couple of widget-benders. The student has learned how to think more critically regarding problems, to be more rigorous in the PDCA process, starting with understanding the problem and current condition. And through the student/leader discussion, the student maintains a sense of ownership of the issue, thus it becomes an engaging and motivating experience as well.

Look for Teaching Moments

This scenario highlights one more teaching/coaching point. Leaders must always be on the lookout for teaching moments. The teaching role of a leader usually doesn't entail arriving at a conference room to teach at a preplanned time. Often it requires the teacher to notice the teaching opportunities, usually in the workplace where they surface during the everyday process of doing the job. Don't miss these golden moments, which can be utilized to expand the organization's problem-solving and improvement capabilities.

Focus on the Process Principle – Be an Improver through Process

Process Principle #1, *Focus on the Process*, also has an altering effect on the leadership role. Responsibility for adherence is with the leader. Commitment to process is really commitment to the long term. In the short term, hoops can be jumped through and fires can be put out to get the job done today, and some improvement can eventually occur through random trial and error. But only by getting back to the process, conducting root-cause analysis, and experimenting our way to effective countermeasures, can we eliminate the cause of the fire and institute improvements which can be sustained and lead to further improvement.

Effective improvement requires a commitment to process, but this takes time and discipline. Therefore, improvement through process must be a clear performance criterion of every leader. The question, *"What was the outcome?"* still applies, but the question, *"How did you produce the outcome?"* must be added. It's the latter question which helps create a sustainable Lean culture of continuous improvement. Being an improver through process, and teacher of this principle, is a responsibility of all leaders.

Optimize the Value Stream Principle – Be a System Coordinator

Process Principle #2, *Optimize the Value Stream*, alters the traditional role of many leaders. Instead of rigorously protecting their departmental turf, the Lean leader understands that the overall system, or value stream, is what ultimately must be optimized. Any local improvements must support the value stream goals. Reference the previously reviewed 9th Waste, *False Improvement Waste – Making a "local" or departmental "improvement," but the waste has simply been moved to a different location in the value stream*. The value stream or system perspective must be a guiding reference point during all improvement activities.

The value stream focus also affects how a leader cooperates with their counterparts from internal suppliers and customers. There is no place in a Lean organization for departmental turf wars and functional silo-building. This is a clear Lean principle violation. Cooperation and coordination at the boundaries is essential and must become part of every leader's job. This is the "boundary manager" role, referring to this coordinating role at the *boundaries* of the leader's responsibility area. On the front line, this means coordination with neighboring departments or work areas. At another level, this means coordination among the director of operations, sales, engineering, etc. This multi-department or cross-functional collaboration throughout the value stream must become a non-negotiable component of the leader role and leader performance criteria.

Teamwork Principle – Be a Team-Builder

People Principle #3, *Teamwork*, requires Lean leaders to be team-builders. Of course there are individual responsibilities and accountabilities, but most work is accomplished within the structure of teams. Teamwork is not only applicable to local work area teams, but also across departments and functions to support the *optimize the value stream* principle. For multi-facility organizations, teamwork is needed across locations. Regardless of leader level, following are five leader actions or behaviors to build an effective team:

1. Model the behavior
2. Provide clarity of purpose and direction
3. Assure alignment
4. Provide resources, tools, and information
5. Incorporate mechanisms for team development

Item #1, leaders must *model the behavior,* is intentionally placed at the top of the list. If a leader is singing the teamwork message to their team, but they don't demonstrate the desired behavior, credibility and trust is severely damaged due to the mixed messages. For example, how does the leader work with peer leaders from internal suppliers and customers? As with all desired Lean-aligned behavior, if a leader wants teamwork, they must model teamwork.

All Lean leaders must *provide clarity of purpose and direction* for the team. Leaders must not allow *clarity voids* to develop which produce confusion and fear, both of which will negatively affect team performance and the Lean transformation. Key performance indicators provide direction for the team. They clarify what is important, and establish improvement goals for the team to strive for. Leaders should also clarify their team's basic purpose, and how this local purpose fits within the overall company purpose and strategy. In a medical instrument company, does the CNC technician view purpose as simply to machine a valve from a chunk of metal, or does the technician feel that the purpose is to produce a component of a life-saving piece of equipment utilized in hospitals across the country? If we are trying to engage the minds and hearts of our employees, the latter purpose is likely more impactful. More will be said about *purpose* during the motivation discussion. A Lean leader must build their team by providing clarity of purpose and direction.

A Lean leader must *assure alignment* with the teamwork principle. Besides the before-mentioned KPIs, do other systems and practices encourage teamwork? Do your recognition practices promote teamwork, or do they unintentionally praise the accomplishments of only a single team member at the expense of the whole team? Leaders must always be watchful for any practices which may damage, rather than build, teamwork.

The leader must also *provide resources, tools, and information* to support the team. It is extremely frustrating when you know *what* to do, know *how* to do it, and *want* to do it and do it well, but you don't have all the means of doing it, whether the missing item is a tool, material, or piece of information. And are these provided in a manner or format where the team can be successful even if the leader is not available? If not, the leader has fallen short on this critical role. The use of visual management methods where the needed information is easily accessible to the team is one mechanism to support an empowered team. It is the role of leaders to assure that these supporting methods, along with all other needed tools and resources, are in place for the team to win.

Leaders must *incorporate mechanisms for team development.* Time must be provided to enable team problem-solving and collaboration on improvement opportunities. The leader must facilitate and coach the team in the PDCA problem-solving process, and promote respectful and open sharing of ideas and problems. As the leader develops the team and the members begin to work interdependently, rather than independently, the power of the team increases far beyond the collection of a group of individual contributors. This is the essence of synergy.

These are a few key responsibilities of Lean leaders required due to the *teamwork* principle of Lean. Leaders have a responsibility to develop effective teams within work areas, throughout the value stream, and even across company facilities.

Scientific Thinking Principle – Be a "Fear-Destroyer"

In Chapter 3, when reviewing the Improvement Principle, *Scientific Thinking (PDCA)*, we considered the redefinition of the word *failure.* Fear of failure is debilitating to a Lean transformation, since it stalls movement through the PDCA process. We may never make it to "Do." In an experimental environment, as long as learning has occurred, the word failure loses its negative meaning. We may even conduct an experiment knowing that there is a high likelihood that it will *fail* in order to learn something regarding a problem.

Failure, along with related words such as *mistakes, problems,* and even *improvement,* often invokes fear. Due to past experiences, this could be a fear of failure or a fear of being reprimanded by the supervisor, or possibly a fear of appearing poorly in front of peers if a proposed idea is rejected.

In the absence of fear, Lean behaviors such as experimentation and surfacing of problems and mistakes can safely and openly occur. A call for improvement is not interpreted as a scolding as if you did something wrong, so therefore you must improve. Rather, improvement becomes an integral part of everyone's job, and the leader has created a *safe* environment to facilitate open discussion and debate. The leader's *own* behavior, not just what they say, is the primary mechanism for removing fear. Consider how a leader reacts to a mistake which the employee highlights.

A Leader Behavior Example – How Do You React?

How does the leader react to a mistake or problem which is brought to their attention? Disgust and blame? Exasperation that the issue was even brought to them? I know; the leader may be a very busy person. That's the last thing they need to hear, another problem. If this is how you react, you're moving in the wrong direction; turn around 180 degrees. This is *anti-Lean leadership* at its best, or maybe I should say *at its worst*.

A better reaction is, if a mistake occurs, work with the employee or team to dig for the root causes with the *5 Whys*. What can be done to change the process to enable the employee to be successful? What have we learned? What's the next step, the next experiment? Problems are opportunities to improve the process, so we need to highlight them and jump onto the PDCA problem-solving cycle.

Since there is a deep fear of failure embedded into many of our psyches, a fear of looking like a fool in front of our peers, it is every leader's responsibility to continually look for teaching moments to eliminate fear. Make it safe for employees to highlight mistakes and problems. Fear freezes us. We often can't speak or move, therefore there's no improvement. Leaders must be *fear-destroyers*.

Supporting Leadership Behaviors and Characteristics

Now we'll look at the following leadership behaviors or characteristics which support the principle-based roles just reviewed:

- Be visible and active
- Be a communicator of the vision
- Be a humble leader
- Be a giver of power
- Be an influencer

These traits apply to any leader level; however, they aren't necessarily currently distributed equally across the leader ranks. For example, due to the nature of the job, the front-line leader is typically already a *visible and active* leader. However, the need for visibility crosses all leader levels and is often severely lacking once we go beyond the plant-floor leader. A practice such as *communicating the vision* is often affiliated with the executive leader level. However, every leader, regardless of rank, must provide their team with clarity of team and company vision. So proceed with the perspective that though these recommended traits are universal, the need for improvement will likely vary amongst leader levels.

Be Visible and Active

The first topic has to do with leader visibility. We've previously discussed the standardized *gemba* walk process, which is one mechanism that supports this leadership role. Visibility is not enough, though. Lean leadership must be both visible and *active*. The word *active* has been added to assure there is no misunderstanding, thinking that making numerous fly-by appearances to the *gemba* is sufficient. The goal isn't simply to become endeared to the troops by high-fiving and fist-pumping your way through the facility. This is appropriate if this gregarious outgoing style is your nature, but not near enough; this may be *visible*, but not quite the *active* we're talking about.

The Purpose of Visible and Active Leadership

As we've done in many places throughout this book, let's start with purpose. What is the purpose of a leader being visible and active in the workplace? Following is a list of a few reasons which answer the purpose question:

- ▪ To listen
- ▪ To show you care
- ▪ To teach
- ▪ To coach
- ▪ To help
- ▪ To identify problems
- ▪ To clarify
- ▪ To get accurate information

Transforming an organization is a tough task. There is no room for assumptions: assuming that once you set the direction for the organization, everything will naturally happen as envisioned. That would be wonderful, but there are too many years of built up inertia and past behavior which stands in the way. The above bulleted list is not meant to be in any order of priority, except for the first two bullets … *to listen and show you care*. These are intentionally listed at the top. Change is not easy for us humans, even when the change is good. Caring and showing empathy is not only the right thing to do from a personal standpoint, but by listening to the concerns and fears of the associates, you can develop countermeasures to address such concerns and fears.

Visible and Active Leadership from Another Place and Time

Lean leadership behaviors can be found outside of the business setting. Visibility, like most Lean leadership behaviors, can simply be considered *good leadership traits*, whether practiced in the factory, office, or some other place of work, such as in government. Chapter 1 of Don Phillips' book, *Lincoln on Leadership: Executive Strategies for Tough Times*, is titled "Get Out of the Office and Circulate Among the Troops."[6] John Nicolay and John Hay, Abraham Lincoln's personal secretaries, reported that he spent 75 percent of his time meeting with people. Lincoln obviously understood the value in being a visible and active leader. An interesting statement from Lincoln regarding his accessibility reveals another leadership trait which can be considered a partner to visibility: the need for *courage* as it relates to communication.

"I tell you," he once said, "that I call these receptions my 'public opinion baths' – for I have little time to read the papers and gather public opinion that way; and though they may not be pleasant in all particulars, the effect, as a whole, is renovating and invigorating."[7]

Another way I interpret Lincoln's words – *"though they may not be pleasant in all particulars"* – is that you may not always like what you hear, but you *do* need to hear it. You can't address a problem, even if it is a misperception, unless you hear it. Someone's perception is reality until *they* choose to change it. This accessibility to people requires a level of courage. Not everyone is comfortable hearing news that *"may not be pleasant in all particulars."* But keep in mind that as a Lean leader, you are asking associates to step out of their comfort zone. It is absolutely critical that you do the same. Visibility does require courage.

The Invisible Leader

What's the downside? What happens if you are not visible and active as a leader? Some might argue that the best leader is one who *is* invisible, just keep signing the checks for what we need. This may have some merit in an extremely Lean-mature organization, but even in this case, I feel that the risks of *invisibility* are far too many. Besides not fulfilling the purpose as described by the bulleted list above, what is the appearance or perception from the workforce of a leader's absence? A leader shouldn't assume that everyone is okay with their truancy, that their nonappearance is viewed positively.

A Story of the Invisible Leader

At the last quarterly all-hands meeting, the leader may have passionately talked about the need for everyone to jump onto the mission of developing a true continuous improvement culture. He may have eloquently described how this will not only put the company in a more competitive position, but how it will create a more fulfilling work experience for everyone. On all counts, a fine Lean vision speech was provided.

Now let's leap forward a few weeks when reality sets in. Work teams are struggling with some initial improvement efforts, and there's confusion everywhere about the KPI/communication boards and the huddle process. The information on the communication board is not easily updated, and the area leaders are frustrated by the amount of time it takes to keep it current. People start believing that the board is only window dressing for management, since they are not exactly sure how it is supposed to be used.

Another frustration is some area leaders' admitted difficulty in facilitating the daily huddle meeting. *"We've never done this before!"* There also have been some issues with finding the time to implement even the small ideas which the teams came up with. And for ideas where the teams needed support, such as from the engineering group, it's nowhere to be found. These are all realistic issues which may surface, especially in the early stages of a Lean transformation, which require coaching, clarification, and support.

While this is all going on, what if the leader is not around? What if he's still basking in the glory of his Lean pronouncement at the last quarterly meeting? What do you think the workforce is thinking? Here are a few possibilities:

> *"Sure would be nice if Mr. Bigwig would at least make an appearance to look at the stupid board we put up for him! He probably wants to show it off to Mr. Corporate Bigwig for when he comes for a tour every once in a blue moon. Plus, maybe he can give me an idea as to how this is going to help the company and my department. I don't think that was really talked about during his big speech."*

> *"Would it kill him to take a few seconds to come out here and at least acknowledge the improvements that we put in place, in spite of the roadblocks in our way? The team really worked hard. Is a little appreciation expecting too much? The team even did some of the work on their own time! Cut me a break!"*

"Maybe we aren't doing the right thing? Maybe his absence means that he doesn't approve? If we're not doing the right thing, what are we supposed to be doing? I know we have other ideas to try, but maybe we should hold off until we get some sort of signal from the powers that be."

At some point, eventually, these workplace frustrations might reach the leadership level that can then help address the situation; however, the key word is *eventually*. Just think of the damage to the morale of the work area leaders and their teams until someone *eventually* helps. Compare this with the visible and active leader approach where there is little to no lag in information flow, both good and bad information. In fact, you want to encourage the sharing of *the bad* so that you can help, or get the help which is needed. Or maybe clarify, educate, and coach as to how the team can help themselves, maybe outside assistance is not required. *"Oh, you mean we're authorized to do that? Thanks, I didn't realize that! That's great; we'll take care of it!"* Leaders must be both visible and active.

Be a Communicator of the Vision

The previous discussion highlighted the inadequacy of simply making a passionate speech at the all-hands meeting; however, this passionate speech should not be discarded. The point is that it is not sufficient. It won't replace visible and active leadership. However, it is your job to set the direction and provide a glimpse into the Lean future, to set expectations, even though the future is admittedly a little foggy. So what should be the tone of a Lean journey speech? First of all, it's acceptable to admit the unknowns of the future. This honesty will make you look human, but also part of your message should be that everyone will play a role in how we find our way through the cloudiness. We'll work together to find the best path that works best for us, not for Toyota, not for Boeing, not for Company X, or whoever else; this is our journey. It's up to us to find our unique path. Sure, we need to learn from as many other organizations as possible, and we will, but we'll take that knowledge and work together and experiment our way to *our own* Lean future.

This message should not only be part of some all-hands public speech on Lean, but should be a constant ongoing message supported by action, not just words. In John Kotter's book, *A Sense of Urgency*, the section titled "be visibly urgent" is aligned with our discussion of visible and active management.[8] Kotter describes the visible/active activities of a plant manager named David Bauman. Following is a statement regarding the consistent and relentless message from Mr. Bauman:

> The oh-so-visible message is oh so clear. "There can be no letting up. The only way we can guarantee job security, keep raises higher than inflation, and maintain a clean, attractive, safe workplace is if we move faster, smarter, and better than the competition. Because the competition does not sit still, this task is very challenging. Yes, we have been successful and should be proud. But our success in meeting the challenges of the past tells us little about a future that constantly throws new problems and opportunities at us."[9]

As for the frequency of this message, Kotter states, "This message is broadcast to every single employee, every single day, every workday in the fifty-two-week year, with words and deeds."[10]

All the words mean absolutely nothing without the deeds to go along with them. The clarity and honesty of this plant manager's message should be emulated, and in no way is it a condescending lecture on past failures. In fact, it expresses recognition of past success, something to be proud of. But the message addresses the fact that the competitive business environment of today requires ongoing improvement.

Any Lean journey message should have a personal component, the *"what's in it for me?"* question. The previous excerpt of David Bauman's message from Kotter's *A Sense of Urgency* addresses this to a certain point.[11] He mentions job security, raises, and a safe work environment. Besides these basic human needs, a few other items worth sharing about the future on a Lean journey are the opportunity to have input into how your job is accomplished and improved, and the increased opportunities for learning and growth. The idea of a work experience where it's challenging, and maybe even fun, might be something to look forward to rather than the current *zombie-like* work environment of too many organizations. Lean can be a life-changing experience for many associates. Every leader, at every leadership level, must appreciate this aspect of Lean and your obligation in being an effective Lean leader. We focus so much on the company transformation and resultant competitive business advantages of Lean, we fail to appreciate arguably the most important outcome of developing a Lean organization – people's lives are changed for the better. This may seem like too soft of an issue for some old-school managers, but these *soft* issues are *leadership* issues which will enable your organization to produce *hard bottom-line results*.

Be a Humble Leader

Let's look at another characteristic of Lean leaders, *humility*. Without this trait, I'm not sure it is even possible for a leader to abide by the *Respect for People* principle.

> humility:[12]
> [hyoo-**mil**-i-tee *or, often*, yoo-]
> noun
> 1. the quality or condition of being humble; modest opinion or
>   estimate of one's own importance, rank, etc.

For some of you, I bet this doesn't sound like the description of many leaders you may have known from your past. Humble, modest, it just doesn't seem to fit, but Lean demands that leaders lead with humility. In fact, that exact wording, *Lead with Humility*, is Principle #2 of the Shingo Prize, the Nobel prize of Lean excellence.[13] This idea of humble leadership shows up in other sources. In Jim Collins' *Good to Great*, he uses the term "Level 5 leader" to represent the highest hierarchy of executive capability found in their research. He describes a Level 5 leader as "an individual who blends extreme personal humility with intense professional will."[14] All *good to great* companies were found to have Level 5 leaders. And in our previous reference to the plant manager, David Bauman, in John Kotter's *A Sense of Urgency*, Kotter writes, "The plant manager has a genuine humility. Yet his mild voice has an intensity that makes you feel he wants to be on the team winning the World Series."[15]

The Purpose of Humility

So what's the purpose? Why the need to be humble when leading in a Lean environment? First of all, no one wants to work for the boss who is the extreme opposite of humble … the vain, arrogant, and conceited jerk. I think most would agree that we like humble, but don't like arrogant; however, this Lean leadership characteristic entails more than simply being a nice person:

- Without a sense of humility, it's impossible for the leader to engage their team and seek input from others. Why would this type of leader do this? He's the smartest guy in the room with all the answers; why waste time engaging the team? *"They just need to do what I, the smart guy, tell them to do."* That type of attitude will not develop the engagement and teamwork that we want.

- Without a sense of humility, a leader is unable to look in the mirror and acknowledge their personal opportunities for improvement. To continuously learn and grow as an organization, we need to continuously learn and grow as a team and as individuals. This requires the ability and courage for self-reflection. Without humility, it would be difficult to understand this idea of personal ongoing learning and growth.

- Without a sense of humility, it's doubtful that a leader will understand that good ideas can come from anyone at any level in the organization. They'll believe that only someone with their stature would be able to produce any ideas of value. In fact, this type of leader will probably try to find a way to be credited for their staff's accomplishments rather than recognizing the deserving individual or team. I bet there are probably at least a few of the readers who have had a boss like this. *Boss* would be the correct label, since *leader* would actually be a misnomer. The resultant effect on employee morale via this behavior is obviously devastating.

- Without a sense of humility a leader won't be modeling Lean leadership behaviors to their staff, and thus they will perpetuate the type of behavior which will stall the transformation.

This is just a partial list. The need for humility is another one of those traits which may seem like a "soft" issue, but we need to start considering this as simply a solid, good leadership characteristic. We need to start getting tough and hard on these so-called "soft" issues. In the past, humility simply hasn't been part of our leadership paradigm. Even in the movies, think about how leaders have been portrayed on the big screen. I don't remember too many humble leaders riding into town on horseback or rushing onto the battlefield to save the day. Back in the workplace, the title "boss" doesn't depict humility, and the label "superior" is unfortunately self-explanatory in its lack of humility.

In a non-Lean environment, humility isn't even a necessary leadership characteristic. A wide range of leadership styles can be successful in an environment of complacency and status quo, but Lean changes everything. The goal is no longer just compliance; it is improvement, *continuous improvement*, with everyone involved. This requires humble leaders who believe in the creativity and potential of all people.

Action Item – *Reflection of Past Leaders*

Think about those few leaders that stand out in your memory who were most effective in engaging their team, whose team always seemed to be enthusiastic, even in challenging times. They somehow performed and improved in all key measures regardless of the existing culture of the organization surrounding them. Maybe this was a team which other employees wanted to be part of since they inexplicably appeared to have more fun while always exceeding performance expectations.

You may have to search your memory for a lower-level leader who led a small department or maybe a maintenance supervisor or manager who had a team of technicians who were as dedicated and creative as any engineering group. If you reflect upon these diamonds of Lean leadership excellence, I bet you'll locate a determined, but humble, leader. Go ahead, put the book down for a moment, and reminisce. It will bring back some memories of good people, and I bet it will add support to the need for humility.

A Lesson from Outside the Factory

As has been demonstrated, I like to step outside of our familiar workplace setting and search for lessons elsewhere which can help us on our Lean transformation journey. Let's take a short diversion out to sea to search for confirmation of the previously reviewed Lean leader traits, and whether additional Lean leader characteristics can be found.

L. David Marquet was a captain of a nuclear-powered submarine, and he successfully turned the USS *Sante Fe* from the very worst in the fleet to the best, worst to first via a cultural transformation initiated by redefining what it means to be a leader. In fact, after their transformation, their inspection score wasn't only the highest in the fleet, it was the highest score ever received! He shared his journey in the book *Turn the Ship Around!*, which should be on everyone's reading and study list.[16] At one point during his and his ship's transformation, Captain Marquet makes a decision which may sound ridiculous, considering that he was the captain of the ship. He vowed *never to give another order.*

Captain Marquet's decision reminded me of what one plant manager told me a few years ago. He said, *"I can't make anyone do anything."* What were Captain Marquet and my plant manager friend talking about? They were the boss; they had the power to direct, but they made a concerted effort not to do so. Historically, a leader often defaulted to the use of their position power. *"I'm the boss, just do what I say!"* It's an easy approach, and it's quick. But at best, you might gain compliance. No one will learn. No one will grow, and no one will have the opportunity to use their creativity and skills for improvement. By vowing not to give orders, it forces the leader to influence others by teaching, coaching, clarifying, modeling the desired behavior, and creating the environment for change and continuous improvement. It's more difficult than simply barking out an order, but much more effective if your goal is to engage and develop the team.

This empowerment mindset does not imply an image of chaos with everybody running around doing their own thing. The appropriate image would be the exact opposite. In *Turn the Ship Around!*, Captain Marquet details how the *competence* and *clarity* pillars must support the *give control* objective to make this work.[17] If we give control or authority to someone without developing their capability and competence or without providing clarity on the goals and objectives, what do you think will happen? The chaos image would likely become reality. There are no shortcuts; they always backfire. In the next chapter we'll see how *giving control, competence, and clarity* parallel key motivational factors.

Be a Giver of Power

This story highlights the paradox of effective leadership today, whether on a nuclear-powered submarine or in our factories. Once you gain the power to control, you must find a way to give away, or at least share, this control. A non-Lean culture of compliance can be dictated, but a culture of continuous improvement cannot be directed and forced. The motivational on-switch resides within the hearts and minds of every single employee; no one else can switch it. This presents leadership challenges that simply didn't exist in the status quo world of compliance. To engage the workforce, once a leader gains power, they must immediately get to work giving away this power to their team. This is empowerment, the giving of power.

Be an Influencer

In spite of my plea for leaders to empower their teams, *position power* does exist. This is something which cannot be given away. The leadership position itself inherently carries some extra weight. Your words and actions have a profound effect on your culture. Whether earned or not, due to the position which you hold, you have this heightened power to influence. Consider it an obligation, an obligation to use this position power as influencing leverage to develop a Lean culture.

All leaders, regardless of rank, should be on the lookout for influencing opportunities which highlight the desired Lean behaviors; however, if the leader is not in touch, not visibly and actively leading the charge, these opportunities to influence will sail right by unnoticed ... opportunities lost! This parallels our earlier discussion of being watchful for teaching moments. Leaders must not only utilize their own personal influencing power, but must create opportunities for social, or peer, influence to occur. Leaders cannot stand on the sideline and expect others to do the heavy lifting of influencing change. They need to be influencers. In the next chapter, much more will be said about the topic of influence and building a critical mass to transform the organization.

Leader Missteps of the Past – What and Why?

Even if the benefits are known, why is there sometimes a reluctance of leadership to practice some of the before-mentioned behaviors? Consider *visibility*, which requires spending time with the value-adding workers in the *gemba*. We've already touched on one reason: some people are just not comfortable doing it. It's one of those comfort-zone issues which leaders must have the courage to face and overcome. But there are other reasons why a leader may be reluctant to embed themselves in *gemba* operations. I'll repeat what was previously stated when reviewing Failure Mechanism #2, *Leaders Aren't Leading. Leaders occasionally try to justify delegating this role in the name of empowerment, or a desire to not micromanage the change, but both of these reasons are usually cop-outs and an abdication of their own critical responsibility.*

A leader using the *micromanage* excuse is somewhat understandable based on engrained past non-Lean behaviors. But the problem is solely with the past behavior itself. If you know of a micromanager who has demoralized their staff by their condescending nature and by overriding most everything which the staff has done, or wanted to do, it's this particular behavior which must be eliminated. *Visible and active* Lean leadership should never remotely be confused with negative anti-Lean micromanaging behaviors and practices.

Let's review a short story depicting other leader missteps which must be avoided. Unfortunately, leaders can abuse, alter, and transform an effective Lean practice into an inept anti-Lean practice by poor execution or their inability to free themselves of behaviors which conflict with Lean principles. The leading character is Mr. Richard McAutocrat.

The Story of Richard McAutocrat

Richard McAutocrat is a plant manager who has recently instituted a *gemba* walk process where he and his staff spend 10–15 minutes at each work area every single day. Mr. McAutocrat was always a hands-on manager and was eager to institute this Lean practice. His background was as a manufacturing engineer, and his effectiveness in this role helped to propel him through the management ranks to the current plant manager position. Mr. McAutocrat appeared to be following the *gemba* walk script fairly well as far as asking questions regarding adherence to schedule, problems, and improvement opportunities; however, it's his reaction to the information where this process took an ugly turn. Instead of providing support by committing resources and/or time that would enable the work area team to address a problem, or taking the time to teach and coach the team leader on how to address a particular problem, Mr. McAutocrat's approach was more of an interrogation. He chastised missed schedules and ordered, *"Get it done, or else!"*

As for improvement activities, he went to the other extreme; I guess his manufacturing engineering background kicked in. He tried to dive into every detail and seemed to alter every single plan or process change which was instituted by the work area team. His personal stamp had to be on everything, at least everything that was positive. This was frustrating for the work area team leader since he was actually hoping to get some recognition, not just for himself, but for one of his team members who worked hard on a particular improvement effort which clearly was a success. Recognition was not part of Mr. McAutocrat's vocabulary, unless it flowed to him.

Through all of his criticisms and directives, there was very little learning taking place. After the initial questioning from Mr. McAutocrat, the whole conversation was one-way, Mr. McAutocrat speaking, everyone else listening.

It was clear that Mr. McAutocrat felt he was the smartest person in the room, or in this case, the *gemba*; and, he seemed to work very hard to make sure that it was clear to everyone that he indeed was the smartest person there. *(This is not the type of clarity that a Lean leader should be providing.)* And besides the damage to the morale of the work area team, the other outcome of Mr. McAutocrat's version of a *gemba* walk was that he was modeling his anti-Lean leadership style for his staff. So, on second thought, there *was* actually employee learning and growth occurring; unfortunately, the wrong kind! He was effectively developing the next generation of Mr. McAutocrats.

What Can We Learn?

Execution Matters!

The above scenario may be a slight exaggeration of the real world, but maybe not. Mr. McAutocrat instituted a solid Lean practice, the *gemba* walk, which enabled visibility; however, his poor execution demonstrated the types of behaviors which we are actually trying to eliminate. So the first lesson is that execution matters. The fault wasn't in the mechanism, the *gemba* walk. If someone says, *"We tried gemba walks before. They didn't work,"* most likely the failure was in the execution of this practice, not the practice itself. It could also be stated that Mr. McAutocrat was a *teacher and coach*, a key role of a Lean leader. Again, the problem was with the execution. Unfortunately, he was teaching and influencing anti-Lean behaviors. Execution matters!

Lean Principles are Standards, not Options!

The other lesson from this story is that Lean principles, and the required leader behaviors which derive from these principles, must *all* be followed. Mr. McAutocrat clearly violated the *respect for people* principle and did not exhibit any indication of *leading with humility*. Until Lean principles become unarguable standards, and not simply "suggested options" which can be opted out of if deemed inconvenient, anti-Lean behaviors such as those by Mr. McAutocrat will continue to thrive, and continue to stall employee engagement and the development of a Lean culture.

Mr. McAutocrat – What Should You Do?

If you currently have tendencies like Mr. McAutocrat which you know must be eliminated, I admire you for acknowledging this problem. Now treat it like any other problem. You know the target behavior, to listen, teach, coach, support, clarify, in alignment with Lean principles, and you know your current condition, an autocratic do-it-my-way approach. Now experiment your way to the desired target. One suggestion is to have your staff and a work area team leader critique you on your *gemba* walk performance. Not only will you improve, but you will be teaching at the same time. You are teaching that the autocratic behavior must be changed, and you are teaching that we all personally have to look in the mirror to see how we can improve. This is not an easy thing for any of us to do. I understand; it does take courage, but the impact will be immeasurable. *"Wow, if Mr. McAutocrat can change, anyone can! Now he'll have to change his name."*

Now let's spend some time focusing on a specific leader category, the front-line leader. It's my experience that this leader group includes some of the most creative and dedicated individuals within an organization. Let's review a few things to help them not only be successful, but to become the real Lean all-stars of the organization.

Front-Line Leaders

Due to the fact that a majority of the workforce reports to a front-line leader, preparing this group of individuals for their role as Lean leaders naturally takes on a heightened importance, but, unfortunately, this preparation has typically been lacking in many organizations. As reviewed in Chapter 2, it's absolutely not their fault. We have made significant changes to their position but we haven't provided effective training and coaching, and often we haven't even provided clarity on the requirements of their capacity as a Lean leader. Roles such as teacher/coach, which include employee engager and idea facilitator, and boundary manager may be totally new concepts for the leader raised in the traditional leadership mold, and the idea of *focusing on the process* may be foreign to someone who is used to operating in a *"just get it done!"* environment. By not providing the clarity, coaching, and ongoing support, we set them up for failure, create frustration, and then act surprised when Front-Line Leader Joe seems to be fighting against the Lean effort, as opposed to supporting and leading. Before we review a few ideas to help address this issue, as with any problem, we should understand its roots.

Why Have We Ignored the Front-Line Leader?

Part of the problem might be that with the leadership focus on the upper and middle leader levels, organizations have been slow in directing their attention to the front-line leader. In many organizations, this critical leadership level has been undervalued for years. When we talk about leadership or company leaders, how often do we envision those who lead at the front line? The individuals who typically come to mind probably have titles like president, CEO, operations manager, or plant manager, seldom the assembly team leader or CNC department foreman. As for the typical selection process of this foreman, we often promote the most experienced CNC machinist to supervise the other CNC department personnel. Seems to make sense, but is this individual qualified or even interested in engaging the team in work area improvements? This is one of the reasons why many companies have *spotty* Lean transformations. Within the same facility, you might see work areas and their leaders who can be described as models of Lean, while other areas, maybe only a few steps away, are great examples of an anti-Lean environment and culture. Observe the behaviors of the respective front-line leaders and you'll likely see the root cause of why this dichotomy exists in a *spotty Lean* environment. Later in this chapter we'll return to this topic of *spotty Lean*.

What Are Some Ideas to Prepare the Front-Line Leader?

Early Involvement in the Change Process

Do not delay involving this critical leadership level. Engage the front-line leaders in the early planning and design stages of the Lean transformation. Any time lag in their involvement will only increase the confusion, fears, and frustrations, and any of their concerns will naturally disperse to their teams. The front-line leader would be totally unprepared to coach and guide their team, and be unable to provide any enlightenment into even the most basic questions regarding Lean and any impending changes. This only adds to the front-line leader unease. The result is that an unintended wall of resistance will be rising higher and higher by any postponement in engaging the front-line leader.

Involve the front-line leaders in activities such as the initial workforce Lean training. Enable them to provide input into the training approach and content for their teams, and encourage them to participate in the delivery of the training. Some early adopters may jump at the opportunity to deliver the training. This visible and active leadership will not only develop the front-line leaders, but will help engage their teams. The priority of the Lean transformation will be obvious. On the other hand, a lack of visible commitment will send the signal that Lean is not a priority. Lean will be viewed as a disruption to the team members' "jobs" since this is how their leader seems to view it, rather than Lean being an integral part of everyone's job.

Training and Coaching

The front-line leader naturally needs a foundation of Lean knowledge and understanding, so Lean principles training and how these principles affect the leadership role must be provided. This includes an understanding of how the role of the front-line employee, who they are leading, is changing. Some of these changes, such as the exposing and highlighting of problems, will require patience, ongoing encouragement, and coaching from the leader.

The traditional *classroom* training approach, by itself, has proven to be only marginally effective. Reference Failure Mechanism #5 – *Lean "Training" Isn't Effective.* Classroom training doesn't need to be replaced, but rather it needs to be supplemented with ongoing teaching and coaching to develop the leadership skills and behaviors required for an effective Lean transformation.

Form a Front-Line Leader Peer Team

Consider utilizing a *peer group* format as a method to develop the front-line leaders. Peer influence is powerful. One-on-one coaching is needed, but there are many benefits to supplementing this with a peer group approach. Some of the heightened *people aspects* of the Lean leader role may seem daunting and invoke an amount of fear. By teaching and coaching in a group setting, fear may be alleviated due to peer support. A peer format provides opportunities for leaders to learn and grow by helping each other. It may even make sense to have them team up to conduct some of the initial basic Lean training for their teams.

In some cases, these leaders are internal suppliers and customers to each other who must learn to work as a value stream team, so getting them together in the same room will facilitate the collaboration required of the *optimize the value stream* principle. Finger-pointing must be replaced with cooperation and teamwork. If there are any internal customer/supplier conflicts, better to get these problems exposed and addressed now. Remember, with Lean, we want to expose and highlight problems, not hide them. The peer format also enables the teacher/coach who is working with the peer team to identify those who require additional coaching and support.

Look for opportunities to take the front-line leaders on benchmarking visits. If you can arrange for the tour leader from the benchmarking site to be from the front-line leader level, you gain the benefit of peer influence via a peer from another organization. Finally, this peer format can be utilized to enable the front-line leaders to participate in redefining their own roles and responsibilities. Very few people resist something which they help to create.

Engagement in Redefining the "Job"

If a front-line leader contributes to the design of their own job, don't you think the chances of support, adherence, and even ongoing improvement would increase? The motivational aspect of this approach is a primary topic of the next chapter. Of course, the Lean principles are non-negotiable and must be the design framework for the Lean strategy, so if someone proposes a practice which is clearly misaligned with these principles and company goals, this is another teaching and coaching opportunity. This may also indicate a weakness or need regarding the Lean training process. The front-line leader roles and responsibilities should be documented as *leader standard work*, which will be reviewed in the next section of this chapter.

Summary – Front-Line Leaders

The idea that it is sufficient to simply gain passive support or "buy-in" from the front-line leader is a completely faulty premise – that is, if developing a Lean culture of continuous improvement is your objective. Front-line leaders must become the Lean leaders who coach, teach, engage, and grow their team members. They must work with the leaders of their internal customers and suppliers to optimize the value stream linkages in order to provide the most value to the external paying customer. And they must become process-focused, almost to a fanatical level, and develop this perspective in their team members as well. This is necessary to consistently obtain the desired results and to have a basis for ongoing improvement.

Some leaders on the front line may consider firefighting and jumping through hoops as a primary component of their jobs. Obviously within a Lean environment, the emphasis is on process improvement to minimize the need for this type of behavior. Rather than a primary element of their jobs, firefighting becomes a process deviation, a signal of a process problem to be addressed with their team. Though undesirable, the firefighting and hoop jumping, in a way, is still welcome. It highlights an opportunity for process improvement and employee engagement.

It is imperative that Lean leadership development at the front line becomes a priority. Following are the items we've reviewed in this past section to specifically help those invaluable leaders at the front line:

1. Early involvement in the change process – don't delay and wait for the execution or "rollout" phase.
2. Training and coaching – this should include multiple personnel development means, including traditional classroom training, ongoing one-on-one coaching and mentoring, and peer team approaches.
3. Form a front-line leader peer team – this approach enables peer learning and support along with accountability.
4. Engagement in redefining the "job" – develop *leader standard work* to provide role clarity, to highlight problems, and to enable continuous improvement and growth.

Leader Standard Work

"Leader standard work" may seem like a bizarre concept to some of you. Standardizing the variabilities of a leader's role into some sort of standard working document may seem like an impossible task; however, the development of leader standard work has multiple benefits and provides opportunities for continuous improvement. David Mann provides excellent guidance on this topic in Chapter 3 of his book, *Creating A Lean Culture: Tools to Sustain Lean Conversions.*[18] He effectively outlines typical standard work activities for various leader levels. What I'd like to focus on here are the benefits and some reasons why you should devote the time and effort in developing standard work for leaders.

Before we go down this path, I do want to address the before-mentioned concern which I know some of you are struggling with: that leader work would seem too irregular for standardization. Obviously, a leader's daily activities are different than the associate working in the assembly workcell. In the assembly worker's case, probably close to 100 percent of the work content can be defined as standard work. Admittedly, even at the front-line leader level, I doubt that 90 percent of the leader activities can be documented onto a standard work sheet which defines the activity content, time required, and sequence/frequency; however, this shouldn't prevent us from standardizing the 75 percent or 80 percent of the items that *can* be detailed and documented. As you develop leader standard work, if you are only at 25 percent or 30 percent of the day standardized, keep working at it. It's like a Pareto chart where the highest bar is the "other" category, and you need to dig into "other" to break it down into identifiable parts. The same applies with your leader standard work. If the "other duties as needed" category accounts for most of your day, take a deep dive into this category. What you will find is that there are items which can actually be standardized as to content and timing, and you'll find other items which don't belong in your standard work plan.

As leader standard work is developed for higher leader levels, the challenge of rigorous standardization becomes even more difficult. In some cases specific activities or activity frequencies and time required are difficult to define; therefore, the format of the leader standard work will be less structured and precise.

Leader Standard Work: Purpose #1 – Role Definition

The theme of this section on leadership is how Lean affects the roles and responsibilities of leaders at all levels. Leader standard work *defines* what the role is! There's no mystery; it's not hidden behind a fuzzy job description or rough outline of expectations. With leader standard work, you define specifically *what* needs to be done, *how long* it should take, *who* does it, and *when*. In the past, maybe this sort of leader responsibility rigor was not required, but now that we are changing the job to be aligned with Lean principles, more role clarity and definition is needed. Equally as important as the definition of what needs to be done is the role clarity provided by what is *not* part of the leader standard work. Past leader practices may conspicuously be missing and replaced with more Lean-aligned activities. The first critical reason to develop leader standard work is role definition.

Leader Standard Work: Purpose #2 – Problem-Surfacing

The next reason is the same as why we standardize anything in a Lean environment: to highlight abnormalities or a gap from where we currently are, to our target condition. If the role is not sufficiently defined, how do we know if the leader is being successful in their job, if expectations are being met? Please pause before jumping to the knee-jerk response of, *"Hey, just look at the results! Is the leader getting the results? It's as simple as that!"* If that is in fact your response, you must have nodded off a bit when reading the section on the *focus on the process* principle and the various references to this principle. *(Note: I apologize for not keeping your interest which led to the nodding-off period.)* Let me provide a quick recap. *Yes*, we absolutely want the *results*, but the *process* of *how* we obtain the results does matter in a Lean environment, otherwise any improved condition is likely non-sustainable. Yes, you should be commended on how you and your team may have accomplished a Herculean task by jumping through various hoops and slaying multiple dragons this past month to obtain the desired results, but obtaining those results via a defined and standardized process is a significantly more effective approach, not to mention less stressful. The process does matter, and leader standard work defines the leader process which helps to generate the desired results. With a standard process, any abnormalities to the standard process can be identified. Problems can be recognized.

Leader Standard Work: Purpose #3 – Improvement and Development

Another reason for developing leader standard work is that it provides a baseline for ongoing improvement. Once problems are recognized, root causes can be investigated to develop experiments and countermeasures for improvement. For example, a front-line leader may have a standard work task which requires them to check whether an operator is having any difficulties in following their standard work on the assembly line. The leader standard work might define that a check is to be completed twice per day. If the leader misses one of these checks, a process deviation, an abnormality, has occurred, and this miss should be treated as any other missed commitment or deviation from the standard. A problem-solving PDCA cycle should begin. The front-line leader's coach can then provide the support needed to enhance the learning and growth of the front-line leader. Leader standard work becomes a tool for leader development.

Leader Standard Work Format

The leader standard work mechanism can be a simple columned document listing the leader activities, how long it should take to complete each activity, and when the task is to be performed or frequency. The document could be put into the format of a checklist. Or, a more visual method can be utilized where the leader standard work information is shown on a large board. A card system could be devised where the color-coded, two-sided task card is flipped over when the task is completed. This is a visual practice often utilized for other types of procedures, such as for equipment maintenance activities. Experiment and develop the method or system that works most effectively for your particular situation.

Leadership – Key Roles and Responsibilities – Concluding Thoughts

The Lean leader roles and responsibilities covered in this section are applicable across all leader levels, from front-line leader to CEO, in spite of the authority and accountability differences among leader ranks. The reviewed items were not meant to form an all-encompassing list of desired leadership traits, but they do provide a solid foundation for Lean leader behavior. Following are the principle-based leader roles and supporting leadership behaviors and characteristics which we reviewed:

1. Teacher and coach
2. Improver through process
3. System coordinator
4. Team-builder
5. Fear-destroyer
6. Visible and active
7. Communicator of the vision
8. Humble
9. Giver of power
10. Influencer

Unfortunately, some of these Lean-aligned behaviors have not been part of the traditional definition of leadership. Even our leader titles have been misaligned with the desired behaviors. *Supervisor* and *boss* don't effectively describe the type of leader needed to develop a Lean culture. The label of *manager* even misses the target. *Team or group leader, coach*, or *team facilitator* would get us closer to the mark.

Even though it will ruin my top 10 format listing, an 11th leader role must be added to the list; all Lean leaders must be *students*. Continuous improvement requires continuous learning and development. Leaders must be scholars not only of Lean principles, but of associated topics such as change, influence, and motivation to become better developers and engagers of people.

The next role which we'll examine is the largest personnel category within an organization, that of the front-line employee. These are the team members whom the front-line leaders are leading. Every role is affected by Lean, and the front-line employee is no exception.

Team Members – Key Roles and Responsibilities

Problem-Detectors

One of the key roles of a front-line employee is the exposing and highlighting of problems. Actually, this is a responsibility of every single employee, regardless of position in an organization. We emphasize it here with respect to the front line since they are often in the best location for problem-detection. The front line is where the value is being added, and any non-value disrupts the process of flowing value to the customer. We may think that detecting problems would be an easy practice to instill. You have a problem, just let someone know about it; however, in reality, it's an extremely challenging behavior to get comfortable with. Exposing problems, especially problems in which we have a connection, and maybe even caused by us, is simply not an easy or natural behavior for many people. An excerpt from *Toyota Culture: The Heart and Soul of the Toyota Way* by Jeffrey Liker and Michael Hoseus emphasizes this point in reference to the start-up of the Toyota facility (TMMK) in Georgetown, Kentucky:[19]

> Hiroyoshi Yoshiki was originally trained in human resources in Japan. He was involved as early as the site selection for the Georgetown plant. We asked him what stood out most about the difference in culture between Toyota in Japan and what he saw when starting up TMMK. He did not hesitate:
>
> *"We were most surprised by the reaction of the people when we asked them about problems. In Toyota we always ask what is the problem? The reactions from Americans were very, very negative. We were surprised. It does not have any negative connotation for us in Japan."*

Due to our negative reaction to problems, we may have a tendency to hide or somehow work around problems rather than expose them. I'd like to think that we don't ever intentionally overlook or ignore problems, but we might quietly do a quick workaround to temporarily repair the issue rather than expose it for other eyes to see. Though we may be satisfied and confident of the "rightness" of our proactive *fix*, this action assures that the problem remains concealed until it resurfaces at another point in time … and it will. If problems aren't exposed, they obviously can't be addressed through a rigorous root-cause analysis approach, and sustainable improvement cannot occur. Surfacing problems is a key front-line role.

The leadership challenge is to turn an unnatural behavior of exposing problems into one which we will do automatically as part of our daily work. We've already discussed how ongoing encouragement and coaching from company leaders is needed to overcome this negative association with problems. But why is this behavior so difficult for us?

Why is Exposing Problems so Difficult?

What is the root cause of our negative association with problems? The *problem* itself isn't the real issue; it's the reaction to the problem that we fear:

> *Will I be blamed for the problem or mistake? Will I look like a fool? Will I get "written up" for the error? Will I get berated for interrupting the boss? Will I get in trouble for stopping my machine for a short while? Will I get one of my friends in trouble?*

I have no idea as to whether this fear is an in-bred characteristic, but I am quite certain that the anti-Lean leadership behaviors of the past have played a significant role in embedding this destructive fear within our employees. Though the front line needs to understand that it is their responsibility and obligation to highlight problems, it won't happen unless the corresponding leadership behavior is in place. Problem-detection must be encouraged and supported, and even welcome. Remember, no problem is a problem; they must be exposed.

Problem-Solvers and Process-Improvers

Along with being problem-detectors, the front-line employees are problem-solvers and process-improvers as well. People Principle #1 – *Everyone,* requires that all employees are players in the continuous improvement game, not mere observers. This is the ongoing challenge of Lean leadership, engaging the minds and hearts of every single employee in the Lean effort. Providing the tools, training, and ongoing support is essential, and the most limited resource of all must be provided … time. This level of involvement is a major transition for some employees. For years they have been told exactly what to do and when to do it, and as long as this was accomplished most of the time, it was a job well done. The job was definitely boring, and kind of demoralizing, *"We don't pay you to think!"* but that was the job as defined in the world of compliance and status quo. Many people not only accept, but actually become comfortable with, this workplace attitude since an alternative was never offered. Lean provides this alternative of a more engaging, fulfilling, and productive work environment.

Sure, improvement occurred occasionally in the status quo workplace, but it was infrequent and typically reactive, such as a change initiated by a customer complaint. Addressing that complaint was usually someone else's job. Front-line involvement was minimal, if at all, until *told* what they had to do differently. Lean puts us in the world of continuous improvement, and now we're asking folks to participate in determining how they do the job, and how to continually make it better. And if there is a customer issue, the front line must be intimately involved in root-cause analysis and countermeasure development. Everyone is *expected* to think and contribute; anything else would be disrespectful. Plus, who knows better about the job than the person doing the job? So it's common sense, besides being respectful, that the front line should be active participants in the Lean strategy.

This expands the role of what we now call the *job* at the front line. There may be years of inertia to overcome. I believe that some of the behavior which we label as resistance to change is simply shock. People are frozen by the shock of finally being asked for their opinions, for finally being listened to and respected as the intelligent, creative people that we all are. Rather than resistance, the initial silence may simply be disbelief in what appears to be going on. The first thought is probably, *"What's the catch? There must be some ulterior motive."*

Developing the problem-solving capability and integrating the front line into the continuous improvement strategy requires a serious commitment of time. This includes time elements such as training and coaching time, problem analysis, idea-generation, and problem-solving and experimentation time. However, the employee engagement aspect of Lean is the greatest investment you'll ever make in your organization; but since this does require time, you have to *design in* this time. As already reviewed, the "fit it in when we have the time" approach seldom works, at least not for long. When considering the time commitment of incorporating Lean into the workday, remember that Lean is *subtractive* with respect to time. As we remove waste from the system, we actually free up time.

Standard Work Followers and Improvers

Another key role of the front-line employee is to follow the standard work. This is a prerequisite of the other two roles. Before you can highlight a deviation from a standard, or improve a standard process, the process must be in some form of a standardized condition which can be followed. It can be argued that this is not really much of a new role for the front line since there have always been standard procedures to follow. This is true, so maybe not a brand new responsibility as a result of Lean, but definitely a heightened role.

In the past, usually the result or outcome was really all that mattered. If you found a technique or trick to improve the way in which you completed a processing step, you might have just kept it to yourself. Not because you aren't a sharing type of person, but rather it's because there wasn't any emphasis placed on distributing your findings. Plus there wasn't a clear method or avenue in getting the word to everyone, especially in a three-shift operation. Mr. Industrial Engineer created the *standard* procedure and it would remain the procedure until he changed it at some point. Anyway, your personally improved process made you look good compared with your coworkers, correct?

This type of behavior is why, when you compare the supposed *standard work* procedure with what actually is going on in the *gemba*, it doesn't always quite match up. Sometimes it's not even close. In the Lean world, it's your *obligation* to share and discuss the proposed change with the team, and if it is, in fact, an improvement, the standard work document and any other associated documents will be changed for all to follow. All team members will be trained in the new method, which becomes the new standard. Not doing this would be a major violation of the *teamwork* principle of Lean. In the Lean world, this team-based behavior will be what makes you, and the team, *look good*.

Value Stream Team Members

The *optimize the value stream* principle is one which should be accentuated during Lean training/coaching sessions with front-line personnel. Just as the front-line supervisors must broaden their "job" perspective beyond their functional area of responsibility and expertise, the front line needs to understand how their work fits into the overall value stream. It is critical that everyone views the next step of the process as their customer, the internal customer. *Everyone* has a customer; some support functions such as maintenance and HR have many internal customers. Cross-training and multi-functional improvement efforts will facilitate this internal customer and value stream viewpoint. Plus, cross-training will provide organizational flexibility. People can move to where the work is needed.

The Front Line – Final Thoughts

Certainly there are numerous other roles and responsibilities of the front-line employee. The goal was to review only a few which are generally impacted by the application of Lean and require ongoing teaching and coaching by company leaders. The roles emphasized here for the front line are applicable to any employee; the obligation to abide by the principles of Lean pertains to everyone. Everyone should be:

- Problem-detectors
- Problem-solvers and process-improvers
- Standard work followers and improvers
- Value stream team members

Through training and coaching, and ongoing involvement in the continuous improvement process, employees grow and develop into better problem-solvers, idea-generators, and process-improvers, so any benefits to the company will increase exponentially over time. (Note: I hate the word "resource" when talking about people. It just sounds a little too inhuman to me. However, I will make an exception in order to emphasize a point.) Another way to put it is that people are a resource which actually appreciates, or increases in worth, over time. And since we know that our work experience has a tendency to carry over into our non-work life, the resultant benefits expand far beyond the walls of our factories.

The final personnel group which I'd like to review in respect to their Lean roles and responsibilities is the Lean support team. This group may be known by other names such as the Lean department, operational excellence team, or CI (continuous improvement) team.

The Lean Support Team

The Lean department, operational excellence team, or CI (continuous improvement) team is a personnel group you'll find within many organizations traveling on the Lean journey. In small organizations, maybe fewer than 50 employees, this team may not actually be a team, but rather a single individual, referred to by labels such as the Lean coordinator or facilitator. Facilitator and coordinator are good descriptors for the role, though a more accurate, though too laborious, title for the Lean facilitator or Lean team member would be Lean teacher/coach/trainer/supporter/ truth-teller, along with facilitator and coordinator. Notice the word which is conspicuously missing … *leader.* As already elaborated on, company leaders must do the leading, though the Lean team often needs to provide coaching and guidance for the leaders. The Lean team provides *support*. It's a critical support role, but clearly a Lean support, not leadership, role. Leaders must lead.

Do We Need a Dedicated Lean Facilitator?

Let's take a step back for a moment, and address the question as to whether a dedicated Lean facilitator or team is actually even needed. Can this position with all of its responsibilities be absorbed by existing internal personnel or maybe a group of people? This is where I have to provide the unsatisfying response of, *"Well, you probably need a dedicated role, but it depends."* Factors such as company size, type of processing, current personnel roles, and existing Lean experience of company personnel, will affect the answer to this question of whether dedicated Lean resources are required. At this point in our history, folks with abundant Lean knowledge and experience have been working for various organizations, and occupying a range of positions within these organizations. This creates the condition where it might be feasible that a company could move forward even without dedicated Lean personnel, especially when supplemented with external Lean support resources. We've progressed from decades ago where many companies didn't employ anyone who knew even the most basic concepts of Lean, let alone be the resident expert.

In many organizations today, even considering the increased Lean awareness and experience, companies find that having internal dedicated Lean expertise is an invaluable component of their Lean organizational structure. Let's look closer at some of the characteristics and roles and responsibilities of a Lean support team or an individual Lean facilitator. You will then be in a better position to decide how you address the responsibilities often held by a Lean team. For simplicity, I will use the term Lean facilitator, whether referring to a single person, or members of a Lean team.

Role of the Lean Facilitator

Subject Matter "Expert"

First of all, the Lean facilitator needs to be a Lean "expert" and student. I usually refrain from using the word expert, since it implies a level of knowledge where learning is no longer required. Even for experts, learning must be ongoing. I consider this attitude a trait of an "expert." This is why I include the word *student* in the description of this characteristic or role. I use the word *expert* to emphasize that the Lean facilitator should try to be three or four steps ahead of everyone else in the organization when it comes to Lean knowledge and expertise. The Lean facilitator is the Lean subject matter expert.

The challenge for every organization is to determine the specific Lean roadmap, paths, and steps which will be most effective for their organization. Culture change is not easy *(an obvious and extreme understatement)*, so having a person or group with only a superficial understanding of Lean serving as teacher and coach would be ill-advised. The Lean facilitator must, through experience, observation, and study, gain a deep understanding of the various approaches, pitfalls, and lessons learned to be an effective advisor and guide for company leaders. The subsequent Lean facilitator role descriptions will provide further clarification as to the knowledge and skills which are needed. I had stated that the Lean facilitator should try to remain three or four steps ahead of everyone else with regards to Lean knowledge. However, if the Lean facilitator fails in this challenge, this may not necessarily indicate that they have underperformed. It may actually mean that they have performed exceptionally well since they have excelled in the transfer of knowledge and expertise, which leads us to the next role of the Lean facilitator, that of being a teacher.

Teacher

The Lean facilitator must be a teacher. During the early stages of the Lean transformation, most of the facilitator's time will be teaching. This teaching can be through multiple mechanisms such as classroom training, kaizen events or projects, or informal discussions to clarify Lean concepts, principles, and the *why* of Lean … why Lean is critical to the success of the organization and all company personnel. It may be beneficial to select a work area to serve as the initial pilot or model of Lean to be the primary learning forum for the teaching by the Lean facilitator. (We'll look at different deployment approaches in Chapter 7.) This teaching spans all levels of the organization.

Coaching, the next Lean facilitator role, is often used interchangeably with teaching, as we did during our previous discussion of leader roles. With respect to the roles of the Lean facilitator, it would also be acceptable to combine the role into "teacher/coach." However, for purposes of this discussion, I detached the roles to place emphasis on the responsibility of providing *ongoing* coaching to help the student apply and develop the learned skills.

Coach

Coaching of Lean involves long-term behavior change, helping the student develop and adjust to their new Lean responsibilities. A critical coaching responsibility of the Lean facilitator is helping company leaders become coaches themselves. As previously reviewed in this chapter, leaders must become teachers and coaches. Some are not prepared, especially at the front-line leader level, so being a developer of coaches is an important Lean facilitator responsibility. As a Lean journey progresses, the Lean facilitator position typically transforms from being heavy on teaching Lean principles, tools, and techniques to more attention on coaching, facilitating, and influencing of behavior change.

Facilitator

The "facilitation" role is probably the most recognized and understood role of the Lean support person or team. It's a responsibility which requires detailed knowledge of Lean tools and techniques along with facilitation skills. For example, if you are to facilitate a team in reducing machine changeover times, you'll want to be familiar with quick changeover techniques and the SMED (Single Minute Exchange of Dies) process. Your objective is to guide the team through the analysis and change process to enable group learning and progress. Facilitation, just as coaching, is *not* providing answers; no one becomes a better problem-solver in that scenario. *(Plus, don't assume your answers would be the best answers, even if you are the "expert.")* Facilitation is guiding the team through a specific process and asking the right questions. The role of coach and facilitator is somewhat blurred. With regards to our Lean discussion, I consider coaching as focused on the individual needs of the employee, or the group as in a peer team coaching format. Facilitating is focused more on a specific organization need and the change process to address that need. SMED, 5S, the value stream mapping process, and cellular design are a few common Lean change processes which the Lean facilitator may facilitate a team through.

There are many other sources which can provide further information on facilitation skills. My intention here is to highlight *facilitator* as one of the multiple roles which the Lean support person or team typically holds. The roles and responsibilities of the Lean facilitator which are described here are often integrated. While facilitating the team, you are teaching and coaching as well. Another role which is embedded within the others is that of Lean influencer.

Influencer

I use the label *Lean influencer* to imply a responsibility to initiate, to be proactive. This is a responsibility which was also included in the role discussion of company leaders. As the internal subject matter expert for Lean, I believe that it is the Lean facilitator's *obligation* to influence others in the needed Lean behavior changes. This is a tall task, since this obligation may require upward influencing of company leaders. If you are a Lean facilitator or a member of a Lean team, this may seem an unfair burden which I am placing on you. However, you can't always wait to be asked to teach or coach or mentor.

Consider the company executive whose behavior is anti-Lean, and thus requires some immediate coaching before they downgrade Lean to another wasted *program of the month*. The request from them for help may never come due to ignorance. I don't mean this as a slight to the executive; rather, they simply *do not know what they don't know*. As the Lean expert, you do know what is required, so the burden is on you. This requires being a student of influence and motivation, the topic of the next chapter.

But you are correct! In the perfect world, you shouldn't have to find a way to influence the leader who is a level or two, or maybe three, above you in the hierarchy. I place no obligation like this on any other functional department, such as the IT department for example. I'm not obligating the IT manager to influence the Lean behavior of the CEO, so I do acknowledge my unfair request to the Lean support person or team. It's not a perfect world! Anyway, if you are a Lean facilitator, what's the alternative?

I guess you can wait for the misguided executive to get their "aha" moment and somehow realize that they need to learn how to become a better Lean leader. Or, maybe they'll leave the company for greener pastures, or if you're very lucky, they'll finally reach retirement age and you can hope and pray that they are replaced with an executive that really understands Lean and "gets it!" In the meantime, while waiting for one of these things to happen, I guess you can continue complaining about the misguided executive that just doesn't understand Lean, even if they think they do, and who continues to make your job difficult and frustrating. In fact, I bet you can probably find a number of cohorts to join you in this leadership bashing exercise and "woe is me" attitude.

However, this approach sounds extremely un-Lean and wasteful to me, definitely not something that a Lean facilitator should consider. So maybe you can do as I suggest and get to work in finding a way to influence, teach, and coach this executive, or maybe even influence the whole leadership team. The Lean steering committee structure is a great forum to do some teaching and coaching. I utilized this *misguided* executive leader example, since to address Failure Mechanism #2, *Leaders Aren't Leading*, someone may have to hold up a mirror to company leaders, and this just may have to be the Lean facilitator. Or, the Lean facilitator may need to locate an executive peer to do the mirror-holding, or garner help from other sources. This is an example of social influence, which will be discussed later.

Role Model

Lean facilitators must model Lean behaviors. Model the behavior which you are trying to teach. This is another role which was mentioned during the leader section of this chapter. If you are trying to teach others to be respectful and open to others' ideas and opinions, you better do the same. If you are the leader of the Lean team, you must exhibit the same Lean leadership behaviors which you are teaching and coaching to other leaders. Without walking the same as you are talking, the obvious hypocrisy will significantly erode your influencing capability. *"Based on your own behavior, you're clearly not serious about the subject, so why should I even listen to you?"*

External Lean Resources

Often, external resources can be invaluable supplements to assist with any or all of the above Lean facilitator roles and provide long-term ongoing support to the organization, but relying too much on external resources can thwart internal learning and development. Company leaders must lead the Lean transformation, and the only thing that is worse than abdicating this leadership responsibility to the internal Lean support team is relinquishing it to an external support resource. External support can be a catalyst for change, provide needed expertise and guidance, and can help instill accountability. The external resources which you should engage will view their role as a builder of internal institutional learning and development rather than cultivating an unhealthy dependence on their services.

Summary of Lean Facilitator Roles

This was just a quick overview of some of the key roles of a typical Lean support person or team. I'm sure we could add to the list of Lean facilitator roles. For example, Lean cheerleader is one that could be added or at least incorporated within the *influencer* role. I listed these roles to help you determine how they will be filled in your organization. Following is a brief summary of the items covered in this section:

- For those traveling on the Lean journey, you will need Lean expertise, *subject matter experts*. I have never heard of any organization blindly and ignorantly stumbling into a successful Lean transformation.

Lean does involve ongoing experimentation, often in a one step backward, two steps forward manner, but clueless trial and error won't work.

■ Lean is an ongoing learning strategy which requires new organizational knowledge and behaviors, so you'll need *teachers and coaches*, who can then develop others to be teachers and coaches.

■ Lean activities require someone to guide the teams through the analysis and improvement processes. So you'll need Lean *facilitators* for these efforts.

■ And you'll need personnel, regardless of company rank, who have the knowledge, tact, courage, and perseverance to be the "truth-tellers" and *influencers* to engage all levels of the organization.

To fill these needs, some organizations have formed Lean teams or departments, but the specific approach is up to you and should be based on your unique situation and needs. For example, maybe some combination of dedicated Lean resources, external help, and other internal personnel within various company functions would be appropriate. And as a company progresses along their Lean journey, needs change, so the approach will likely have to change over time.

Before we close out this section, I'd like to review what typically happens when the Lean team is actually viewed as the *leader of Lean*. This may be a re-examination of earlier discussions, but it's a critical topic which has often stalled the development of a true Lean culture, thus it warrants a little extra elaboration and repetition.

NOT the Role of the Lean Support Team

Once he hears about the wonders of Lean, it sounds so inviting and straightforward to the CEO. *"I'll hire a top notch Lean guy with tons of experience and make him responsible for making us Lean. To show how serious I am, I'm willing to pay him the big bucks to make it happen! I'll put my money where my mouth is!"* When you read that comment, it actually does sound kind of reasonable, almost common sense; however, hiring a Lean guy or gal isn't the same as hiring a new shipping manager to lead the shipping department. Lean changes everything. It's an alteration to the company culture, and placing the Lean leadership and culture change burden on the Lean department is definitely not common sense. Let's look at just a couple of the Lean principles and see whether this "Lean department as Lean leader" is aligned with these principles.

Misalignment with Lean Principles

Lean is largely a numbers game. You can have a few smart folks running around making improvements, or you can engage the creativity of the whole workforce. We're trying to utilize *everyone's* brainpower with Lean. Does it really make sense to place this responsibility on the Lean department to increase these engagement numbers while company leaders simply watch from the sidelines and their direct reports may, or may not, decide to participate in the transformation? Some of the leaders themselves may have already decided to opt out of Lean. *"It sounds a little risky to me! No thanks. I'm doing just fine."* Therefore some leaders may actually try to block the efforts of the Lean team. *"My folks have absolutely no time to attend any training or participate in this kaizen event thing you are referring to!"* From the Lean team's perspective, one of the words which comes to mind is *frustration.*

Or take another key Lean principle, the idea that to optimize the whole value stream, the various functions and departments which make up the value stream must work as an integrated team. In many organizations, these functional departmental silos may be quite extensive, and the lack of coordination across work areas or departments is the cause of much waste. Does it make sense to place the burden of breaking down these silos squarely on the shoulders of the Lean team? Of course not; this only increases the frustration level of the Lean team even more.

This highlights just a couple of the reasons why assigning Lean leadership to the Lean department doesn't make sense, even though it may initially sound logical. However, I surely have not let the Lean team off the hook in this story. Remember, previously, I placed the burden of influencing and coaching company executives as a key responsibility of the Lean support team. So if your CEO is misinformed on how Lean leadership is different than many traditional leadership behaviors, the Lean team needs to get to work and figure out a way to address this misunderstanding. Admittedly, during the early stages of Lean, where the Lean facilitator may be the only individual with any Lean knowledge, it's hard to make it appear that the Lean facilitator is *not* leading the effort; however, the Lean facilitator must set aside their ego and remain focused on key Lean principles and transferring

Lean leadership to its proper owners, company leaders at all levels of the organization.

Misplaced Lean Leadership

But what actually happens when the Lean team *is* anointed the leader of Lean, responsible for the Lean transformation where it's their job on the line if Lean doesn't take hold and produce the expected outcomes. Often, in the beginning, everything is fantastic. There's usually enlightened leaders somewhere in the organization that are open, and maybe even enthusiastic, regarding Lean and getting their team involved. Training occurs, some pilot projects are successful, KPIs start showing up on communication boards, and some daily practices like huddles may be initiated. The hope is that this model area of Lean will shine a light, and all other leaders will see the bright light and jump on board. Some may, and the Lean movement expands, but typically, some leaders won't even acknowledge the bright Lean light. They'll take what they feel is the safe route, and distance themselves from Lean. We'll dig into the various reasons why people resist change in the next chapter. For those leaders who choose to opt out, they can always point to the Lean team who is responsible for Lean, *"Hey, it's not my job! I'm not on the Lean team!"*

Spotty Lean versus Cultural Lean

This creates what I refer to as *spotty Lean*. There will be progress in some areas, seldom throughout the whole value stream, so any performance gains are limited. However, I want to be clear that a strong Lean team can drive a lot of improvement even without the desired company leadership, but there is a solid ceiling on the improvement potential. Spotty Lean is not even in the same league as *cultural transformation Lean*. Only a portion of the workforce is engaged in spotty Lean, and the lack of real commitment is obvious to everyone by allowing leaders and others to opt out of Lean. And since some company leaders are watching from the periphery, there is a real risk of misalignment between overall business strategies with the Lean department's objectives and goals.

After the initial spike, a spotty Lean environment seldom grows and expands; rather, it usually erodes over time as the few Lean leader zealots leave the organization, and/or due to frustration with the inability to affect the whole organization, the Lean team members take their skills elsewhere.

Or, unfortunately, the company leader simply does not see the anticipated results, and decides to close the Lean department.

You can recognize companies who have backslid from their spotty Lean past. You'll see remnants of Lean, such as worn location indicators, or maybe an old whiteboard no longer being used for performance communication or recording of ideas. If you close your eyes, you can almost envision their past daily huddles where information was shared, problems surfaced, and ideas generated. All of this has been discontinued. Now, everyone appears semiconscious as they drag themselves through the workday. Lean never grew cultural roots to enable sustainability.

The Lean team can be an invaluable resource, and we've covered a number of critical Lean facilitator roles, but culture change is a leadership activity. I believe there is a lot of truth in the following words of Ram Charan: "The culture of any organization is simply the collective behavior of its leaders. If you want to change your culture, change the collective behavior of your leaders."[20] Don't make the mistake of placing the Lean culture change load on the shoulders of the Lean team. Leaders must lead; however, the Lean team may have to teach and coach the leaders in how to excel in their Lean leadership role.

Chapter Summary – Key Roles and Responsibilities

In this chapter we've reviewed some of the key roles and responsibilities of individuals in positions ranging from the front line to the C-Suite. We've also looked at the roles of a couple teams, the Lean steering committee and the Lean team. My purpose was not to provide an extensive job description for membership into any of these groups, but rather, the focus was on how Lean and the guiding Lean principles affect each of these roles.

In the leadership section, there were only a few distinctions made among the various leader ranks. This intentional lack of separation was to emphasize the need for certain *Lean-principle-aligned* behaviors, regardless of leader position within the organization hierarchy.

The difference between a status-quo, minimal-change environment to a Lean, continuous improvement culture is obviously significant. The need for role and responsibility adjustments to affect this transformation almost falls into the category of common sense. However, we must realize that not everyone currently has the skills and capabilities to effectively perform in their new roles. This is why ongoing teaching, coaching, and support in helping personnel transition to a new way of working is a common theme in this chapter.

One example is the leader responsibility of being an *improver through process*. For the manager raised in the paradigm that leader success is solely based on the *outcome* regardless of *process* utilized, they'll likely require ongoing teaching, coaching, and practice to develop this new habit and mindset. And as the *continuous improvement* principle dictates, the roles and responsibilities covered in this chapter should not be viewed as stationary standards to obtain. Rather, everyone should continually strive to improve in their new Lean-aligned roles, and as the organization progresses on the Lean journey, the roles may require further adjustment.

Action Item – *Roles and Responsibilities Review*

1. During the next Lean steering committee meeting, reflect on this chapter and whether the roles and responsibilities which were reviewed are effectively being addressed. If not, develop a plan to address the gap. Consider both internal and external resources along with dedicated and partial responsibilities.
2. If you are a manager of a Lean team, or even the single Lean facilitator for the organization, reflect on the reviewed roles and compare with your current condition. If adjustments to roles and responsibilities would be beneficial, take action. Since you are the Lean subject matter expert, you hold a crucial position in helping others transform to their new roles.

Notes

1. Kotter, John P., and Dan S. Cohen. "Introduction." In *The Heart of Change: Real-life Stories of How People Change Their Organizations*, 1–14. Boston, MA: Harvard Business Review Press, 2002.
2. Deming, Edwards W. "Principles for Transformation of Western Management." In *Out of the Crisis*, 24–6. Cambridge, MA: Massachusetts Institute of Technology, 2000. Originally published in 1982.
3. Pyzdek, Thomas. "Building the Six Sigma Infrastructure." In *The Six Sigma Handbook*, 39. New York, NY: McGraw-Hill, 2003.

4. Liker, Jeffrey K. "Principle 9: Grow Leaders Who Thoroughly Understand the Work, Live the Philosophy, and Teach It to Others." In *The Toyota Way: 14 Management Principles from the World's Greatest Manufacturer*, 171–83. New York, NY: McGraw-Hill, 2004.

5. Rother, Mike. *Toyota Kata: Managing People for Improvement, Adaptiveness and Superior Results*. New York, NY: McGraw-Hill, 2010.

6. Phillips, Donald T. "Get Out of the Office and Circulate Among the Troops." In *Lincoln on Leadership*, 13. New York, NY: Warner Books, 1992.

7. Ibid., 17.

8. Kotter, John P. "Tactic Two: Behave with Urgency Every Day." In *A Sense of Urgency*, 97. Boston, MA: Harvard Business Press, 2008.

9. Ibid., 112–13.

10. Ibid., 113–14.

11. Ibid., 112–13.

12. "Humility." Dictionary.com. Accessed January 6, 2019. www.dictionary.com/browse/humility.

13. Shingo Institute, and Utah State University. "The Shingo Model." Shingo Institute. Accessed January 6, 2019. www.shingo.org/model.

14. Collins, James C. "Level 5 Leadership." In *Good to Great: Why Some Companies Make the Leap ... and Others Don't*, 21. New York, NY: HarperCollins, 2001.

15. Kotter, John P. "Tactic Two: Behave with Urgency Every Day." In *A Sense of Urgency*, 113. Boston, MA: Harvard Business Press, 2008.

16. Marquet, Louis David. *Turn the Ship Around! A True Story of Turning Followers into Leaders*. New York, NY: Portfolio Penguin, 2012.

17. Ibid.

18. Mann, David. "Standard Work for Leaders." In *Creating a Lean Culture: Tools to Sustain Lean Conversations*, 51–74. Boca Raton, FL: CRC Press, 2015.

19. Liker, Jeffrey K., and Michael Hoseus. "Engaging Competent and Willing People in Continuous Improvement." In *Toyota Culture: The Heart and Soul of the Toyota Way*, 165–6. New York, NY: McGraw-Hill, 2008.

20. "Leadership Development." Advanced Business Coaching. Accessed January 6, 2019. www.abcbizcoach.com/leadership-development/.

Chapter 6

Resistance, Demotivation, and Motivation

Before we dive into the primary topics of this chapter, I'd like to briefly review some information presented in Chapter 3. In the introduction to the "People Principles," we discussed McGregor's Theory X and Y perspectives of human nature, and the need for all Lean leaders to be heavily biased toward the Theory Y end of the Theory X/Y continuum. My intent is not to judge anyone's perspective as right or wrong, or good versus bad; however, engagement of the workforce in continuous improvement activities is dependent on a belief that people are inherently creative, responsible, and have the ability to learn and grow. People will utilize their creativity and brainpower for the betterment of the company when the right motivational environment is in place *and* where *demotivators* are removed. Does this imply a fantasyland where all personnel issues have vanished? This sure would be nice, but this nirvana is probably best considered an ideal vision and a direction to move towards, not the next target condition to obtain. However, this basic belief in the power and potential of people is a foundational element of Lean principles and aligned behaviors, and the following discussion of *people issues* is based on this perspective.

Resistance to Change

The first indications of resistance often surface during the initial introduction of the Lean transformation strategy, or maybe even prior to the introduction, when the rumor mill picks up a signal that some sort of change is on the way; however, resistance can and will occur at any point throughout the Lean journey. A Lean principle such as *one-piece flow* may be so foreign to the workforce that a resistance spike may occur when initially introduced. Resistance should be considered an ongoing part of the change process. Even the most engaged and enthusiastic employees will at times exhibit some resistance to a proposed change. Don't be shocked, but rather, as with any problem, try to get to the root causes of the issue.

Changing or Being Changed

The following short quote from Peter M. Senge provides a great deal of wisdom regarding why people resist change:

> People don't resist change.
> They resist being changed.[1]
>
> – *Peter M. Senge*

As was noted previously, the motivational on-switch resides within the hearts and minds of every single employee. Leaders do not have access to their employees' switches. This is why we get frustrated by our efforts in trying to change people. We need to give people a reason to change, a reason for them to keep their motivational switches flipped to "on." Sure, we can force a change and explain that this is just the way it has to be, and hopefully over time, everyone will see the wisdom of this decision. In some rare cases this approach may actually work, but unfortunately in most cases this isn't going to happen. The forced change will more likely create or further embed a disengaged workforce which simply goes through the motions, and at best only does what they are told to do, no more, no less. This *compliance* environment is not quite the engaging, proactive, and innovative continuous improvement workplace we are striving for.

The decision to create a Lean organization does have a directive, maybe even *forced*, aspect. We must move in the Lean direction; however, *how* we move in this direction and who is involved is what makes all the difference. Are we going to try the easy, anti-Lean, route and force the change down everyone's throats? *"Get on board or get out! That's all I need to say!"* Or the more challenging, but more effective, Lean approach where the *why* of the change is addressed from the employee, company, and customer perspectives. Expectations are set and the workforce becomes an integral part of the change process. Change doesn't feel like it is being imposed upon everyone. Granted, realistically, a major change such as a Lean transformation will always create some feeling of *imposition* upon people; however, the more everyone feels part of the change process, even with its inherent challenges, stumbles, and frustrations, the less resistance will surface.

From a Lean principle perspective, the attempt to force and dictate change would be a violation of the *respect for people* principle. *"We have the right and capability to understand the need for the Lean transformation. And since we are directly affected by the changes, by not engaging us in this process, not communicating expectations and progress, not soliciting input, nor adequately preparing us for the impending changes, you clearly are disrespecting us."* In a moment we will review multiple reasons why people resist change, but they all can be considered subcategories of resistance resulting from people feeling that they are not in control of the change, the feeling of *being changed*, as Mr. Senge has so aptly stated.

The Root Causes of Resistance

Rick Maurer lists three reasons for resistance to change in his book, *Beyond the Wall of Resistance: Why 70% of All Changes STILL Fail – and What You Can Do About It*.[2] These three categories provide significant insight as to the root causes of why people resist change, and we'll use them as a kick-starter for our discussion. Maurer's three reasons or levels are stated in three simple statements:

> Level 1 – I Don't Get It
> Level 2 – I Don't Like It
> Level 3 – I Don't Like You[3]

I Don't Understand

"I just don't get it! I'm confused about what this Lean thing is, and I simply do not understand why we need to do this!" A lack of Lean transformation understanding could be with respect to how Lean affects the company or the customer, or the confusion could be for more personal reasons. It is difficult to support something if I don't understand the logic behind it, even if there is an honest attempt to engage me in the process. I feel that part of our DNA as humans, at least for a majority of us, is that we want to know

why. If this need isn't satisfied, there's a feeling of someone just trying to tell us what to do, trying to change us. *"Please help me understand WHY!"* Otherwise, expect resistance. Employees deserve to understand the purpose and rationale behind any change that affects them. This is a requirement of the *respect for people* principle.

It's Not Just Logic, It's Personal

I don't believe that a lack of understanding is purely a logical issue. It also has an emotional component. With us humans, simply providing the logical reasons and facts of an impending change will not necessarily alleviate the resistance based on our need to understand. We don't make decisions solely based on logic; we are emotional beings. John Kotter, who has devoted his career to studying and teaching us about change, states that:

> People change what they do less because they are given *analysis* that shifts their thinking than because they are shown a truth that influences their *feelings*.[4]
>
> *– John Kotter*

This need to "influence feelings" is not independent from the unemotional logical reasons for the change. Rather, it forces us to consider *how* we present the logic of facts and data to engender an emotional impact. How can we create this gut-feel, emotional understanding for the need for change? What is it that will make us say, *"Now I really get this Lean stuff, makes total sense! Now let's get to work making this change happen!"* The most emotionally impactful reasons for a change would be those factors dealing with us personally. *"How does this Lean transformation change my job? What are the benefits to me personally and to my family?"*

So how can we guard against resistance resulting from a lack of understanding at a personal level? Communicate, communicate, communicate would be a good start, but futile if not followed up by action aligned with the words. People need to understand the empowering aspect of the Lean transformation and the learning and growth opportunities it provides; and then when this understanding is experienced through actual involvement, it creates a deep commitment for the change process. *"We're doing it! It's not being done to us! I'm helping to decide how we do this!"* However, if we perceive the change to be some sort of threat to us personally, we'll naturally resist.

Look for ways for associates to meet with peers from other organizations who are further along on their Lean journey. Resistance can be eased by employees talking to others who initially had the exact same concerns. The personal and emotionally filled *"How does this affect me, and what's in it for me?"* issues always have, and always will, be on everyone's mind when any change is introduced, so make sure you provide clarity of understanding through your words and especially your deeds.

I Don't Understand – the Company and Customer Need

An emotional impact can also derive from our understanding of the need for change from the organizational and customer perspectives. If we fail to see this need, we may resist the change since we just don't get the point. *"Why are we doing this?"* An understanding of the challenging, maybe even dire, business situation can rally the workforce. Don't have your CFO present the emotionless financial facts in a 45-minute sermon of numbers. If you do, you'll also need to plan some time to wake everyone up and to summarize what was missed. Sure, these are the facts, the bottom line, but unless you have an organization of accountants, I doubt that the emotional impact needle will be moved much. Financial transparency is critical, but be creative in developing ways for the workforce to gain an understanding of the business conditions and competitive threats in ways which are emotionally impactful.

If feasible for your type of product and industry, consider taking a group of employees to a customer to see and hear firsthand what the customer's needs and concerns are. Or invite a customer to one of your all-hands meetings to say a few words. Besides the emotional impact of listening to the concerns of someone who is actually purchasing what you produce, the "employee to external customer" interaction can provide other benefits as well. The external customer is given an actual face. For companies who sell directly to the public, the customer connection is rather easy. The next customer is the final customer. The next customer may even be the employees themselves. But for companies who are located in the earlier stages of the supply chain, the customer could be less relatable. When people start to view the customer as a real person who has expectations and commitments which they are being held to, it can create a whole new perspective on why we do our jobs. We don't just make parts for Company X, but rather, we make parts for Jim and Jane. This can add to the motivational aspect of *purpose*, which we'll delve into later in this chapter, and it may create an understanding of why our organization needs to continuously improve.

If face-to-face interaction is not feasible, consider a video of a customer – better yet if this is a customer who is not exactly thrilled with your past performance. Our Lean improvement efforts have taught us the power of video for both process analysis and impactful before/after comparisons. Where feasible, expand the use of video to raise awareness of customer issues to lessen the change resistance. In *The Heart of Change: Real-Life Stories of How People Change Their Organizations*, authors John P. Kotter and Dan S. Cohen highlight a story which demonstrates how a video of an angry customer was utilized to increase the urgency for change.[5] An increase in urgency naturally will help melt away the wall of resistance. Kotter's story highlights how the video of the angry customer enabled more people to hear and see the frustrations of the customer. In many organizations, company issues aren't broadly shared, thus any impact for reducing resistance to change is isolated.

My suggested use of video is not to present a threatening, demotivating image of severe gloom and despair on the big screen which could result in wasteful panic and non-effective action. Rather, video can be a tool to educate the workforce on the reality of the business environment and raise customer awareness, and thus support your message of the need for change. *(At least I find this more impactful than trying to decipher a stream of declining sales numbers from our friendly accountant.)* The desired response from the video is a motivating, *"Let's keep making things better!"* or, *"Let's work together and get this fixed now!"* NOT, *"We're doomed! I quit!"* Video can be just as effective in presenting *positive* customer feedback to increase morale. In fact, I suggest this use of video, as much or more so, than for sharing "less-than-positive" news.

How about your competitors? Does the workforce have an awareness of who they are, and how their products or services stack up to yours? This not only can support the understanding of the need for change, but since most people have some level of competitiveness in them, this competitor-awareness can be a motivational catalyst. Remember, understanding the need for change is not solely a logical exercise, it's also an emotional challenge if we are to understand deeply, and it's only when we understand deeply that we'll then commit our hearts and minds to the effort. Then any resistance to the change will begin to crumble.

I'm Afraid

Now let's address Maurer's second reason why we resist change, his Level 2 reason, "I Don't Like It." Maurer states:

> Level 2 resistance is an emotional reaction to the change. Blood pressure rises, adrenaline flows, pulse rate increases. It is based on fear. People are afraid that this change will cause them to lose face, status, control – maybe even their jobs.[6]

Without a concerted effort in addressing the debilitating effects of fear, this can freeze your Lean progress, because it can freeze your workforce. Everyone's focus and energy is on how the change will cause something devastating to occur. Obviously, this is not helpful in getting everyone engaged in the continuous improvement process.

The Unknown

One fear which most everyone can relate to is the basic fear of the unknown. This fear can tie back to the previously reviewed resistance resulting from a lack of understanding. Of course we'll probably never totally eliminate the fear of the unknown since we can't foresee and guarantee the future; however, we can provide enough of a future vision to minimize the fear, and thus permit us to move forward.

What can we do? We can utilize the countermeasure previously noted … communicating, communicating some more, and then a little more. It seems like any communication void always gets filled with a negative consequence which creates fear, and the rumor mill rapidly distributes this fear throughout the organization. Very seldom is the communication void filled with a positive rumor which excites the workforce. If the issue of job security has not been discussed and addressed adequately, I never hear, *"Hey, I bet this change will guarantee our job security, and I'm also betting we'll immediately be getting a nice big raise and bonus!"* Rather, the information void usually results in something like, *"Well, when do you think the layoffs will begin? This Lean stuff, it's just another way to Lean us out of a job. I hear that's what happened at the place where Jane used to work."* Don't wait for someone to verbally express this concern; it may never be spoken. And interpreting silence as something positive would be a huge mistake. Even though it may not be verbalized, the job security issue will be on a majority of employee minds; I guarantee it. Be proactive in addressing this fear, which has the capability of building a thick wall of resistance.

My Job Has Changed

The same proactive approach is required to relieve other fears. For example, Lean does change everyone's job to some degree; this can be scary, especially when someone has been doing the same job, the same way, for a number of years. So provide definition of the new roles and responsibilities, and how training and ongoing coaching will be part of the change process to enable everyone to be successful. There still will likely be some fear, or at least apprehension; but if the job changes start to appear more like growth opportunities, rather than opportunities for failure, resistance can fade away and the transformation can move forward.

Since employee fears may not initially be expressed or evident, ask! Use multiple communication methods such as all-hands meetings, small group discussions, and one-on-one feedback, both formal and informal practices. Fear can be debilitating to a Lean transformation. Fear can spread imperceptibly, divert the attention and energy of the workforce, and hinder vital Lean behaviors; it cannot be ignored.

I Don't Trust You

Maurer's third reason category as to why we resist change, his Level 3 reason, is "I Don't Like You." Maurer states, "Maybe they do like you, but they don't trust or have confidence in your leadership."[7] Lack of trust is the basis for this reason for resisting change.

Trust has multiple components to consider. Honesty is one element which we all can probably relate to. If I have reason to believe that you might not be telling me the truth, I'm not going to trust you and will naturally resist whatever you are trying to sell me or whatever the subject of your attempted influence.

Another component of trust is competence. I may believe that my doctor is a man of great integrity and honesty, but if I have doubts in his ability to diagnose and treat my ailment, I'm not going to trust him. The same applies to our Lean transformation discussion. Honesty may not be in question, but if the workforce feels that the leader has no idea as to what they are talking about, they'll listen with skepticism and resistance will result.

There's a third element to trust which is a little more difficult to describe. Empathy or sincerity may be close descriptors, or maybe the speaker's *intent*. For major change efforts such as a Lean transformation, if I doubt whether you have really considered how the change affects me, or if there is some other uncertainty in my mind which makes me question your intentions or motives, I probably won't trust you. I'll resist because I'm not quite sure where you are coming from, what your real intentions are, and how they affect me.

You May Have Inherited This

Besides the multiple aspects of trust which, when lacking, can contribute to the *resistance to change* challenge, another complicating factor is that the lack of trust may be based on false information. The reasons for not trusting you may be totally unfounded, not true. This lack of trust may have nothing to do with you as the leader. This may just be a carryover from the prior leader who was a real bona fide jerk, and a classic autocratic non-Lean leader. I know, this isn't fair, but perception is the current reality, so we have to deal with it.

Repairing Lost Trust

So how can we deal with these challenging trust issues to minimize resistance to the Lean strategy, especially considering that we may have done absolutely nothing to create these issues? Let's take a look at a few scenarios. We do have to accept the fact that it's usually going to take some time to put a significant dent into repairing lost trust. Words can only provide so much healing. Trust issues outside of the workplace have taught us this. Action over time is what builds trust. Most people aren't convinced of another person's honesty by listening to a speech; this can only be gained through demonstrated honest behavior. However, there are short-term things which can be said and done to reduce the resistance due to trust issues.

The Competence Problem

Take the situation where you are not trusted due to a perceived lack of competence. Remember, this does not need to be true. Simply by virtue of being a young person or someone new to the organization or the last manager was incompetent so you must be the same, a portion of the workforce may resist the change effort. They simply don't trust that you really know what you are doing. You may be considered an honest person, and possibly well liked, but in spite of this, your lack of experience or knowledge, whether real or perceived, is creating resistance to your Lean message.

So what do you do? You can try explaining your past accomplishments or how you are different than the previous idiotic manager; however,

I doubt that this approach will change many minds. Also, speaking ill of others can be considered a character flaw and a violation of the *respect for people* principle. Be open and honest; don't try to fake it and violate the honesty component of trust. You'll be found out and the perception of your incompetence will be magnified. You'll dig an even deeper lack-of-trust hole due to your *tweaking* of the truth.

It's okay to admit that you don't have all the answers as to how exactly this Lean journey will play out; nobody does. Lean is a journey of ongoing learning, improvement, and adjustment, and everyone is on this journey together. This honesty and demonstrated humanity is critical, but unfortunately, sometimes trust is so depleted that any of your words aren't going to budge the trust needle. So you might have to accept this fact that, right now, they don't trust you, and there's probably nothing you can say to change this perception; however, consider *who they do trust*. Spend time recruiting the *key influencers* within the organization. A key influencer may be a manager or maybe a front-line operator who has been with the company for a number of years and is well respected by their peers. Key influencers aren't determined by title; they are well respected and socially connected individuals throughout the organization. The workforce may not trust you, but they unquestionably trust them. Spend some one-on-one time with these folks. Help them understand the need for the change. Maybe take them on tours to other places. Listen intently and address any concerns which they may have. Get them to support the proposed change, or at least be willing to listen to you, and then a majority of the workforce will be willing to listen to you, regardless of any trust issues with you personally. Again, these trust issues may be imagined. Provide opportunities where these influential converts can share what they have learned. We will expand further on the power of peer influence later in this chapter.

The Past Failure Reason

How about the situation where there is an understandable reason for a trust issue. Maybe your first attempt at Lean ten years ago faded away, or worse, maybe Lean was blamed for the layoffs which occurred during the time period of this initial Lean volley. I think the worst thing you can do is to ignore the past; pretend that it didn't happen. Your thinking may be, *anyway that was a long time ago. Some people left or retired, and those that did remain may not remember this failed attempt from years ago.* Nice try, but they definitely will remember (wouldn't you?), especially if some of their friends were hit by the layoffs. People don't forget when you mess with their lives, or the lives of their friends. Again I ask, do you?

So what can you possibly do in this situation? If you and your team did screw up the first time, how about admitting it? How about discussing what was learned through that failed experiment? And, as was noted earlier, clarify the job security issue since this will always be a concern of major change.

I believe our experiences have taught us that all the different reasons for resisting change are not independent from each other. If we do a good job in making sure there is clarity and understanding, and we provide ongoing support to reduce the fears of change, we will automatically move the trust needle in the positive direction. However, this works both ways. If we do a poor job of providing understanding, and we allow fear to envelop the workforce, workforce trust will likely erode.

The Golden Countermeasure – Early Involvement

We've reviewed a few approaches to addressing the resistance to change issues; however, the single most powerful countermeasure of all is early employee involvement, which will be the catalyst for long-term engagement. Eli Goldratt, in his book *Theory of Constraints*, explains the logic of this robust approach. Goldratt states:

Any improvement is a change.

Leading to:

Any change is a perceived threat to security.

Leading to:

Any threat to security gives rise to emotional resistance.

Leading to:

Emotional resistance can only be overcome by a stronger emotion.

Goldratt defines this stronger emotion as the "Emotion of the Inventor."[8]

Just think about it. Who's the one person who we can guarantee will not resist the change? It's the inventor or creator of the change. Seldom will someone resist what they helped to create. This logic is so simple yet so powerful. If we can create a workforce of *inventors* of the change, our resistance problem naturally fades away. Well, at least it decreases. Granted, this is easier said than done, but it provides a clear strategy to follow. We can't simply force everyone to be inventors. It's their choice.

Motivation is the topic of the rest of this chapter; however, I would like to emphasize something from Goldratt's logic. He stated the emotion of the *inventor*; notice this is not the emotion of the *implementer* or *reviewer.* It is the emotion of the *inventor.* It's this early involvement, if at all possible, in the design stage of a change, which provides the greatest emotional impact. This destroys resistance and builds ownership and commitment. Too many companies miss this opportunity by only incorporating later stage involvement where most of the power has been depleted. Create a workforce of *inventors* by early involvement in any changes affecting them, and watch resistance disappear.

Summary – Resistance to Change

Rick Maurer's categories of resistance, which are based on understanding, fear, and trust, capture the various root causes well.[9] Address them all, but pay special attention to lack-of-trust factors. Any trust issues will divert attention away from your Lean message. For further insight on the topic of resistance to change, I strongly recommend diving into Maurer's *Beyond the Wall of Resistance: Why 70% of All Changes STILL Fail – and What You Can Do About It.*[10]

Probably the quickest path to discovery of the root causes of resistance is the empathy path. Put yourself in their shoes. You may not always have insight as to their past experiences which may be contributing factors to the resistance; but by trying to view the world through the eyeglasses of others, you'll learn a lot. Stephen Covey said it best:

Seek first to understand, then to be understood.[11]

By following Covey's suggestion, you'll gain an awareness which will enable you to be more effective by targeting specific concerns. Also, this empathic approach shows respect and builds trust. Others are more willing to listen to you if you demonstrate a sincere willingness to listen to others. Resistance to change is not a characteristic of a flawed individual; rather it's simply a characteristic of us humans.

Demotivation

Keep in mind that our goal is to *engage* the workforce, not just to reduce resistance to a point where folks will quit blocking progress. A Lean culture is where everyone participates and drives the progress. To facilitate employee engagement we must address motivational factors. Though before we focus on what motivates us, let's take a look at what *demotivates* us. If there are enough demotivators at your place of work, engagement is impossible. Everyone's focus is diverted. The product of a demotivating environment is not always resistance to change. At times, *indifference or apathy* might be a better descriptor of the result. In either case, you will have a disengaged workforce, the opposite of our intent.

What is Demotivation?

Let's begin with a quick review of motivation versus demotivation. The topic of demotivation was originally introduced in Chapter 2 as one of the failure mechanisms, *demotivation is tolerated*, where we noted Frederick Herzberg's work, which taught us that motivation and demotivation are separate and distinct factors, not simply opposites.[12] There is some overlap. They are not totally distinct, but for the most part, there are things that are good at motivating us, and then there are some different things that are good at demotivating us. However, our challenge is not a balancing act between the two where all we have to do is pile up enough motivators on the scale to outweigh any demotivators. Unfortunately motivators lose most of their power if demotivators exist. I contend that demotivators will always trump motivators, and if ignored, will destroy your Lean culture-building efforts regardless of your motivational attempts. Another way to think of it ... demotivators make people hard of hearing; they're not listening any more.

Some of the more recent literature on motivation appears to support Herzberg's original motivation/demotivation distinction, though with different terminology. And the same literature provides support for my "demotivators trump motivators" claim. For example, in Daniel Pink's fascinating book *Drive: The Surprising Truth about What Motivates Us*, which draws upon decades of scientific research on human motivation, he uses the terminology "baseline rewards."[13]

Pink places items like salary and benefits within this group, and he states, "If someone's baseline rewards aren't adequate or equitable, her focus will

be on the unfairness of her situation and the anxiety of her circumstance ...
You'll get very little motivation at all."[14]

I believe the two key words in this statement are *equitable* and *unfairness.*
I don't believe any amount of motivating factors will overcome the
crushing effect of a lack of equity and fairness. This can be with regards to
compensation, promotions, or any number of company policies and practices,
or just simply the unfairness of not providing a safe and respectful work
environment that all employees should expect as givens, or *baseline* conditions.

Let's look at this motivation/demotivation distinction from a different
reference angle ... the results of hundreds of employee surveys. In David
Sirota's *The Enthusiastic Employee: How Companies Profit by Giving Workers
What They Want*, he and his team provide data and research results from
years of employee surveys from around the world. The first factor of his
"Three Factor Theory of Human Motivation in the Workplace" is *equity*:
"To be treated justly in relation to the basic conditions of employment."[15]
Following are some examples of what is included in Sirota's equity list:

- Safe working environment
- Treated respectfully
- Workload that does not damage physical/emotional health
- Reasonably comfortable physical working conditions
- Reasonable degree of job security
- Satisfactory compensation and fringe benefits
- Credible and consistent management
- Fair hearing for complaints
- Reasonable accommodation made for personal and family needs[16]

He makes a particular point about this first of his three factors of motivation.
Sirota states, "if people are not satisfied with the fairness with which they
are treated, satisfaction of either of the other two needs has a relatively
minor effect on morale."[17] Sirota does not refer to these equity items as
demotivators. This is his first factor of the "Three Factor Theory of Human
Motivation in the Workplace."[18] However, if *equity* is lacking, the other
two are weakened significantly. In other words, Factor 1 has the power to
minimize or deplete the power of Factors 2 and 3. This seems to provide
some credence to my "demotivators trump motivators" assertion, though the
demotivator/motivator distinction is not actually made.

Regardless of the terminology, when there is a perceived lack of equity,
fairness, or respect, the focus is diverted away from where we want it, which

is on continuous improvement activities to create ever increasing value for the customer. Equity is intimately related to our previous discussion of trust. A lack of equity will naturally erode trust. This can totally stall your Lean transformation progress, and this is why one of the Lean failure mechanisms reviewed in Chapter 2 is *demotivation is tolerated.* Due to the overriding power of demotivators, the first step in creating a motivational environment should be to quit demotivating.

What and Who Demotivates?

Policies, Procedures, and Practices

The previously listed equity and fairness conditions all have associated policies, procedures, and practices which define their current condition. For purposes of our discussion, policies can be considered direction-setting statements, procedures are the specific instructions or steps, and the practices relate to application. Actual practices may, or may not, be aligned and follow written policies and procedures, or a practice may not even be based on any documented policy or procedure. *"It's just the way things are done around here. It's one of those unwritten rules."*

An apparent inequity in a current condition can result from either an external or internal comparison. For example, compensation policies may be deemed unfair when compared with other organizations in the area. Or, the comparison may be internal, such as when "Department A" has a higher pay scale than all other departments even though the work is similar. The inequities related to factors such as compensation, safety, and working conditions are typically the most damaging to morale since they're personal.

There are some inequities which may not individually be as damaging since they don't affect us on such a personal level; nevertheless, they still can have a demotivating effect. For example, a company purchasing procedure can demotivate. It may not seem fair when one work area team must go through a laborious approval process which requires multiple signatures and justifications, but another individual or department easily gets whatever they want, seemingly with no questions asked. It's not only the resulting aggravation which affects morale; most of us can deal with a manageable level of aggravation in our jobs. Rather, inequities like this erode trust since they veer away from our Lean principles such as *respect for people* and *teamwork*. I believe that this expands the demotivating effect of what many would consider minor inequities.

Let's take a look at another *insignificant* policy, the parking policy that reserves prime parking spots for executives. Doesn't this policy have the potential to create or reinforce an *us/them*, non-teamwork, non-respectful, non-Lean environment? I always ask what the business justification is for a policy like this. I've never received a compelling response. Why create an opportunity to demotivate, even if considered a minor infraction? If I'm the employee with a broken leg, or the pregnant woman who must make the long journey from the back of the lot, this parking policy may seem a lot more than a minor inequity infraction. Please don't ignore *minor* fairness issues in policies, procedures, and practices; they may not seem minor to all.

We always need to be on the lookout for any situation which invokes an emotional, *"Hey, that's just not fair!"* reaction. Demotivators create noise or static in our Lean message. There may be times when the static is minor, just a trivial irritant, so our positive Lean message can still work its way through. But at other times, similar to a bad phone connection, the static is so loud that any communication is impossible. Don't allow annoying demotivating static to derail your Lean culture-building activities.

People

We must quit tolerating the behaviors of the very skilled demotivators who reside within our organization. I'm not talking about the skeptics; we need the skeptics. They help assure thoroughness and rigor. They question everything; though annoying at times, this is a good thing. Rather, I'm referring to the demotivating individual whose arrogance and negative attitude spews a constant flow of disrespect towards teammates and the organization. Of course, we must teach and coach these individuals toward the desired behaviors, but they simply refuse to divert from their current mode of operation. They reject the premise of your attempted coaching, thus they won't even try. These folks just wear you down and can sap the energy from the team; however, even more damaging is the effect from the obvious lack of fairness. Everyone else's behavior is guided by the principles and values of Lean, but Mr. or Mrs. Demotivator's behavior is misaligned with multiple Lean principles such as *respect for people* and *teamwork*. Their behavior is *tolerated* by leadership. I know what you're thinking, *"But Leslie has been with the company for many years, and she is one of our best designers. Admittedly, she is a little 'rough' with how she communicates with her teammates, and there's always drama when she is on a team, but, but*

but...." If we value *respect for people* and *teamwork*, but we allow Leslie and a few other select prima donnas to be exempt from the principles and behavior standards which we have committed to, we have created the prime conditions for *organizational hypocrisy.* We're saying one thing, but allowing just the opposite. These mixed messages will destroy trust in company leadership and the Lean transformation strategy. The unintended clear message is that we are not really serious about Lean, so why should anyone invest their time, hearts, and brains to this effort.

Behavior lapses will always occur. This is understandable, probably even more so in a Lean environment where individuals are passionate about their jobs and improvement ideas. We're not talking about the majority of us who hit behavioral potholes now and then. We're talking about the *serial demotivator,* and if appropriate coaching and mentoring fails, and a suitable position within the organization cannot be found where this individual would be successful, employment elsewhere would probably be best for the organization and also for the *serial demotivator.* There's likely a non-Lean organization around which won't mind their demotivating nature; hopefully, a competitor will pick them up! Let the serial demotivator drain the energy from them.

We're All Different

Though it is an obvious point, one thing to keep in mind as we delve deeper into motivation is that people are different. Some resist change more than others, some learn new roles sooner than others, and whatever motivates me significantly may motivate you less, and a strong demotivator in your mind may be a small annoyance in mine. However, even the small demotivating annoyances, when piled on top of each other, can still become Lean culture destroying weapons. You make enough pinholes in the boat, it will sink the same as from a single massive hole. Even with the recognition of the differences in us human beings, there does seem to be some basic agreement on this topic of motivation, whether looking at past psychological studies, employee surveys, or our own experiences. It is too simplistic to suggest that motivators and demotivating factors are totally separate and not interrelated; however, the evidence does clearly indicate that there are some factors, whether we call them demotivators, or missing baseline rewards, or unfairness and lack of respect issues, which, if allowed to exist in the workplace, can significantly reduce or maybe even eliminate our ability to create the motivating and engaging workplace of a Lean culture.

Before we dive deeper into the topic of motivation, let's break away from this somewhat academic discussion and bring it back to something we all are more personally familiar with, our own experiences. At this point, let's stick with the topic of demotivation.

Action Item – *Demotivation: Try to Identify with a Past Personal Experience*

Can you identify a situation in your past where demotivators had a strong negative effect on your morale and how you felt about your job and organization? A time when your motivation senses were turned off since you basically quit listening, even to things that may have actually enhanced your motivation if you only had the desire to pay attention?

Maybe you've been extremely fortunate, and you cannot relate to this scenario at all. You should feel blessed. But if you can relate, were there lack-of-equity or unfairness issues at the root of your morale drop? Would you agree that these demotivators seem to minimize the effect of any motivators which may have existed within the organization, that demotivators, do in fact, trump motivators? (If you are having difficulty identifying motivators, it may be best to return to this exercise after our next section on motivation.)

The purpose of this exercise is that though we definitely need to learn from the research of experts, don't forget to learn from your own life's experiences. You've invested a lot of time and effort in life's training and education process. Reflect upon what you've experienced and learned along the way and how you can utilize this knowledge in the future.

Action Item – *Demotivation: A Lean Steering Committee Exercise*

At your next Lean steering committee meeting, create your own list of demotivators. Start with some of the items presented here. Review Sirota's equity list[19] and consider the demotivating effect when any of these are lacking. Don't forget to consider policies, procedures, or practices which may seem insignificant since they're not directly tied to personal issues like pay and safety; they too can damage workforce morale. Then have an honest discussion as to whether any of these demotivators are allowed to fester within your organization. If so, determine what you are going to do about it. The next step may be to gather more information and data. You could incorporate questions regarding demotivators into your employee engagement survey process to flush out any issues. Or, put together a cross-functional focus group to delve into this topic. Or maybe there is an obvious policy which was created years ago to address an issue with a single employee, but all it did was demotivate every other employee due to its unfairness. Immediately modify or destroy it completely. If the demotivating policy or practice is clear, don't waste time overanalyzing it. Remove it. Demotivators have the ability to pull the plug on your Lean efforts. They deflect our energy and focus away from our objectives, so ignore at extreme risk.

Motivation

We began our motivational discussion, not by specifically focusing on motivation, but rather by focusing on those things that sap the motivational energy away from us, the demotivators. This sequence was intentional since, without recognition of the devastating power of demotivators, any motivational approach could prove futile.

Key Definitions

Before moving any further, let's assure we are clear on what we really mean by the word motivation. Motivation is a personal, internal decision. It can't be dictated, coerced, or forced upon me by someone else. Sure, you can force or coerce me to do something, but if I don't *want to*, but only do so since I *have to*, there's no motivation on my part, at least not the type of motivation we are driving for in developing a Lean culture.

"I Want To"

I believe the *want-to* feeling is the key aspect of our working definition of motivation. A *have-to* action is short-lived; there's nothing to incite me to use my creativity and brainpower to do more or to even think critically regarding the task at hand. A *want-to* action has the complete opposite effect. *Want-to* is emotional, proactive, and alive. This clarity of definition is important since our motivational standard is much higher than one may initially assume. We are not simply trying to impel or incite an action, which a dictionary definition of motivate may indicate. An outside force can *impel* an action, but only an internal decision can create the motivational *want-to* power which fuels the energy of the Lean environment. A quote from Stephen Covey states this point well: "Motivation is a fire from within. If someone else tries to light that fire under you, chances are it will burn very briefly."[20]

Since our brand of motivation is internal, *you* can't really do or say anything to directly motivate me. You can only create the motivating environment where I, and only I, choose to be motivated. That's the daunting motivational challenge before all leaders when developing a Lean culture.

Engagement

The other word that requires definition clarity is *engagement*. Following is an excerpt from a white paper by Ken Scarlett, President of Scarlett Surveys:

> Scarlett Surveys technically defines employee engagement as *an individual's degree of positive or negative emotional attachment to their organization, their job and their colleagues.*[21]

As this definition states, engagement is emotional. You might have noticed that this emotional facet is an underlying theme of this chapter. Motivation is about people, and we're emotional creatures. As noted in Chapter 3 during our discussion of the *everyone* principle, the word involvement is often used interchangeably with engagement; however, involvement does not guarantee engagement. You can throw a dozen people onto a project team and probably get away with saying that you have a dozen folks *involved* in the project; however, if a portion of the team is basically just taking up a seat, maybe tossing out an occasional comment now and then, you'd be amiss by calling this a fully engaged team. Engagement is emotional and is enabled by motivation, the *want-to* in people. Since we do have a tendency to use involvement and engagement interchangeably, we should at least recognize engagement as a deep, emotional level of involvement, not just filling a seat. And we need to be honest and assess whether we are simply involving our employees in the Lean strategy, or whether we are enabling a deep, emotional involvement, i.e., engagement. The latter is what we want.

People

Now that we have a little more clarity on some key definitions, let's take a look at the ultimate subject of all of this motivation stuff: people! The normal or bell curve is often utilized to depict the various attitudes of people with respect to change. Refer to Figure 6.1 for the people curve.

The curve highlights three groups of people, the two extremes, which typically represent a very small percentage of the workforce, and the third group in the center, which depicts the majority, where most of us reside. It's this majority group which is the target of the bulk of our motivation discussion.

C.A.V.E. People

First let's look at the extremes. The far left extreme represents a small group of folks affectionately referred to as "concrete heads," or "C.A.V.E. people, **C**itizens **A**gainst **V**irtually **E**verything." (Note: These labels are to be taken tongue-in-cheek. This language would be a major violation of the *respect for people* principle. Even concrete heads deserve our utmost respect.) For many of you, someone probably comes to mind. These folks will refuse to participate. They have their internal motivational switches locked in the

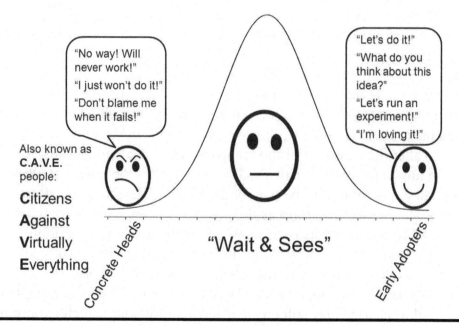

Figure 6.1   The People Curve

off position. In most organizations, there are at least a few individuals who will maintain a firm death grip on the status quo, even when it becomes evident to them that they are part of an extremely small group within the workforce. The reasons for this headstrong attitude could be many. Possibly due to past experiences, the fear of change is too overwhelming, or maybe some folks just think they know better than everyone else. Regardless of the root causes, the fact is that this small faction has chosen not to be actively participating in the continuous improvement process in spite of tireless efforts of teaching and coaching.

Is there a place in a Lean organization for the few concrete heads in the ranks? I apologize, but I'll have to answer that question with the wishy-washy response of *maybe, but probably not, well it all depends.* It depends on their specific behavior.

If a person, regardless of position, is actively working to derail the Lean strategy and culture which you are trying to develop, and they feel that abiding by Lean principles is optional for special folks like them, their behavior cannot be ignored. The *serial demotivator* previously discussed would fit into this category, so the advice will be the same. They should either be put into a position where they can be successful and unable to continue their damaging behavior, or if no such position exists, a new place of employment may be the only, and best, option for all. Whether considered *serial demotivators* or *obstructionists* due to their desire to obstruct the development of a Lean culture, they can cause irreparable damage to the future of the organization, and their behavior is unfair and disrespectful to the rest of the workforce.

There is another type of concrete head who is usually not quite as damaging to the company. These folks are every bit as headstrong as the obstructionists in their refusal to change and participate in spite of the benefits to them personally; however, this group doesn't proactively attempt to alter the direction of the company. They adamantly refuse to engage in any improvement activities, but they really don't mind at all if you do. They don't stand in the way of their teammates; they just don't join them. I'll refer to this group as the *passive refusers.* They'll continue to do the basic requirements of the job, minus the active participation in the continuous improvement effort, but they won't try to knock you off course. You'll have to determine whether there still is a place for any *passive refusers* in your organization. They may not be obstructionists, but their refusal to change may still create a sense of inequity which cannot be tolerated. In some cases, peer influence eventually convinces them to find employment elsewhere. Or, since Lean participation is now a component of the performance expectations of the job, they may fail to perform to an adequate level to warrant continued employment.

There is one situation where I am much less wishy-washy when it comes to concrete heads. A concrete head, whether obstructionist or passive refuser, cannot be allowed to hold a leadership position in a Lean organization. This would be blatant organizational hypocrisy, and diminished workforce trust would be the result due to the mixed signals. *"We're supposed to improve our processes. We want to improve our processes, but our boss refuses to participate, doesn't help us, and doesn't even give us a few minutes to talk about the problems we need to solve. What a joke!"* There may be a very rare anomaly which escapes me, but I've never experienced, nor can I imagine, the situation where there is justification for having a concrete head in any leadership role within a Lean organization. There's a chance that there may be a place for them to land within the company and be successful, but definitely not as a leader of others, whether with a staff of 1 or 1,001.

Keep in mind, the concrete head mindset is typically held by a very small minority; however, due to the havoc which they can create, we cannot ignore them. If you allow them to thrive and influence the majority group, the "wait and sees," the overall engagement level will suffer.

Early Adopters

Let's look at the other extreme depicted on Figure 6.1, the "early adopters." This is also typically a very small club, but regardless of the dire conditions of the current culture, this group is ready to roll. They naturally want to try something new. It's as if they were born engaged and their enthusiasm has only grown exponentially over the years. *"Let's get started!"* This group is vital in shaking off the company inertia from years of status quo thinking. Find these folks and get them engaged. You probably already know who they are; they're obvious by their energy and *can-do* attitudes. However, don't take them for granted. Making the first leap in any endeavor always takes a level of courage, even for some of the early adopters. Be sure to thank and recognize them, along with the brave "wait and sees" who broke rank and have joined them.

The most potent individuals within the early adopter group are those which we mentioned during our discussion of the root causes of resistance. These would be the *key influencers* or *opinion leaders* in the organization.

Key influencers can reside throughout the change attitude spectrum, but you are fortunate when you have a few in the early adopter troop. Others respect and trust the key influencers, so if they say *go*, others will follow or at least be paying attention. This key influencer faction is critical in the development of the Lean culture. We'll return to these individuals later.

Wait and Sees

The center group in Figure 6.1, representing the largest body of employees, is the "wait and see" group. This group is the prime target of our motivational efforts. An engaging environment is needed for these folks to make the personal decision to turn on their internal motivation switch. The early adopters are hardwired to *on*, and the concrete heads have padlocked their switches to *off*. But the majority of folks in the middle need a reason to give their time, hearts, and brains to the Lean transformation effort. They need to know *why*. So how do we influence this majority to join us on the Lean journey? What are the characteristics of the motivating environment which we've alluded to?

Intrinsic and Extrinsic Motivation

We have described motivation for our purposes as the *want-to* in people and as an internal personal decision, as compared with *having to do* something which is externally driven by somebody else. Probably the most common method of describing these internal versus external drivers is by the two categories, *intrinsic motivators* versus *extrinsic motivators*. They both impel us to do something, though via different means. The following describes the difference:

- Intrinsic motivation involves engaging in a behavior because it is personally rewarding; essentially, performing an activity for its own sake rather than the desire for some external reward.
- Extrinsic motivation occurs when we are motivated to perform a behavior or engage in an activity to earn a reward or avoid punishment.[22]

Intrinsic motivation is internally driven. Extrinsic is externally driven. Intrinsic rewards will be our primary motivation focus for developing the *want-to* in people; however, extrinsic rewards also have a role. Refer back to Dan Pink's "baseline rewards"[23] and David Sirota's "equity"[24] motivation category, and you'll find externally driven, extrinsic rewards such as compensation and benefits.

These externally driven items do have some motivational effect; however, when viewed as unfair or unequitable, their most potent power is as demotivators. Another example of an externally driven reward which most people desire is recognition. However, as with compensation, if recognition practices are considered unfair or unequitable, the demotivating effect takes hold and diverts attention and energy. Extrinsic rewards have their place in the motivation spectrum, but it's the intrinsic rewards that generate most of the momentum and passion of the *want-to* since they come from within. Ed Deming had a couple of statements which put the intrinsic/extrinsic discussion in perspective:

> … intrinsic motivation, which is the key to quality and improvement.

> It's true that insufficient extrinsic rewards can kill motivation too. If you have to worry about paying the mortgage and have to moonlight, you can't possibly work at your best. But after a point, extrinsic rewards become useless and may even backfire.[25]
>
> – *Ed Deming*

Motivation Drivers

I know it has taken a while to get here, but now let's look at the specifics of what motivates us. We previously noted Dan Pink's "baseline rewards" from *Drive: The Surprising Truth about What Motivates Us*. He identifies three primary motivational drivers:

1. Autonomy – the desire to direct our own lives
2. Mastery – the desire to continually improve at something that matters
3. Purpose – the desire to do things in service of something larger than ourselves.[26]

We'll use Pink's drivers as the starting point of our motivation discussion, and we'll delve into the relevancy and alignment of these drivers with our goal of developing a Lean culture of continuous improvement.

Autonomy and Ownership

I think we all can relate to the autonomy driver. We all want control over our own lives; however, this does not imply an image of everyone running around doing their own thing, unaware and unconcerned about the activities of their teammates. In a business environment this would create chaos and violate multiple Lean principles, such as *teamwork* and *focus on the process*. This doesn't minimize or restrict the autonomy factor, but rather it puts parameters around which autonomy is applied. Pink notes the work of Deci and Ryan, who make an important distinction, "Autonomy, as they see it, is different from independence. It's not the rugged, go-it-alone, rely-on-nobody individualism of the American cowboy. It means acting with choice – which means we can be both autonomous and happily interdependent with others."[27] Autonomy is aligned with Goldratt's "emotion of the inventor"[28] and Senge's statement that "people don't resist change; they resist being changed."[29] *Being changed* is the opposite of autonomy.

In an environment where we are able to act with autonomy, ownership develops. When autonomy is thwarted, where you have no choice, the *have-to* feeling makes it difficult to develop any ownership of the change. Someone else wants it and owns it. Ownership creates an emotional attachment to a change which provides the motivational impact of autonomy. With ownership comes commitment, and once an individual or team becomes committed to a cause, there is no limit to what can be accomplished.

A Short Story – The Power of Ownership

Following is a short story titled "The Power of Ownership," where two different improvement approaches are compared, one led by Michael Myway, and the other led by Flo Facilitator.

The Power of Ownership

Ownership has power. And though its place within the change process may be acknowledged, it is almost always undervalued. Even if we do involve those affected by the change, do we really spend the necessary time to assure that the team owns the issue, the proposed change, and its implementation, or do we expediently move forward, satisfied that we did our part in trying to involve and empower the team?

When no one takes ownership of a change or improvement challenge, failure is the typical result; however, this total lack of ownership is usually not the problem, but rather it's a question of *who* specifically owns the challenge. Let's look at this situation by reviewing two different approaches to implementing a type of change which occurs during some Lean transformations, the design and implementation of a workcell. Then we'll look at the advantages and disadvantages of each approach and delve into the role played by ownership.

A company leadership team has determined that a transformation to a one-piece flow, cellular processing design would shorten lead times, and thus create significant growth opportunities for the organization. In our first scenario, one of the Lean department experts, Michael Myway, was tasked with the challenge of instituting the initial pilot workcell. Michael was excited about this opportunity and ready to get started, so he quickly got to work gathering the customer demand information and processing data from historical records; and when data he needed wasn't readily available, he grabbed his handy stopwatch and went to work time-studying the operations on the production floor. Some of the folks weren't too thrilled with Mr. Myway looking over their shoulder with stopwatch in hand, but Michael did get the needed processing data in spite of some sideways glances.

Michael then went to work planning the cell configuration. He came up with a textbook U-shaped cell. He beamed with pride. If a workcell could ever be described as beautiful, this was the one; he couldn't wait to get it implemented. However, Michael remembered his boss telling him that he was supposed to do a better job in getting other people involved in his improvement projects, so he figured he better call a short meeting to show the folks what their new workplace would look like. Admittedly, he usually forgot to do this involvement step, but he planned on doing it right this time.

Michael had his meeting and presented the design. For some strange reason, the folks didn't seem as thrilled and enthusiastic as he had expected. Not much was said, but maybe they were speechless due to their amazement over his grand design; it must have been that *too-good-to-be-true* reaction. Anyway, no one had questions, so he adjourned the meeting after a few minutes, satisfied that he had *involved* the team. Check off that box on his to-do list. The only thing left to do was to implement the new design, and wait for the "attaboys" and pats on the back. He was confident that he really nailed this one!

Now let's take a look at how another member of the Lean team, Florence Facilitator (everyone just called her Flo), handled the same challenge of designing and implementing a workcell. Flo took quite a different path. First of all, she paid a visit to the production floor to discuss the cellular idea with Tilly the team leader. Flo not only wanted to get Tilly's thoughts on what she thought would be needed to make a cell work effectively in her area, but she also knew good processing data was needed for an effective cell design process, and that Tilly would have some good ideas as to the best way to gather this data and make sure it was good representative data.

Tilly and Flo agreed that it would be best to get the whole team involved in the analysis and design since they work the process every day, and they could also help in gathering any data which was needed. Based on some rough numbers which Tilly shared with her, Flo did create some preliminary cell design concepts to show the team, but during the meeting the concepts were presented only as a means to jumpstart the team's thinking, not as any sort of finished product. Also, Flo used the cell concepts she created to teach and reinforce some Lean principles to the team to assure that they were looking at the design challenge from a Lean perspective.

In fact, when Tilly and Flo met with the team, Flo provided some training on the cell design process, and then the team went to work. They split up the assignments and gathered the needed processing data. Then Flo helped them work through the other design steps. The team had plenty of great ideas which modified Flo's original concepts. She helped the team evaluate the ideas and decide which ideas to incorporate into the cell plan. In order to gather the data, develop and evaluate the multiple cell designs, and then agree on a design to implement, the original meeting actually turned into three separate meetings. However, at the end of the third meeting, the team was excited and ready to implement the new cellular layout. They anticipated that once they started running it, they would have some fine-tuning to do. Plus some other opportunities would surely surface to make it even better than the initial plan.

Comparing the Michael Myway and Flo Facilitator Approaches

In both of the above scenarios, someone clearly feels ownership of the cell design. Neither case is a "no one owns it" situation. Michael Myway's cell design is clearly owned by only one person, obviously that would be Mr. Michael Myway himself. In the second scenario, Flo brought her expertise into the design challenge, but each team member felt ownership of the developed cell. As her name indicates, Flo Facilitator acted more like a facilitator, teacher, and coach, rather than the all-knowing Lean expert. And Tilly the team leader also played more of a support and coordinating role for the team. For example, the team wanted a few dollars to purchase a new workstation, and Tilly somehow found a way to make this happen without the need for the typical ten-page (maybe a slight exaggeration) justification for approval, and there were a few other small hurdles which Tilly and Flo managed to get moved out of the way for the team.

Let's evaluate the two different approaches based on the three factors of *speed*, *risk*, and *potential*. *Speed* is selected as a factor not only since everyone is busy and has limited time, but the sooner we implement the improvement, the sooner we reap the improved results. *Risk* should always be considered since any change depending on multiple contributing factors bears some level of risk as to whether it will meet performance expectations. And the *potential* category is based on the longer-term opportunity of the change. Does the change facilitate or somehow encourage ongoing improvement opportunities, or is it limited in its capability to grow?

Speed

In our two scenarios, the approach of Michael Myway would seem to be the obvious winner when considering the category of speed. If we define speed as the time to reach initial start-up of the change, not considering the effectiveness of the implementation, I think we can all agree to give Michael the *speed* trophy. He didn't spend the time talking to Tilly the team leader or holding multiple meetings with the work team. In Michael's mind, why do all that stuff, which would have only delayed implementation of his great design?

However, before we hand over the *speed* trophy to Michael, if we want to consider speed as it relates to reaching a desired performance level, we need to look at our second element, *risk*. If the risk of failure is high, getting first to the initial implementation stage doesn't mean a whole lot. This would be like arriving first at the starting line for a race, only to finish the race dead last. We should be reminded that in the PDCA experimental process of Lean, failure is almost an irrelevant term as long as learning has occurred. For purposes of our story, *failure* denotes process performance issues which would put the customer at risk due to our inability to provide a quality product when needed. Additional time would be required to address these performance issues.

Risk

To evaluate risk, we need to make some assumptions about the types of changes and the complexity of changes which we encounter along our Lean journey. Some changes are very simple, and regardless of design approach, the risk is minimal. However, as with our story involving a cell design, many changes have multiple factors which integrate people, equipment, materials, and information, and therefore have multiple error opportunities. Often it is only through monitoring the new process that we can work through the learning curve of the change. So with this perspective in mind, think about the risk of having only Michael Myway *owning* the newly developed cell. Since the work team was not intimately involved in the design process, they likely wouldn't be capable of effectively monitoring the process, even if they had the desire to do so. Therefore, for the most part, Michael was pretty much on his own in making sure the cell operated as he had planned. Since Michael doesn't work in the cell every day like the team, we have to assign some level of risk to his approach since there's only so much process monitoring and observation that he practically can do.

Due to the team's sparse knowledge of Mr. Myway's cell design, limited to only *what* to do, and without any insight into critical process changes or *why* something was done a certain way, a great amount of time may elapse before a problem is even discovered. Michael could possibly notice something while checking up on the team, or unfortunately, it may be the customer who informs us of a problem resulting from a single detail which Michael failed to take into account. The team wouldn't purposely miss this detail; it's only that they wouldn't be knowledgeable enough about the changes to know what to look for. Traveling through the learning curve may end up being a rather painful experience. When considering other details such as Michael relying on historical data, and gathering time study data without input from the team, additional risks are introduced. So, for the Michael Myway approach, a grading of "moderate to great risk" would seem appropriate when gathering all risk factors.

Now let's look at the risk associated with Flo's approach. First of all, it's worth repeating that Flo didn't just show up and tell the team, *"Go to it! You own it! It's yours! Good luck,"* and then walk away. No, she clearly shared her expertise to teach, guide, and facilitate. The risk of failure with Flo's approach would be minimal, if any, for a couple reasons. The first reason is that Flo took the time to teach and coach the team to focus the team's design efforts to assure alignment with Lean principles, and by involving the people who work the process every single day, the chances of missing any key details is greatly minimized. Who knows better regarding the current process than those who work it every single day? The second reason for a minimal-risk grading is that once implemented, you have a team which is emotionally invested in the cell design. They *own* it.

What happens when you are emotionally invested? You will do whatever you possibly can to assure a successful outcome. And the work team members, who operate the cell every single day, are in the best position to affect the outcome, not any single individual like Michael Myway. Even if a detail was missed during the design process, the team will find it quickly and take care of the situation. Basically, an engaged team will *refuse to let it fail*. They simply will not allow it. There may be things outside the control of the team which may derail the plan; otherwise, an argument for a no-risk rating, rather than minimal, could be made.

Potential

The third comparison category, *potential*, asks us to look into the future and visualize the best possible outcome of the change. In Michael's case, the cell's performance limit is compliance to the original design. The team neither has the knowledge nor desire to push the potential beyond this limit. In fact, with all the risks involved, the chances of reaching this potential are not that great, but having the process operate exactly as Michael intended would be the performance ceiling.

Now with Flo's approach, we need to consider both the knowledge of the team and their emotional attachment. Since Flo worked with them on how to analyze and design the cell, they were able to look at the process and their work with a more discerning "Lean eye." Also, another funny thing happens when you become emotionally attached to something. You not only want to make it work, but you just can't help but think about how to make it work even better. Since it is now *your* design, you want it to be the best that it can be. You know *why* something is done, so you're able to think about ways to do it differently. This goes well beyond basic compliance of the initial design plan, but into the category of continuous improvement … which has no limit. So the upper ceiling with Flo's approach is a moving ceiling. There actually is no upper limit. In addition, the gained problem-solving skills of the team will prove beneficial in other problem-solving and improvement challenges, so the benefits are both deep and broad.

Comparison Summary

So in summary of our evaluation, Michael's approach may appear to win the speed race, at least to the start-up phase, but it comes with a great amount of failure risk which will end up adding significant recovery time; thus, so much for Michael's speed award. Sorry about that Michael! In addition, his approach is limited in its potential for ongoing development and improvement. Flo's approach of gaining ownership by those who are directly affected by the change definitely takes more time in the development phase, but the engaged team eliminates most of the failure risks, and the improvement potential is limitless.

In addition to the evaluation factors of *speed*, *risk*, and *potential*, we should add a fourth evaluation category, *alignment with the Lean culture* which we are trying to develop. Flo's approach is the clear winner. In fact, Michael's approach is a major violation of the *respect for people* principle. Lack of involvement in a change which directly affects you is not respectful. Sorry again, Michael, but having a short meeting to present your plan to the team is not sufficient. This approach never developed any ownership by the team.

Looking at these two different change approaches, one led by Michael Myway, the other led by Flo Facilitator, hopefully enables us to grasp the power of ownership – specifically, ownership by those directly affected by the change. With the Flo approach, team member resistance to the change is virtually eliminated. Why would anyone on the team resist the implementation of the new workcell if the team was part of the design process? Who is going to resist something which they, themselves, created and thus now *own*?

Action Item – *Improvement Approach Review:* *Michael Myway or Flo Facilitator*

At the next Lean steering committee meeting, review the last half dozen or so improvement efforts and determine if an approach was used similar to how Michael Myway would have done it, or if more of a Flo Facilitator approach was utilized. Don't just look at the short-term results and jump to the conclusion as to which approach was utilized. Go to the *gemba* and talk to the people who were most affected by the change. You'll be able to determine rather quickly whether Michael or Flo took part in the change.

In either case, you should plan on being there for a while. If Michael was involved, be prepared to listen to a litany of concerns. If Flo was involved, you should also be prepared to listen for a while. You'll not only hear about how the initial change process was carried out, but also all of the improvements that have taken place since start-up. Or, maybe you'll hear how something cropped up in the early implementation stages which surprised the team, but they banded together and made some needed adjustments to prevent any real damage. The pride will be obvious. You see, they are emotionally invested in the change … they own it! They won't allow it to fail, and they'll keep making it better.

Other Ownership Applications

The previous story of ownership focused on an application where a manufacturing process was being improved; however, ownership and the resulting emotional commitment has applications in other processes and areas of our Lean journey. Consider the hiring process. During the interviewing process for a new hire in a work area team, such as the production team as described in the previous story, how often do we involve the team members in the process? The team members would be the peers with which the new hire would be working. If you are a team member, and you actually contributed to the evaluation and hiring of the new person, wouldn't you gain some level of emotional commitment to the new hire? Just as the team involved with Flo's improvement approach would do just about anything to make sure the new cell was successful, if I were part of the hiring process, I'd be inclined to do whatever I possibly could to help the new hire be successful. Through my participation in the hiring process, I became emotionally invested in this person.

Never undervalue the power of ownership, which has various applications during a Lean journey. Autonomy, acting with choice, enables this ownership and its motivational power. Now let's look at Dan Pink's other two motivational factors to see how they may apply to our Lean journey.

Mastery

"Mastery, the desire to continually improve at something that matters," is the second motivational driver from Dan Pink's *Drive: The Surprising Truth about What Motivates Us*.[30] Lean is firmly aligned with this motivational component. Our ongoing experiments, or PDCA cycles, of learning and improvement practically define the mastery driver, and the teaching and coaching role of Lean leaders can be considered a mastery responsibility. We previously reviewed one of David Sirota's motivational factors, *equity*, of his "Three Factor Theory of Human Motivation in the Workplace." Another of the three factors, *achievement*, has characteristics aligned with Pink's *mastery*. Within this factor is *challenge of the work itself, acquiring new skills*, and the *ability to perform well*.[31]

An undervalued aspect of mastery is the competitive nature in all of us which was mentioned earlier. We want to win! We want to get better to assure that we will win! Appeal to the innate competitiveness in all of us as a catalyst for action.

Consider your own personal motivational drivers. Would mastery or achievement be on the list? I believe that most people can be positively motivated by the challenge of the job, the ability to be successful and win, and the opportunity to improve and gain new skills. This desire to excel seems as natural to us humans as autonomy, our desire to control our own lives. We are hard-wired with this performance desire. You can argue that some folks may not be interested in learning anything new and are quite satisfied in their current job situation; even so, don't people in this category still want to excel in what they do? People don't come to work with the mindset of, *"I plan on doing a mediocre job, maybe even a poor job, today! I'll likely screw up, no problem!"* I know you probably have an individual in mind who you think does have this mindset. Somehow their hard-wired performance desire has been short-circuited. This person would likely be more comfortable working elsewhere. For the overwhelming majority, though, we want to do a good job. Many of us want to do a really great job. It is self-fulfilling; as we progress, more motivational power is created to drive us further.

The Mastery Environment

So, what does the environment look like to initiate the mastery or achievement motivational driver? Many Lean principles and behaviors of a Lean culture already reviewed in this book are mastery-supportive, but what are some specific conditions which are required for this factor to take hold?

First of all, to be successful, we need to know the rules of the game, i.e., the Lean principles, and we need to know how success is determined. Are the goals of the company, team, and individual understood? Is it clear whether we are winning or losing today, and if losing, what can we do to get back on track? Is the feedback timely, both from a team/process performance standpoint and from a personal performance perspective? Is it clear whether, or not, we are improving over time? This ties back to our review of key performance indicators, or KPIs; also, refer back to the visual communication board discussion. This communication mechanism supports a number of the mastery-related needs:

- Are we given the time for improvement?
- Do I have the materials, tools, and information to be successful in my job and to make it better?
- Do I have the process knowledge required?
- If I have a problem, is there a clear mechanism for requesting and obtaining help?
- Does my manager/mentor help me develop and grow, and if I want to expand my skills beyond my current work role, do they provide guidance and support?
- Are there opportunities to grow and expand my skills beyond my current job function?
- Am I, and the team, recognized for our achievements?

An affirmative answer to these questions provides a glimpse into the type of workplace which enables and serves as a catalyst for the mastery motivational driver.

However, let's consider a work environment where some of the above questions elicit a negative response. What are the ramifications of *not* creating the mastery-supporting environment?

There are some cases where the absence of a motivational factor can produce the environment for demotivation to breed. If the tools, training, and information which I need to be successful in my job are not provided, or if my desire to improve is stifled in my current work environment, what is my reaction? It might be *apathy*, simply a motivational void. Or I might react with the feeling that this lack of mastery support is unfair and maybe even *disrespectful* to me?

An environment where it seems that roadblocks are placed in front of me every day, definitely not removed for me, not only creates frustration, but maybe a sense of being ignored and disrespected. If so, now we have entered the damaging world of demotivation which was discussed earlier. Of course we all are different, so our reactions will vary. The question is whether something is viewed as only absent, or rather, viewed as unfair.

Alignment with Lean Principles and Behaviors

On a positive note, the message that we should glean from even a cursory understanding of currently accepted principles of workplace motivation is that there is total alignment with Lean principles and behaviors. The first sentence in this section included the words *continually improve*. "Mastery, the desire to continually improve at something that matters," is the second motivational driver from Dan Pink's *Drive: The Surprising Truth about What Motivates Us*.[32] Right from the start, this sounded kind of Lean.

Lean leaders at all levels are focused on creating a motivating environment, and a core responsibility is to teach and coach to develop workforce capability, or mastery. The purpose of most Lean tools is to expose problems for subsequent improvement towards our next target condition, directly feeding our desire for mastery. Also, systems such as our KPI system, practices such as huddles and *gemba* walks, and even mechanisms such as visual communication boards, are all supportive of a motivational environment where both autonomy and mastery can thrive. But there's one more motivational factor to review which Dan Pink identifies. But before we move on, let's take a time out to reflect upon our own experiences with the mastery factor of motivation.

Action Item – *Mastery*

Think about mastery in your own life, situations where you individually, or as a member of an organization or work team, improved at something over time. Not a one-time big hit, but an effort where you made an improvement which then motivated you to improve further. And when the next target condition was obtained, you felt compelled to go even further ... repeated PDCA cycles. This is the mastery driver at work. Isn't this what kaizen is all about?

Maybe you've experienced this with a hobby of yours. I'm a runner, and each progression of improvement on my 5k times urged me to get even better. My motivation did not stay the same; it actually increased. *(Admittedly, at a certain age, the challenge became not to lessen my 5k times, but to minimize my speed loss due to the root cause of age. If anyone has a good countermeasure for this root cause, please contact me.)* With motivational factors, don't forget to reference your most familiar source, you and your own personal experiences.

Purpose

"Purpose, the desire to do things in service of something larger than ourselves," is Dan Pink's factor number three.[33] As with Pink's first two motivational drivers, David Sirota's "Three Factor Theory of Motivation in the Workplace" has some similarities. "Working for a company of which the employee can be proud" is a component of Sirota's *achievement* category, and "opportunity to interact as a team on the job in the service of common performance goals," describing his *camaraderie* factor, would also relate to our desire for purpose.[34] We've talked a lot about purpose throughout this book, such as the purpose of tools or systems, but let's spend a little time delving into how purpose, as a motivational factor, aligns with a Lean culture.

An argument can be made that the *purpose* driver is stronger as we approach the twilight of our careers, where we start questioning what we have accomplished with our working lives. Others will link a stronger *purpose* focus with our younger generation, who are less concerned with the profit motive and more concerned with saving our planet. I do not dispute either of these assertions; however, I believe that the purpose factor transcends career maturity and generation. Isn't it motivating knowing that we are making some sort of impact, that our work has real purpose beyond our personal need to obtain an income? If your experience tells you the opposite, that people really don't care that much, and purpose as a motivational factor is limited to only a small cohort of zealots amongst us, you are likely just observing the natural result of the current non-Lean work environment. People may appear not to care much since they were never given something to care about. Just as autonomy and mastery are basic human desires, isn't purpose in the same category? I think it is.

The Big Picture

Purpose can be viewed from both a localized and broad holistic perspective. Let's first consider the big picture. An organization which makes medical products which save people's lives has a clear company purpose that gives work significant meaning. A similar case can be made for those organizations which make products for our heroes in the military. In these cases, purpose would seem obvious; however, clearly not everyone works for a company that makes life-saving products or products for soldiers who defend the freedoms of our country. Even so, all organizations are providing some type of product or service which a customer values.

Help your employees understand this value, not only from the context of our overriding Lean principle of adding ever increasing value for the customer, but at an even deeper emotional level if possible. What does using your product really mean to the customer? How is the product used? Why do they like your product over the competition? We seem to spend a lot of time explaining to prospective customers as to how our product or service will provide value to them by addressing a need, but do we spend enough time explaining this to our employees, to give purpose to the work? Shouldn't we? As has already been suggested, if feasible, take a road trip and have employees meet a customer, or invite a customer to say a few words at your quarterly all-hands meeting. Or utilize video to introduce the customer. Give the customer a face that people can relate to rather than a stale company name on a sales order. Help your employees become more emotionally connected to your product or service and customer to initiate the *purpose* driver of motivation.

From Chapter 5, remember the CNC technician who worked for a medical product manufacturer. Does the technician view their purpose as machining a chunk of metal, or producing a piece of life-saving equipment? Now, you tell me which perspective indicates a greater sense of motivational *purpose*, and an employee who is more likely to be engaged in meeting the goals and objectives of the organization?

Other Purpose Drivers

Purpose is not only tied to an organization's overall mission or product value; purpose or meaning can be derived from efforts at the departmental or work area level as well. A worthwhile goal or challenge in front of a project team can provide purpose that motivates the team to meet and even surpass their goals. The challenge of ongoing improvements via repeated PDCA cycles can provide a reason for being, a purpose which is tied to the mastery motivational driver, the desire to get better and better. Consider the local-level improvement reviewed in the previous short story, "The Power of Ownership," and what took place with the work team in the Flo Facilitator approach. Wouldn't you think that this whole cell design project created some sense of purpose for the team?

A purpose driver, unrelated to a company's product or service, can be a company's contributions to their community, such as charitable activities. Being part of an organization which does good for society in this manner can add meaning to work. When being a successful company not only means that we are enhancing value for our customers, but also enhancing the lives of people in the community, the purpose motivational driver can be initiated. For most people, I doubt that this single factor would create the *want-to* in people to be engaged in the Lean journey. But when combined with other factors, a sense of company pride can be an invaluable contributor to the overall motivational landscape. When you involve the workforce in determining which community projects to participate in, you add an autonomy component to this purpose driver.

Motivation Summary

For a detailed analysis and review of motivational factors or drivers, both of the references utilized in this section, the works of Dan Pink and David Sirota, are highly recommended. I believe that Lean leaders and Lean support staff should be students of motivation, and these two sources are invaluable. My intention was to highlight a few of the key motivational components covered in these sources and use them as our discussion starting point. The objective was to review motivational factors as to their alignment with the Lean philosophy of employee engagement and how a Lean work environment must enable these motivational drivers.

Change is difficult; even good change can invoke resistance due to a lack of understanding, fear, or trust. We don't simply want people to quit pushing back, resisting the change, but rather we want people to become motivated to invest their heads and hearts and become engaged in the change process. With any daunting endeavor, it is wise to search for points of leverage, those things which provide a disproportionate amount of impact or a significant movement towards our goals. In the next section we'll investigate leverage factors which can increase our chances of success in our quest of a Lean culture of continuous improvement. But before we get there, let's reflect upon motivation in our own lives, both inside and outside of the workplace. Though we definitely need to learn from the research and wisdom of the experts, we should never forget to gain insight from our own life experiences.

Action Item – *Motivation Reflection*

Think deeply again regarding the one data point that we all can relate to: ourselves. What makes us love our job, hobby, or any venture? Try to think of experiences which may have had some unpleasant aspects, but these unpleasantries still didn't deter you from being passionate about the endeavor. What made you emotionally invested in the task, whether on the job or outside of the workplace? Did the combined effects of autonomy, mastery, and purpose create the motivational impact? Think of things that you really want to do, not just have to do.

Consider your hobbies: which activities do you spend excessive hours on even with the negative side effects? For example, if you are an avid gardener, in spite of your sore lower back from spending hours tending to your garden, why do you still love it and want to do more? Why do you keep at it even though your body is telling you that it's time for a break? Or in the workplace, have you ever really loved your job or maybe some part of your job and actually looked forward to getting to work? Why? What made you feel that way?

A good guideline for company leaders to follow regarding motivation/demotivation might be to think of all the things in your past which personally demotivated you, which sucked the energy right out of you. Then make sure that you *don't ever* do any of these things to others, and don't tolerate this demotivating behavior from others. Then reflect upon the times when you were passionately motivated and engaged in some undertaking, regardless of any difficulties which surfaced along the way. Then work real hard to create the conditions and environment where others can feel the exact same way, and make "building a motivating environment" a primary responsibility of all leaders.

Building the Critical Mass

In this section I'd like to discuss methods of leverage to help us engage the workforce in our Lean journey, not simply to be observers, but rather to be active participants and drivers of ongoing improvement. What actions can we take to broaden and accelerate employee engagement? To search for some answers, as is often the case, we should not limit ourselves to considering only our workplace situation in which we are familiar. We should study behavior change challenges from any type of environment. In those situations which were successful, were there a set of techniques or approaches used regardless of the specifics of the challenge? If so, maybe we can incorporate these practices to provide leverage in our Lean transformational efforts.

Influence

The bestselling book *Influencer: The New Science of Leading Change* by Joseph Grenny and his co-authors provides valuable insight into a number of daunting behavior change challenges where influencers were somehow able to beat overwhelming odds against them and obtain success.[35] There are a few business examples cited, but many of the stories are from outside the world of business: for example, an international effort to eliminate the guinea worm parasite, a terrible disease where people ingest the larva of the worm; and there's Delancey Street, an organization in San Francisco with an amazing record of turning people with extensive criminal records and a history of drug use into productive and valuable citizens. Then there are the efforts to reduce HIV cases in Thailand. These are just a few of the formidable influencing challenges which were researched. The authors identified three keys to success which all of the influencers heeded:

1. Focus and measure
2. Find vital behaviors
3. Engage all six sources of influence[36]

The first one clearly is applicable to our Lean transformation challenge, and we've previously reviewed KPIs extensively in Chapter 4. Let's consider the second key to success, "find vital behaviors," and determine if there is something to learn which we can utilize during our Lean transformation.

Vital Behaviors

The influencers who were studied didn't get overwhelmed by the task of modifying a large number of behaviors in people. They applied the Pareto principle to their influence effort. They focused on just a few, maybe only two or three, critical high-leverage behaviors.[37]

Think about how this may apply with respect to our Lean transformation. Consider "high-leverage" not only those behaviors that will provide the most significant forward impact, but also those behaviors, if not instilled, that will significantly slow progress. Depending on your particular situation, your short list of leveraging behaviors may vary slightly compared with other organizations. Let's consider one specific case, the changing role of the front-line employee. We previously reviewed this role change in Chapter 5, and each of the key Lean roles and responsibilities could be a direct source of a vital behavior. Let's look at the critical role of being a *problem-detector*, and narrow our attention to what we would consider the *vital* behavior(s) resulting from this role.

Detecting problems could be considered a vital behavior in itself, but if we think deeper about the type of behavior which will provide the most leveraging effect on our Lean culture, I feel that we need to add a related behavior which doesn't come naturally to many of us. We need to *highlight the problems*, not just detect them. Many of us are reluctant to raise our hand and say, *"I need help. I may have screwed up."* There's often a hesitance to speak up even if we weren't the individual causing the infraction. Past *anti-Lean* leadership practices likely have contributed to this reaction. This topic was covered in previous pages, but I repeat it here since, when searching for those few Lean cultural leverage points, we need to make sure that we dig deep enough to identify the key behaviors which are most impactful. When we laser-focus on a vital behavior such as *highlighting problems*, we'll also make sure that our Lean tools are supportive in drawing attention to any deviations from the standard. Mechanisms will be put in place to make it easy and convenient to take action to highlight problems, e.g., your version of the Andon Cord, popularized by Toyota, which enabled workers to stop the line when a problem occurred. There will be an emphasis on leader behaviors to assure alignment with the front-line vital behavior. These are just a few examples of how the vital behavior is elevated to enable the most impact.

The same type of behavior analysis can be applied to the second front-line employee role reviewed in Chapter 5, being a *problem-solver and process-improver*. We don't only want people to become better problem-identifiers and highlighters, but we also want to develop a workforce of problem-solvers and improvers. Again, the leader is a key cog in influencing this vital behavior. Training and coaching are critical, but also, do we have various practices in place to provide the opportunity for idea input? These may include the daily huddles, kaizen events, a formal idea system, dedicated daily improvement time, or informal one-on-one discussions. Utilize a variety of mechanisms to encourage this vital behavior. People are different, so apply multiple methods to reach everyone. Monitor the idea contributions of the workforce. When the engagement level is declining, do we currently even pay attention to this trend? Do we even notice it? When we elevate the vital behavior, we put things in place to assure that we continue to pay attention.

My objective isn't to elaborate again on the critical need for highlighting problems and generating ideas. The intent is for us to consider breaking down our seemingly insurmountable behavior change challenges of a Lean transformation. Search for those few vital behaviors. Then, laser-focus on these vital behaviors. Elevate them and assure alignment, and use them as leverage mechanisms to accelerate the development of a Lean culture of continuous improvement.

Action Item – *Vital Behaviors*

At the next Lean steering committee meeting, discuss your most difficult Lean behavior change challenges. Reference the Lean role changes covered in Chapter 5. Maybe it's the front line, as was used as an example above, or maybe it's a leadership position such as the front-line supervisors or possibly the mid-level leaders don't appear to be grasping their new responsibilities. What are the vital behaviors which you want to see demonstrated, and discuss how you can help instill these behaviors. Regardless of the specific behavior change challenge in front of you, try to break it down to a few key behaviors for focus, behaviors which provide a disproportionate amount of transformational impact. We routinely utilize the Pareto principle for solving a variety of company problems, so why not try to utilize this same concept with our behavior challenges as well?

Sources of Influence

The third key success factor from *Influencer: The New Science of Leading Change* is to "engage all six sources of influence." In forming their six-source influence matrix, the authors do not only focus on the motivational requirements of influence, but they include another dimension, *ability*.[38]

What can be more disheartening than having the desire, the *want-to*, to make something happen, but not yet having the capability to do so, nor a clear path to obtaining the required skills? This situation is a good definition of the word *frustration*! Think back to our fictional, but based on true events, story of Michael Myway and Flo Facilitator. Flo didn't only provide the motivational component by enabling a sense of autonomy for the team. She also provided the training and support to develop the capability in the team to effectively move forward on their mission. This *ability* component of the influencer matrix aligns well with Pink's second motivational factor which we reviewed, *mastery*.[39]

The *Influencer* authors look at these two components, *motivation* and *ability*, across three influence sources, *personal*, *social*, and *structural*. One of the main themes of the book is that all of the influencers featured in the book addressed their daunting challenges, not by focusing on a single, or a select few, influence sources, but rather by employing the whole matrix.[40]

Addressing the challenge by building motivation and ability across all three sources, personal, social, and structural, is what provides the leverage to overcome the odds. It's this deep *and* broad attack which lengthens our lever arm for change. Many of our previously reviewed topics would fit well within the *Influencer* matrix, but now I'd like to dive deeper into one particular sector, the *social* component, to explore how this source of influence has leveraging capabilities which can help propel us along our Lean journeys.

Social Influence

The influencing or persuasive power which others have over us is sometimes so subtle we're not even aware when we are being influenced. Why do you think bartenders toss a few bucks of their own into the tip jar? They know that bar patrons will be more inclined to tip the bartender if they believe that their drinking peers have already shown their generosity to the bartender. Yes, strange, but that's just the way we think and behave at times. The *Influencer* authors state, "No source of influence is more powerful and accessible than the persuasive power of the people who make up our social networks. None."[41] In the tip jar example, the social network includes the patron's drinking peers.

Opinion Leaders

A few times in this chapter I've mentioned a group of people who I referred to as "key influencers." I was referring to individuals who are well respected and socially connected to their peers. They could be from any position within the organization, from a front-line employee to the CEO. Their influence is not based on position. It is based on who they are and the respect and connections which they have fostered with others. The *Influencer* authors refer to this group as *opinion leaders*. Here's a shocking statement from their book which has huge ramifications as to our Lean transformation:

> The rest of the population – over 85 percent – will not adopt the new practices *until opinion leaders do*.[42]

Eighty-five percent! Think about that for a moment. You may think that you are hitting all the right motivational buttons, but for some reason, folks just aren't getting on board and engaging. Maybe, just maybe, the opinion leaders haven't boarded the ship yet, and until they do, others will refuse to join in. Even if you feel that your organization is *different*, and you want to lower the 85 percent number to 50 percent, half of the workforce is keeping a close eye on the opinion leaders. That's still a significant cohort. They are wondering what the opinion leaders feel about this Lean stuff. They don't know them as *opinion leaders* or *key influencers*, just associates who they respect and whose judgment they trust. The thinking might be, *"If Jane isn't behind it, something must be wrong or shady. I'll just sit this out for a while and see what happens."* I'm not suggesting that our culture-building struggles are all due to our failure to win over the opinion leaders amongst us; however, I *am* suggesting that we should pay special attention to this powerful group.

Many years ago, as a young manufacturing engineer and internal Lean facilitator, I was confronted with an influence challenge during our early Lean endeavors. I had no concept of *early adopter* or *opinion leader* or *key influencer* at the time. All I knew was that I wanted the pilot project to be successful. My thought process at that time was, *"how could I stack the deck in my favor to increase our chances of success?"* Basically, do I have any leveraging options? I knew quite well that even though I was respected and well liked within the organization, I was still the young guy, *"well-meaning, but you know, not yet really aware of how things work around here. We're much different than other companies!"* I remember a conversation where someone gently and respectfully stated this viewpoint to me. I was pretty confident that this perspective was not an anomaly. So, bottom line, even though my plan was to use the effective Flo Facilitator approach, even this wouldn't work if no one was willing to listen to me. *"Poor young inexperienced fella, he just doesn't get it!"* So what did I do? Well, the team may not be ready to listen to me no matter how much they liked me, but I knew they would listen to Jim. Jim was definitely an opinion leader, but he was not one to immediately volunteer to get on the ship. He was probably closer to the *wait and see* category, but I knew if Jim was on the team, at least the other team members would be listening. *"Sure, if Jim is here, let's at least pay attention. Jim isn't one to waste his time on a futile effort. Maybe something of value will come out of this project. Probably not, but you never know. Again, Jim is here!"* Once this thought about Jim came to my mind, I realized that I needed to spend some time with Jim to talk about the plan, address any concerns, and ask (beg may be a more accurate word) him to be on the team. The outcome: he agreed, and the pilot project was successful. Again, I had no concept of opinion leader. I only knew that I needed some help and I figured Jim might be able to provide some assistance.

Some readers may be thinking that you shouldn't have to spend the extra time and effort to encourage the Jims or Janes to be on the team and to help in the change process. People should take more initiative and volunteer to participate, so why should the burden be on someone to solicit involvement. I guess in the perfect world, you'd be right; however, as I've pointed out the obvious before, there is no perfect world. So to be successful, we absolutely do have to continue to focus and spend the extra time on the human aspect of Lean. As the Lean environment grows and matures, hopefully there actually will be more initiative shown throughout the workforce, lessening the need for *encouragement.*

Just like we don't seem to notice the preloading of the bartender tip jar and how it subconsciously influences us, I contend that we don't always notice the opinion leaders and their influential power. We therefore miss a huge opportunity to accelerate the building of the Lean culture, and we may not recognize a root cause of some of the workforce resistance. We may acknowledge that there appears to be a trust issue which is stalling our progress, but what are the reasons, or root causes, of the trust issue? If a portion of the workforce believes that the opinion leaders don't trust something about the proposed Lean strategy, they will also feel that something must be wrong.

The good news about opinion leader power and leveraging capability is that we don't necessarily have to figure out how to engage the whole workforce, but rather, once we engage the opinion leaders, they'll help pull the others onto the Lean ship. *Pulling* may not be quite the appropriate word to describe what happens, since once the opinion leaders are on board, others will naturally follow and a positive snowballing effect begins. Little if any pulling or pushing is required. As for the typical size of this opinion leader group, of course it's one of those things which will vary from organization to organization, but the *Influencer* authors state that this group represents about 13.5 percent of the population.[43] My unscientific, anecdotal, study would approach this number. In general, for every group of 8–12 folks, there's likely an opinion leader in the mix.

Action Item – *Opinion Leaders*

It's time again to reflect upon our past. Can you think of any past "opinion leaders" that appeared to have influencing power, whether or not they held position power by virtue of their role within the organization? They were well-respected individuals who others naturally sought out for opinions and were fully trusted. They may have been, but weren't necessarily, outgoing and vocal individuals. They could have been very quiet, but when they spoke, everyone paid attention and was curious as to their viewpoint. Often these are folks who have been with the organization for a number of years, but that's not a prerequisite. Also, think of opinion leaders from organizations you've been a part of outside the workplace.

In your current work situation, can you identify the opinion leaders? If not, spend more time in the *gemba* and you'll probably figure out who they are. If not, ask around. If you are forming a project team to improve a particular process, ask some team members who else should be recruited. Possibly, when talking to one of the volunteer team members, you may be staring right into the eyes of one of the opinion leaders. Consider initial pilot or model projects to be in areas where one or more opinion leaders reside. Engage the opinion leaders to leverage your Lean efforts, and be sure to recognize them for their support and help. A simple *thanks* would be much appreciated, and when you tell them, *"We couldn't have done it without you,"* you really should mean it, because it's likely a true statement.

The Obstructionist Opinion Leader

Now what do you do if one of the opinion leaders is a card-carrying member of the *Lean obstructionist* club? They don't just refuse to engage, but they are proactively working to dismantle or disrupt any Lean efforts. This takes us back to previous discussions regarding *serial demotivators* and *obstructionists* and the damage which they can inflict on your Lean culture-building activities. Any individual who is actively trying to steer the bus in the opposite direction of your business and Lean strategy cannot be ignored.

If teaching and coaching has proven futile, and an *obstructionist* opinion leader must leave the organization, others in their social network will definitely be paying attention to what has happened. Due to the strong social connections of the opinion leader, you may have a portion of the workforce suddenly confused, fearful, and likely angered by what happened. Lean engagement can't grow under these conditions. Plan on committing the necessary time to answer any non-personal/non-confidential questions about the situation and why this individual had to move on. Be empathetic to the concerns and fears which will flare up. Again, without disclosing anything of a personal or confidential nature, of course, consider providing a general summary of the process utilized in attempting to gain alignment of this person's behavior with the company strategy and guiding principles. The goal is to have the process viewed as fair, even if there still may be disagreement on the outcome. It should be understood that if this individual would have remained within the organization, they would have negatively affected company performance and workforce morale, thus putting everyone's future at risk. Consider engaging your Lean-minded opinion leaders to help in this effort during this fragile period.

Consider what would happen if you took the apparent easy route, and ignored the behavior of the obstructionist opinion leader, and allowed their anti-Lean influence to spread throughout their well-connected social network. Even if you're lucky and the obstructionist club doesn't grow any larger, some of the *wait and see* group will enter a frozen state of *wait* due to the influence of their anti-Lean opinion leader. For other *wait and sees*, the *organizational hypocrisy* will become obvious where the obstructionist opinion leader is being allowed to derail the business and Lean strategy. More trust will be lost and the hole you are digging continues to get deeper, and don't be shocked when some invaluable employees decide to be employed elsewhere. So what you may end up with is the damaging *obstructionist* still gainfully employed and continuing to spew anti-Lean rhetoric, but the Lean-minded individuals who you were relying on to counterbalance the obstructionist camp have left the organization. That's not a good outcome. If you are serious about developing a Lean culture of continuous improvement, this is not the option to choose. *(Reminder – no one said this journey was going to be easy or always comfortable!)*

To end this section on a positive note, consider if, as a result of your effective teaching and coaching, the obstructionist opinion leader successfully transforms into a Lean advocate. They are still opinion leaders, but no longer even close to the obstructionist or concrete head club. They tore up their membership card and quit paying dues. Think about the emotional impact of this attitudinal transformation on others who respect this person. This will produce a profound positive cultural impact.

Opinion leaders, those respected and socially connected employees who can be residing anywhere in the organization, are individuals who you must engage in the Lean journey. We've elaborated on how leaders at every level must create the right environment to enable individuals to personally turn on their own internal motivational switches; however, we must be cognizant of the influencing power of opinion leaders. Identify the members of this group and spend extra time with them so they will use their leverage to help in developing the desired Lean culture, not hinder it.

Peer Learning, Coaching, and Accountability

Another social influence factor which I would like to delve into involves peer learning, coaching, and accountability. Failure mechanism #5 stated that *Lean training isn't effective.* The core weakness of traditional, mostly classroom, Lean training methods has been the failure to be effective in changing behavior. The problem hasn't necessarily been the venue of the training. An effective ongoing training and development plan involves learning in the *gemba* along with some training more suitable to a classroom setting. (Though, even classroom training should have a "visit to the *gemba*" component if feasible.) We've already elaborated on the critical leadership roles of being teachers, coaches, and mentors, but also consider how workforce peer groups can also enhance learning and behavior change.

We began this peer group discussion in Chapter 5 when reviewing the role of the front-line leader. This was one specific application of a peer group. On the production floor, the natural work group, the cell or work area team, can also be considered a peer group. In general, a peer group can be considered any group of individuals who have a similar purpose, needs, and goals. It's possible that titles, roles, and even organization may be different. Though the group's members may be diverse in a variety of ways, it's the unity of purpose which provides the focus. This creates the situation where peer learning and influence can occur.

With any change, there's a natural degree of uncertainty in the future and what this all means. An equally natural reaction is to look at our peers for clarification and support. Any training provided to a peer group will enhance the training since specific discussions can occur which target the needs of the group, as compared with a more general audience. It is also assured that everyone hears the same uniform message from the teacher or facilitator of the group, possibly their mentor. The more significant benefit of forming and collectively developing a group of peers is with respect to how they can help each other in transitioning to new roles and behaviors. Sharing challenges, experiments, and best practices enhances the capability and confidence of the whole group.

By no means does this replace one-on-one teaching and coaching from a mentor (typically the immediate manager/leader), but rather it expands it.

The peer group creates its own mentoring group. They learn together, teach each other, and hold each other accountable. As noted during the front-line leader discussion, always look for every opportunity to involve a peer group in redesigning their own roles. Remember, the one person, or group, who is guaranteed not to resist a change is the one who came up with the change.

Action Item – *Social Influence*

Contemplate the power of social influence and relevance to your organization. Along with the identification and utilization of individual key influencers or opinion leaders, also consider if you are maximizing the use of peer groups and their inherent influential power. There are many easily identifiable peer groups within all organizations, but these groups need a plan, structure, teacher/guide, and the supportive environment in order to be an effective team rather than a group of individuals.

Structural Influence

An additional influence source besides *personal* and *social* from *Influencer: The New Science of Leading Change* is *structural* influence.[44] Where the first two sources are focused on the influencing power of people, this third category is focused on how *things* influence us. We've previously reviewed Lean structural elements, such as an organization's key performance indicator (KPI) system. If any policy or system is misaligned with Lean principles, the wrong, not right, behaviors will be encouraged. We've also reviewed how visual communication mechanisms should be part of the workplace environment to support continuous improvement activities. The previous discussion of policies, procedures, and practices and their contributions to demotivation would fit into the structural category. In this section, there's one specific aspect of structural motivation which I'd like to review, and that is the physical location of operations, the geography of the workplace.

On the factory floor, many of you are likely familiar with the multiple wastes attributed to the physical location of operations along the value stream. Of course there is the waste of transportation and motion, but excessive travel distance also forces increased inventory and potential quality issues. A case can be made that the facility geography can have an effect on every single one of the wastes. The principle of *continuous flow* reviewed in Chapter 3 demands that workplace and facility layout must be a primary consideration during a Lean transformation. Too often we limit this awareness solely to the factory floor; however, this applies to an office or administrative environment as well. In the office, distance may not always result in an increase of administrative inventory, e.g., invoices, quotations, purchase orders, engineering change requests, etc., but rather a significant delay in processing may be the result. For processing of items such as quotations, production work orders, or purchase orders, this delay could have serious negative consequences. A delayed quote may mean a lost opportunity. A long lead time in order processing may contribute to a missed customer delivery. The time lag can result in some of the same quality issues that occur on the factory floor. Feedback is delayed and it becomes difficult to address issues in a timely manner.

In the office, consider the advantages of co-locating personnel based on the flow of information, similar to the co-location of manufacturing operations into workcells on the production floor based on the flow of material.

Another structural office environment consideration is whether you have an open office design with either no walls or low partitions, or does everyone have their own closed-in office space? If the job requires collaboration, an open office design would influence this type of behavior. The purpose here is not to do an extensive review of the various approaches to office layout and design, but when developing strategies to encourage the workforce towards the desired Lean behaviors, be sure to consider the influential power of the workplace environment to supplement the personal and social facets of influence.

Action Item – *Structural Influence*

In this last section we briefly reviewed the influencing power of workplace geography, a critical consideration for alignment with the principle of *continuous flow*. But as was noted, we often limit our perspective to the factory floor. At the next Lean steering committee meeting, assess whether you have effectively utilized the physical location of items to influence behavior throughout the whole organization. Don't limit your review to the factory floor, where layout optimization and cell design is a standard practice and a primary Lean transformation target. Does your office layout influence the right behaviors? If two departments must collaborate to enable the flow of information, are they located where teamwork is encouraged or discouraged? Are these two distinct departments even needed? Should they be broken down into workcells similar to what we routinely do on the factory floor? Also consider the design of the office space as to whether walled offices or more of an open layout would be effective. When's the last time you actually experimented with the office layout and design to improve flow and collaboration? We'll return to *administrative Lean* in the next chapter for a few more points, but for now, consider issues regarding the geography of the office environment and whether we're influencing, or discouraging, Lean behaviors.

Further Reading

Throughout this chapter, I've cited multiple sources which take a deep dive into the topics of resistance to change, motivation, and influence. My goal was to reference a few of the key points from these extensive sources in order to delve into how these points apply to our topic at hand, developing a Lean culture of continuous improvement. Sustainable Lean success is largely defined by your ability to align and engage the workforce in this endeavor. Studying the cited sources will expand your knowledge of these *people topics* far beyond what I highlighted in this chapter. As stated in the *Introduction* of this book, one of my goals is for you to want to learn more, to become a Lean scholar. Learning should be a continuous process. The primary references cited in this chapter, and listed below, will help you *learn more*. One way to learn more from these books is to utilize them in an internal book club format. Consider inserting a book club component into your Lean steering committee or leadership team meetings. All of the following should be considered for this purpose:

1. *Beyond the Wall of Resistance: Why 70% of All Changes STILL Fail – and What You Can Do About It*[45]
2. *The Heart of Change: Real-life Stories of How People Change Their Organizations*[46]
3. *Drive: The Surprising Truth about What Motivates Us*[47]
4. *The Enthusiastic Employee: How Companies Profit by Giving Workers What They Want*[48]
5. *Influencer: The New Science of Leading Change*[49]

Notes

1. "Peter M. Senge Quotes (Author of The Fifth Discipline)." Goodreads. Accessed January 6, 2019. www.goodreads.com/author/quotes/21072.Peter_M_Senge.
2. Maurer, Rick. "Why People Support You and Why They Resist." In *Beyond the Wall of Resistance: Why 70% of All Changes Still Fail – And What You Can Do about It*, 33–51. Austin, TX: Bard Press, 2010.
3. Ibid.
4. Kotter, John P., and Dan S. Cohen. "Introduction." In *The Heart of Change: Real-life Stories of How People Change Their Organizations*, 1. Boston, MA: Harvard Business Review Press, 2002.
5. Kotter, John P., and Dan S. Cohen. "Increase Urgency." In *The Heart of Change: Real-life Stories of How People Change Their Organizations*, 18–20. Boston, MA: Harvard Business Review Press, 2002.
6. Maurer, Rick. "Why People Support You and Why They Resist." In *Beyond the Wall of Resistance: Why 70% of All Changes Still Fail – And What You Can Do about It*, 39. Austin, TX: Bard Press, 2010.
7. Ibid., 41.
8. Goldratt, E.M. "The Process of Change." In *Theory of Constraints: What Is This Thing Called and How Should It Be Implemented?*, 9–21. Great Barrington, MA: North River Press, 1990.
9. Maurer, Rick. "Why People Support You and Why They Resist." In *Beyond the Wall of Resistance: Why 70% of All Changes Still Fail–And What You Can Do about It*, 33–51. Austin, TX: Bard Press, 2010.
10. Maurer, Rick. *Beyond the Wall of Resistance: Why 70% of All Changes Still Fail–And What You Can Do about It*. Austin, TX: Bard Press, 2010.
11. Covey, Stephen R. "Habit 5: Seek First to Understand, then to be Understood." In *The 7 Habits of Highly Effective People: Powerful Lessons in Personal Change*, 235–60. New York, NY: Simon & Schuster, 1989.
12. Herzberg, Frederick. "One More Time: How Do You Motivate Employees?" *Harvard Business Review*. August 25, 2015. Accessed January 3, 2019. https://hbr.org/2003/01/one-more-time-how-do-you-motivate-employees.
13. Pink, Daniel H. "Seven Reasons Carrots and Sticks (Often) Don't Work …" In *DRIVE: The Surprising Truth about What Motivates Us*, 35. New York, NY: Penguin Group, 2009. Also pages 60, 66, 209.
14. Ibid., 35.
15. Sirota, David, Louis A. Mischkind, and Michael Irwin Meltzer. "What Workers Want – The Big Picture." In *The Enthusiastic Employee: How Companies Profit by Giving Workers What They Want*, 10–11. Upper Saddle River, NJ: Wharton School Publishing, 2005.
16. Ibid., 11.

17. Ibid., 28.

18. Ibid., 9.

19. Ibid., 10–11.

20. "A Quote by Stephen R. Covey." Goodreads. Accessed January 7, 2019. www.goodreads.com/quotes/126096-motivation-is-a-fire-from-within-if-someone-else-tries.

21. "What Is Employee Engagement from Scarlett Employee Surveys." Scarlett Employee Surveys. Accessed January 7, 2019. www.scarlettsurveys.com/define-employee-engagement.html.

22. Cherry, Kendra. "Extrinsic vs. Intrinsic Motivation: What's the Difference?" Verywell Mind. Accessed January 7, 2019. www.verywellmind.com/differences-between-extrinsic-and-intrinsic-motivation-2795384.

23. Pink, Daniel H. "Seven Reasons Carrots and Sticks (Often) Don't Work …" In *DRIVE: The Surprising Truth about What Motivates Us*, 35. New York, NY: Penguin Group, 2009. Also pages 60, 66, 209.

24. Sirota, David, Louis A. Mischkind, and Michael Irwin Meltzer. "What Workers Want – The Big Picture." In *The Enthusiastic Employee: How Companies Profit by Giving Workers What They Want*, 11. Upper Saddle River, NJ: Wharton School Pub, 2005.

25. Aguayo, Rafael. "Enhancing Pride and Joy in Work." In *Dr. Deming: The American Who Taught the Japanese about Quality*, 200. New York, NY: Simon & Schuster, 1990.

26. Pink, Daniel H. *DRIVE: The Surprising Truth about What Motivates Us*. New York, NY: Penguin Group, 2009.

27. Pink, Daniel H. "Autonomy." In *DRIVE: The Surprising Truth about What Motivates Us*, 90. New York, NY: Penguin Group, 2009.

28. Goldratt, E.M. "The Process of Change." In *Theory of Constraints: What Is This Thing Called and How Should It Be Implemented?*, 9–21. Great Barrington, MA: North River Press, 1990.

29. "Peter M. Senge Quotes (Author of The Fifth Discipline)." Goodreads. Accessed January 6, 2019. www.goodreads.com/author/quotes/21072. Peter_M_Senge.

30. Pink, Daniel H. "Mastery." In *DRIVE: The Surprising Truth about What Motivates Us*, 109–30. New York, NY: Penguin Group, 2009.

31. Sirota, David, Louis A. Mischkind, and Michael Irwin Meltzer. "Enthusiastic Workforces, Motivated by *Achievement*." In *The Enthusiastic Employee: How Companies Profit by Giving Workers What They Want*, 137–237. Upper Saddle River, NJ: Wharton School Pub, 2005.

32. Pink, Daniel H. "Mastery." In *DRIVE: The Surprising Truth about What Motivates Us*, 109–30. New York, NY: Penguin Group, 2009.

33. Pink, Daniel H. "Purpose." In *DRIVE: The Surprising Truth about What Motivates Us*, 131–46. New York, NY: Penguin Group, 2009.

34. Sirota, David, Louis A. Mischkind, and Michael Irwin Meltzer. "Enthusiastic Workforces, Motivated by *Camaraderie*." In *The Enthusiastic Employee: How Companies Profit by Giving Workers What They Want*, 239–61. Upper Saddle River, NJ: Wharton School Pub, 2005. Also pages 137–237.

35. Grenny, Joseph, Kerry Patterson, David Maxfield, Ron McMillan, and Al Switzler. *Influencer: The New Science of Leading Change*. Second ed. New York, NY: McGraw-Hill Education, 2013.

36. Grenny, Joseph, Kerry Patterson, David Maxfield, Ron McMillan, and Al Switzler. "The Three Keys to Influence." In *Influencer: The New Science of Leading Change*, 13–14. New York, NY: McGraw-Hill Education, 2013.

37. Grenny, Joseph, Kerry Patterson, David Maxfield, Ron McMillan, and Al Switzler. "Find Vital Behaviors." In *Influencer: The New Science of Leading Change*, 35–63. New York, NY: McGraw-Hill Education, 2013.

38. Grenny, Joseph, Kerry Patterson, David Maxfield, Ron McMillan, and Al Switzler. "PART 2. Engage Six Sources." In *Influencer: The New Science of Leading Change*, 65–299. New York, NY: McGraw-Hill Education, 2013.

39. Pink, Daniel H. "Mastery." In *DRIVE: The Surprising Truth about What Motivates Us*, 109–30. New York, NY: Penguin Group, 2009.

40. Grenny, Joseph, Kerry Patterson, David Maxfield, Ron McMillan, and Al Switzler. "Engage Six Sources." In *Influencer: The New Science of Leading Change*, 70. New York, NY: McGraw-Hill Education, 2013.

41. Grenny, Joseph, Kerry Patterson, David Maxfield, Ron McMillan, and Al Switzler. "Provide Encouragement: SOCIAL MOTIVATION." In *Influencer: The New Science of Leading Change*, 146. New York, NY: McGraw-Hill Education, 2013.

42. Ibid., 166.

43. Ibid.

44. Grenny, Joseph, Kerry Patterson, David Maxfield, Ron McMillan, and Al Switzler. "Change Their Economy: STRUCTURAL MOTIVATION." In *Influencer: The New Science of Leading Change*, 217–45. New York, NY: McGraw-Hill Education, 2013. Also pages 247–85.

45. Maurer, Rick. *Beyond the Wall of Resistance: Why 70% of All Changes Still Fail – And What You Can Do about It*. Austin, TX: Bard Press, 2010.

46. Kotter, John P., and Dan S. Cohen. *The Heart of Change: Real-life Stories of How People Change Their Organizations*. Boston, MA: Harvard Business Review Press, 2002.

47. Pink, Daniel H. *DRIVE: The Surprising Truth about What Motivates Us*. New York, NY: Penguin Group, 2009.

48. Sirota, David, Louis A. Mischkind, and Michael Irwin Meltzer. *The Enthusiastic Employee: How Companies Profit by Giving Workers What They Want.* Upper Saddle River, NJ: Wharton School Pub, 2005
49. Grenny, Joseph, Kerry Patterson, David Maxfield, Ron McMillan, and Al Switzler. *Influencer: The New Science of Leading Change.* Second ed. New York, NY: McGraw-Hill Education, 2013.

Chapter 7

Making it Happen

In the previous pages we have reviewed the Lean principles which serve as the infrastructure onto which all else is built. We've examined how roles and responsibilities must become aligned with these principles, and we've focused on motivational aspects required to engender workforce engagement. The purpose of this solid foundation and cultural strength is to develop an organizational habit of improvement, everybody, every day. But what is our application plan, our sequence of activities, our roadmap? Every organization must develop and implement their specific Lean roadmap or transformation plan through ongoing experimentation and learning. There is no universal Lean cookbook that applies to everyone and every single situation; however, this does not imply that you must blindly try to figure it all out for the first time. We can learn from the journeys of others and approaches which have proven effective, and there are application aspects which are similar across varied strategies. In this chapter I'll review some of the key points for *making it happen* and provide some guidelines for consideration. We'll look at some "blocking and tackling" issues that all Lean organizations are always focusing on, and we'll compare three general Lean application strategies. My intention is not to provide a descriptive roadmap for you to follow, but rather to provide some insights to help *you* develop a path for your Lean transformation journey.

But We're Different!

We'll start this discussion by addressing a phrase which has been used to express why someone's organization, facility, or department *will not* be able to make it happen. I'm sure many of you have heard it, and possibly even stated it at some point, *"But we're different!"* The idea that our situation is different than all of those Lean companies; therefore, Lean is something which would be difficult, if not impossible, to apply. This topic could have fit well within the previous *resistance to change* discussion; however, I saved it for this section on application topics since this typically is where the *"But we're different!"* chants will be loudest, when we start developing and committing to the implementation plan. There obviously is some truth in what the *"But we're different!"* cohort is chanting. There are some differences and unique aspects to our processes, people, and challenges. However, any uniqueness should never be accepted as a valid justification as to why Lean is not appropriate. Let's challenge the *"But we're different!"* mantra by exploring the *logic of Lean.*

Of course, logic isn't enough! If it were, we'd all exercise more, eat better, and if we have addictions such as smoking, we'd immediately quit. It takes more than logic to propel us into action. As has been highlighted in previous chapters, we're emotional creatures. However, even though logic is insufficient, it usually is a good starting point. If something doesn't appear logical, if it just doesn't make sense, we're probably not even getting out of the starting gate. It's not worth our time. We're definitely not going to feel compelled to make anything happen.

The Logic of Lean

Let's look at some logical statements of Lean which build a case for why, regardless of industry, product, or type of processing environment, Lean makes sense:

1. We add value for the customer by providing products and/or services to the customer. These products and services are created by a system of processes.
   - Therefore, we need to focus on company processes. (Lean Principle – Focus on the Process)
2. Wastes in processes cause delays and increased costs. Wastes hinder us from adding value for the customer. Waste is the enemy!
   - Therefore, we should eliminate and reduce waste from company processes to satisfy customers and remain competitive. (Lean Principle – Eliminate Waste)

3. The overall process or value stream cuts across functions and departments.
   - Therefore, internal suppliers and customers must work together as a team to eliminate waste and improve the value stream. We must think systemically. (Lean Principles – Teamwork and Optimize the Value Stream)
4. We are in a competitive business environment.
   - Therefore, to beat the competition, we should strive for perfection and continuously try to improve our processes through continuous experimentation. (Lean Principle – Continuous Improvement), and we should work towards engaging everyone in order to utilize the brainpower and creativity of the whole workforce, not just a few designated Lean folks. (Lean Principle – Everyone)
5. We should experiment "efficiently" to effectively utilize our limited resources.
   - Therefore, we should experiment by following a scientific process, PDCA, otherwise even more chaos and waste will develop. (Lean Principle – Scientific Thinking (PDCA))
6. We must make improvement sustainable and continuous.
   - Therefore, we must embed Lean into our culture where improvement and learning is ongoing. Otherwise, it will fade away like past "programs" and "initiatives." (Lean Culture of Continuous Improvement)
7. Culture change, and sustainability, requires committed and engaged leadership.
   - Therefore, developing Lean leaders must be a priority. (Key Role – Leaders, at all levels, must lead the Lean transformation)

There's nothing magical or deceptive about the above. They're simple statements; most would agree to their validity. As a whole, they provide the basis for the logical conclusion that Lean applies to any organization. Of course there are Lean tools and techniques which may not apply everywhere. For example, if I make a single product and never change over my equipment, at least for now, quick changeover (SMED) techniques won't be on the top of my needs list. Lean practices should always be designed and improved to fit your specific situation. Again, we *are* different. But at the basic question of applicability of Lean, and whether it makes logical sense to strive to develop a Lean culture regardless of industry or processing environment, I feel that an affirmative answer is unarguable.

But We're a Job Shop!

Even if a doubter is generally convinced of the logic of Lean, you still might hear the following comment:

> *Well, I guess it kind of makes sense from a theoretical, big picture, perspective, but because of our real-life situation where we are more of a job shop, where we produce so many different products, Lean is going to be a whole lot more difficult, and maybe not even feasible, than at other places!*

This is just another verse of the *"But we're different!"* song. I get the point. In certain processing environments some Lean tools and techniques will be more challenging to apply, such as the creation of a workcell which will approach the ideal of one-piece continuous flow; however, first of all, we shouldn't be so quick to jump to this conclusion. Second of all, from a different perspective, I believe that these heightened challenges actually make Lean *easier* to apply, not harder! Lean is about engaging the workforce to address problems to add ever increasing value for our customers. We need to surface and expose problems (a "blocking and tackling" issue) so that we can address them. *No problem is a problem!* When the obstacles are many, there's no need to work too hard in surfacing problems. It's actually easier!

Think of the opposite situation, a company which makes a zillion of only one product on a single workcell every single day, where each machine in the workcell is perfectly timed with the others. Forget for a moment that a company in this situation of high-volume, no-mix, perfect balance, is difficult to find, but the *"But we're a job shop!"* crowd will point to this imaginary company to explain their own Herculean challenge. The high-volume, no-mix condition may have enabled the creation of a perfectly balanced, one-piece flow cellular processing design, but what's next? How do they continually improve? Surfacing problems is an extreme challenge in this simplified scenario. Significantly more digging is required. It's harder!

So the next time you hear the *"But we're different!"* song, or the second verse *"But we're a job shop!"* think about the basic logic of Lean and what Lean is really all about. Then you'll recognize those verses for what they usually represent, not a well-thought-out counterargument to Lean, but rather an expression of resistance to change. Then, get to work in addressing the root causes of this resistance in order to gather more help in *making it happen!*

Now that we've addressed any concerns of Lean applicability from the *"But we're different!"* group, let's look at the core capabilities that all Lean organizations are building throughout their Lean transformation journeys.

The Blocking and Tackling of Lean

Sports analogies to Lean are sometimes used *(maybe overused by some of us)*, even though Lean is definitely not an event with a finite timeframe such as a 60-minute game. But the fact is that Lean, and business in general, is a team sport (Lean Principle – Teamwork), so sports analogies are often appropriate and effective in clarifying Lean topics. Therefore, to use a football reference, in this next section I'm going to review the "blocking and tackling" of Lean, the application fundamentals which every organization should be practicing. I feel that the words of the great Green Bay Packers coach, Vince Lombardi, are applicable: "Some people try to find things in this game that don't exist, but football is only two things – blocking and tackling."[1] I can't aggregate Lean fundamentals down to only two, but I do believe there are a few core capability categories which should be developed and strengthened throughout your Lean journey. The Lean capabilities I'll review are:

- Develop stable and standardized processes
- Surface problems
- Experiment
- Engage everyone
- Keep score

These topics were reviewed in past chapters, and some capability categories embed multiple Lean principles which were reviewed in Chapter 3, so only summary comments and key points are covered here.

Develop Stable and Standardized Processes

Since Lean involves improving processes by removing waste, we naturally need the foundation of stable and standardized processes to serve as our target for improvement. It's tough enough aiming at a moving target, let alone multiple moving targets. This topic was reviewed in the Chapter 3 section on *Process Principle #1 – Focus on the Process*. Having a stable process is often described as a prerequisite for improvement (address stability first, and then improve). I consider the stability step as an actual method or action for improvement, not simply a prerequisite to progress. As you stabilize and reduce excessive process variations, wastes are being removed from the process which will result in performance gains. Isn't this improvement?

This capability not only involves the method for how you determine the standard process, but also how you document the process into usable work procedures. Involving the *experts*, those who use and follow the developed procedures every day, in the development process is essential. For documentation, where feasible, more visuals and fewer words is a good policy. This approach improves clarity due to the old adage that *a picture is worth a thousand words*, but it also addresses situations where multiple languages are spoken within the workplace. Visuals are a universal language.

This *standard process* capability would seem to be most critical in the early stages of a Lean transformation where process instability is likely most prevalent; however, this capability is even more critical as the Lean transformation progresses. Every improvement must become part of the new standard; otherwise, variability develops and becomes amplified due to the ongoing improvements. This requires a disciplined change process which is part of the "experiment" core capability of Lean.

Surface Problems

If we want to improve processes, we need to see the problems and wastes. They need to be exposed and highlighted. This is the second fundamental of Lean: surfacing problems and opportunities for improvement. We need to put mechanisms in place to facilitate this problem exposure, and we need to encourage the highlighting of problems by all company personnel. Problems can be considered deviations from the current standard, and also the gap from our current condition to our next target condition, but if problems remain hidden, there's nothing to improve. The competition will *out-improve* us and we'll lose our competitive position; therefore, surfacing and exposing problems must be a fundamental core capability.

Most of the tools of Lean are mechanisms for surfacing problems. For example, standard work and visual standard locations are necessary to determine whether there has actually been a deviation from a standard, and an effective workcell design or visual kanban/pull system will quickly expose any process imbalances and associated wastes.

A complicating factor is that since many of us don't naturally and comfortably highlight problems, issues remain hidden or short-term fixes are quietly applied and root causes are never addressed. Encouraging the unnatural behavior of immediately highlighting problems is a key challenge for all leaders. Problems must be exposed!

Experiment

If we have standard processes, and we have exposed problems to solve, what's the basic approach to problem-solving? This is where experimentation and the PDCA process come into play. This is our third fundamental of Lean. Lean companies experiment their way to progress. Rather than becoming paralyzed by the inability to agree on the *best* countermeasure which will provide the greatest benefit, Lean companies start *doing* and scientifically experimenting (PDCA). They *learn their way* to an improvement. In some cases, you may even anticipate that the experiment will not be successful as far as solving the problem or making an improvement, but we try, and learn, and then repeat the PDCA process to learn and improve, over and over again.

A disciplined experimentation approach should be evident in structured improvement events such as kaizen events or other formal project approaches, but also in the daily improvements which occur in the *gemba*. Developing this scientific thinking mindset throughout the workforce is an ongoing process where everyone becomes a process scientist and inventor. Lapses will occur, such as when the root-cause analysis step was insufficient, evident by a recurring problem, or when a change was not incorporated into the standard work, evident by the surfacing of process variability, but these lapses should be viewed as learning opportunities to further strengthen this core capability of *experimentation*.

Engage Everyone

The fourth fundamental capability of Lean is to engage everyone. This is an expansive category which is a primary theme of this book. It has multiple facets which span from people issues such as resistance and motivation to structural issues such as standard practices like daily huddles and improvement events, but the topic of *"How do we more effectively engage everyone?"* must be an ongoing focus during the Lean transformation. This should be a priority topic of every single Lean steering committee meeting.

There are a number of methods utilized to engage company personnel, such as kaizen events or projects, huddles, *gemba* walks, formal idea systems, dedicated improvement time, discussions of problems as they occur, and informal one-on-one conversations. But regardless of the mechanism, Lean companies realize that utilizing and developing the creativity and brainpower of the whole workforce is much better than relying on only a few smart folks from the Lean team. Lean companies don't wait for the opportune time to get folks involved; time never seems to be *opportune*. They find ways of *designing in* multiple methods for engagement; both formal and informal means are employed.

Keep Score

The final core capability is the ability to keep score. This is an area where my sports analogy breaks down a bit. Keeping score is not a "blocking and tackling" issue in the sports world. The score-keeping rules are well established, but in the business world, it's a little more complicated. We need to continually improve our methods of selecting, gathering, and utilizing performance metrics and processing data. KPI systems clarify direction, monitor performance status, indicate needs for course adjustments, and determine effectiveness of improvement activities. If you don't measure, how do you know you're really improving? Refer back to Chapter 4 for elaboration on this topic.

Those are the key capabilities that Lean companies are developing. I've referred to them at times as capability *categories* since there are dozens of capabilities and skills embedded within each of the five listed. They are not applied only at a particular stage of the transformation journey. They span all phases, and we're always trying to get better and better at doing them. Of course everything begins with value as defined by the customer:

- Then we focus on understanding the current standard process
- And we expose problems and waste in the standard process
- Then we solve these problems with continual PDCA experimentation
- By engaging everyone in this process
- And we use data and measurement to monitor and continuously improve.

I can hear some of you saying, *"How in the world can you possibly not include 'eliminating the eight wastes' as one of the core Lean capabilities?"*

That's a valid point, but combatting the eight wastes is engrained in the other capabilities, so it's not listed separately. It's a similar argument for the customer: the only reason to have the core capabilities is to add value for and to satisfy the customer. By all means, feel free to include "add value for the customer" and "eliminate the eight wastes" as Lean core capabilities if you feel that this would complete the list.

Now let's dive a little deeper and look at some key points and strategies for deploying Lean to enable the never-ending development of the "blocking and tackling" capabilities.

Lean Deployment

I need to remind you once again that every organization must develop their specific Lean roadmap or transformation plan. We do need to beg, borrow, and "steal" ideas from everywhere, and we should consider proven strategies and roadmaps that others have utilized, but you'll fall short with a simple *copy strategy* for your Lean transformation. You won't gain the knowledge needed to enable you to recognize and make any course adjustments along the journey. Here we'll review some Lean deployment issues to consider.

Engage Leaders

Regardless of who initiated the Lean journey, or whatever the catalyst for change, right from the start I'd suggest engaging the leadership team. Don't let Failure Mechanism #2, *Leaders Aren't Leading*, grow any roots. Of course, this group needs guidance and coaching from the Lean subject matter expert(s). (Refer back to Chapter 5 for key roles and responsibilities of the Lean steering committee and the Lean support team.) This is also the time to squash Lean Failure Mechanism #1, *Wrong or Incomplete Definition of Lean*. The leadership team must gain an understanding of the Lean principles that will serve as the foundation and bedrock beliefs of the Lean and business strategy; however, understanding is not enough. They must publicly commit to building the Lean strategy with Lean principles as the founding framework.

Commit to the Principles

Think of these principles as your Lean constitution. Just as a country's constitution captures the fundamental principles by which the government was formed and continues to be administered, the Lean principles should serve a similar foundational role for your Lean journey. From these agreed-upon principles, everything else is built and aligned. Every leader must commit to the establishment of Lean principles as the continuous improvement framework. You would think that this starting point of Lean definition and purpose agreement would fall into the category of common sense and would naturally occur; however, the reality is, due to the prevalence of organizations working from a starting point of a faulty Lean definition, or an incomplete definition, or multiple conflicting definitions, it has gained recognition as one of the Lean failure mechanisms reviewed in Chapter 2.

We won't repeat all of the roles and responsibilities of the leadership team or Lean steering committee which were reviewed in Chapter 5, but in addition to planning the initial rollout to the workforce, which will involve some Lean awareness education to address the "what" of Lean, and more importantly the "why" of Lean, the leadership team needs to decide on the overall transformational approach. We'll now review three general paths to take. A fourth approach is some hybrid of the three.

Model Value Stream Approach

This strategy involves focusing on a single value stream to develop a model of Lean. The goal at this point isn't widespread organizational transformation, but rather a deep dive into the application of Lean principles and practices in a specific value stream. A key decision is the selection of which value stream to serve as the target for our learning and improvement efforts.

Target Area Selection

The target value stream should be selected carefully. A significant amount of time and resources will be devoted to the change effort, so you want to gain as much benefit from the model as possible. You want a target value stream which will:

- Produce noticeable impact. This is the time to stack the deck in your favor; you are trying to change mindsets, so set the organization up for success. A value stream producing a product family which will be discontinued within a year won't grab much attention; one with rapidly increasing sales will.
- Have Lean-supportive personnel throughout key areas of the value stream, ideally "opinion leaders," which were reviewed in Chapter 6. This will exponentially increase the leveraging power of the model.
- Produce lessons learned which are transferrable to other areas of the organization. Otherwise, it will have little effect in converting the *"But we're different!"* contingent unless they happen to work in the model area.

Advantages and Limitations

By focusing on a single value stream, a deep dive into the application of Lean tools and techniques is possible. For the moment, you're not diverting attention by the need for enterprise-wide application. Development and learning is more focused, and this concentration of effort should yield quantifiable results since the complete system is being addressed.

A downside or limitation of this approach is that only a portion of the workforce is involved. Everyone else is watching from the sidelines, if they're even watching. Without a solid plan for expanding the transformation, this could inadvertently encourage the creation of the common "spotty Lean" condition where Lean practices are present in only some areas of an organization, but not integrated and evident organization-wide.

A lengthy value stream can take an extended period of time to streamline, so it's critical to remain focused on creating flow throughout the whole system. Otherwise, the disjointed condition significantly limits impact due to the broken connections where wastes can thrive. This is why a rigorous deployment plan must be created from the analysis of the value stream. Obviously, value stream mapping is a key tool of this phase and approach. When utilizing a lengthy value stream as your model, attempt to begin parallel activities in other value streams. Learn from the lessons of the initial target, but don't wait for the development of a mature model before expansion to other value streams. (In a sense, the model is *never completed*; it is continuously improved; however, completion of key milestones could serve as the definition of *complete or mature*.)

Another potential downside is that a *project* or *event* mentality may form since the model line is a defined *project* and likely involves a series of discrete implementation events. It may not initially be apparent that we need to get to the point where Lean practices are ingrained into the daily activities of the work. The end of the *project* does not mean the end of Lean activities! This misperception creates the *Lean-by-project* mentality. The Lean journey will always involve projects, but it's the *dependence* on projects or events which is the issue, and also the defined timeframe of a project or event.

A *project* mindset exists when people are waiting around for the next improvement *event* to make any changes. Think of this as improvement *batching* rather than *continuous* improvement. To combat this potential downside, it is critical that Lean daily management practices are instituted as part of the implementation plan of the model value stream. Rather than a potential downside, maybe we should view this as a concern or caution, since effective application will eliminate the "concern."

Broad Engagement Approach

The other transformational approach takes the opposite tack, and can also be referred to as a "mile wide, inch deep" approach. This involves a more expansive facility-wide introduction and implementation of Lean practices. This may include plant-wide training and implementation of stability-building practices, such as developing standard work and the application of the 5S/workplace organization system. If not already in place, maybe an early action is the development of KPIs throughout the organization, or a communication mechanism is put in place such as a daily huddle system to initiate improvement discussions in addition to the daily production conversations which would typically take place in workgroup meetings.

Advantages and Limitations

This broader approach attempts to engage everyone in Lean learning and improvement and pick up some quick wins. So from an overall cultural perspective, this approach is strong in encouraging continuous improvement practices everywhere, not just in a chosen model value stream or pilot area. The clear message being sent to the organization is that Lean applies everywhere. Another advantage is that a broad approach typically relies heavily on front-line leadership, since they are the ones leading their team's improvement discussions. As we reviewed in Chapter 5, this will be a new and uncomfortable role for some, so teaching, coaching, and ongoing support from company leaders and Lean support personnel is critical, and peer support during this transition can be impactful. This approach facilitates the leader learning process; I consider this an advantage.

"Improvement Habit" Development

Another advantage of this broad-based approach is that it can be effective in developing a habit of improvement throughout the whole organization. I think of it as creating *improvement muscles*, building a little more strength day after day. You gain the ability to see the waste in company processes. You begin to automatically notice the opportunities; it becomes a habit. Prior to developing this Lean habit, the opportunities aren't perceived. For example, in the early stages of the Lean journey, there are typically small changes which invoke comments like, *"It's so simple; why didn't we do this years ago?"* Many of the workplace organization improvements resulting from application of the 5S process would fit into this category. We didn't all of a sudden get smart! Identifying a standard location for our materials and tools was *always* common sense, so why didn't we do something about it in the past? The problem was that *seeing* the opportunity wasn't a habit. Or if we occasionally did happen to notice that we were participating in a wasteful activity, we didn't have a mechanism to change anything. Seeing waste and having a means of eliminating the waste was not a developed capability.

The culture we are trying to develop is where everyone, every day, sees the opportunities to eliminate waste for improvement towards our objectives. It becomes a habit where we would feel uncomfortable if we didn't do it. When we develop habits outside of the workplace we start small. We don't begin training for a marathon by trying to run 20 miles on day one. We start small and develop a running habit to build strength and stamina. When starting on our Lean journey, by dedicating a short amount of time every day to improvement, a habit of seeing and eliminating waste can form throughout the whole organization. This is an advantage of a broad, company-wide, deployment approach.

The downside is that a broad implementation of Lean practices likely just scratches the surface of Lean learning. A deep dive employing multiple tools and techniques is difficult to do while simultaneously applying a broad organization-wide strategy. Often, a limiting factor is available resources to teach and guide the organization-wide Lean efforts. However, this shallow application of Lean should not be assumed a sloppy or unstructured application route. Rather, it's simply a broader approach which covers more territory, but probably will be slower in producing significant visible impact since the application is shallow.

The small wins noticed in each area will grow support, and a large number of small wins can produce considerable benefit. So, even though the resulting impact may be considered a weakness of this broad engagement approach when compared with a rigorous value stream deployment plan, don't *overminimize* the potential of a series of small, shallow, improvements.

Many of these small wins are eliminating workplace frustrations, such as why someone needs to travel the length of a football field just to obtain their tools ... the waste of excess motion. Frustration-eliminating activities are those which anyone can get behind and support! It may not be practical to track the number of workplace frustrations *(though I would love it if someone would accept this challenge!)*; however, if it were tracked, hopefully the frustration trend line would have a steep downward trend. (Unless, of course, you're tracking the total number of frustrations *eliminated*, then a steep upward trend is desired.) Refer to Figure 7.1 for an imaginary frustration run chart.

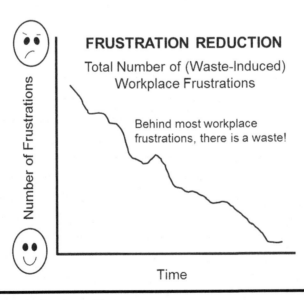

Figure 7.1 Frustration Run Chart

Pilot Area Approach

This third approach is where a focus *area*, not a complete value stream, is chosen as an improvement target. The focus area would typically be one particular work area within an overall value stream, such as a fabrication or assembly department. If the department is large, the focus area may be a segment of the department, for example, Assembly Area A is the target, though the department includes Assembly Areas A–F. Though system optimization is always the goal, this approach does not search for the best value stream to serve as a model, but rather the target area is selected for more specific reasons. Due to the limited scope of the pilot area, this approach is often associated with the term "point solutions" as compared with a system-wide strategy.

Target Area Selection

As with the selection of the value stream in the *model value stream approach*, a pilot should produce noticeable impact, ideally have Lean-supportive individuals involved, and should develop skills and lessons which are transferrable to other areas of the organization. However, with the *pilot area approach*, along with these considerations, a target area is often chosen for more specific reasons, such as:

■ To develop a particular capability for competitive reasons. For example, quick changeover (SMED) techniques are often an initial application target in job-shop organizations where processing would be described as low-volume, high-mix. Being the quick-change artists of their industry could create a competitive advantage. Even though a value stream analysis will highlight the greatest impact area for a quick changeover effort, and system optimization is always the goal, the primary purpose of the pilot might be to learn and develop quick changeover capability. Selecting an assembly area for developing cellular design, one-piece flow processing capability is another common pilot area selection, to then be replicated throughout the facility.

■ To address an existing performance problem. The actual problem will dictate the emphasis on particular Lean tools and techniques. The focus will be to relieve the immediate pain resulting from a quality problem, a bottleneck operation, or a piece of equipment which has more unplanned downtime than actual run time, resulting in missed deliveries.

- To address a longer-term need, such as a sales volume increase which will require a capacity upgrade in an area. Focusing here will address this capacity need, and since it is a product with increasing sales, the pilot will likely get noticed.
- To build capability on a specific tool or technique, such as the application of the 5S system. This is an even narrower scope than any of the before-mentioned pilots. This model can then be a showcase for reference as this capability is expanded throughout the organization.

Advantages and Limitations

Since this effort is more limited in scope as compared with the *model value stream approach*, the implementation timeframe and resources required are significantly less. Results, at least at the local, work area level, will occur quickly. Since the target area is often selected due to a high priority need, the pilot will naturally get a lot of attention. This will help grow support for Lean methods. Though the scope is limited, focusing on a single work area enables a rigorous deep dive into applying and learning various Lean tools and practices.

The limited scope of a work area focus presents a number of potential downsides – one being that only a small portion of the workforce is involved. Also, since this pilot is centered on a narrow target, looking for a *point solution*, the risk is that the overall value stream is not optimized. However, this potential downside can be minimized by strict adherence to the *optimize the value stream* principle. I believe that the often negative connotation of *point solutions* is unwarranted. All local area improvements should be evaluated against the effect on the whole system, the value stream. It's this lack of systems thinking which is at the root of the problem, not the limited scope of the *pilot area approach*.

Which Approach is Best?

The bottom line is that you want to develop *both* broad and deep capability, so don't limit your thinking to an *either-or* debate; you want to get to *and*. You can begin with a broad approach to gain support, get multiple quick wins, develop *improvement muscles*, and build basic stability throughout the organization, but then you can isolate a specific value stream to serve as your Lean showcase. The narrower *pilot area approach* could actually be considered a component of the *model value stream approach* since the value stream is improved through a series of discrete improvement efforts. You don't eat the value stream all at once; you take one bite at a time. So these three approaches should not be considered separate and discrete paths. Again, you want it all. You want deep learning across the entire organization while at the same time addressing specific challenges which may warrant a *point solution.* However, it's the value stream which provides the product or service to the paying customer, so any approach must be deployed with the *optimize the value stream* principle in mind.

As was reviewed, there are many factors which may affect your decision. If you have a value stream with a significant sales increase on the horizon, or possibly a work area experiencing a number of problems, using these as Lean model targets can produce impact that gets noticed. Or from a strategic perspective, you may have a product line which could double sales volumes if lead time could be reduced by X percent. This might be a good place to focus.

Company size can have a major effect on your decision. A *value stream approach* in a small company can also provide the benefits of the broader method since most everyone can be involved. At the other extreme, an expansive facility with dozens of value streams would probably make a *broad engagement approach* covering the whole facility impractical. So as I've repeated multiple times, you need to develop your own path and learn and adjust via continuous experimentation.

Regardless of transformational approach, what we're trying to do is develop a culture of continuous improvement. Most of this book has focused on critical elements for developing this Lean culture, but how does this fit within the overall strategy. As part of your Lean deployment plan, what are the timing considerations of embedding Lean into the culture of your organization? This is the subject of our next Lean deployment topic.

Embedding Lean into the Culture

Many change experts state that embedding Lean into the company culture is a final stage on the transformation roadmap. This advice can easily be misinterpreted to suggest that consideration of any cultural concerns should be delayed until some point in the future after a lengthy period of transformational activity. Of course culture-building takes time, but this doesn't imply that it should be a late-stage step of the change process. We should utilize the early education and implementation activities to *drive* the desired cultural change. Overlooking cultural issues during the early stages of change could halt the transformation right at the starting line. For example, any current practices or policies which are in direct misalignment with Lean principles cannot be ignored. If so, trust will be lost due to the mixed messages. When this occurs, there might be a lot of head nodding and passive support for Lean, but only in the amount perceived to be required to maintain employment. This is similar to our discussion of the first step of motivation, which is to quit *demotivating*. Lean will be perceived as another *program* which many assume will come and go. *"Just wait it out."* The obvious misalignment with Lean principles will justify this belief and grow the culture killing disease of *organizational hypocrisy*.

The other reason for putting culture in the forefront is to assure that you effectively plan and execute in a way which will build the desired culture. How you implement changes, who is involved, what approach is utilized, all can facilitate or thwart cultural progress. Refer back to Chapter 6, where the Michael Myway implementation approach is described versus how Flo Facilitator supported the identical change.

It would be nice if the stages of a Lean transformation were totally discrete events where you completed step 1, put that aside, moved on to step 2, closed the book on step 2, time for step 3, etc.; however, this is too simplistic of a vision. Since a Lean culture is the desired outcome of the transformation efforts, listing it at the final stage of a Lean roadmap may be appropriate; however, culture-building actions should be embedded within each stage of your roadmap. A culture needs to develop and grow over time. It's not something which suddenly appears after completing a magical culture-creating task.

Administrative Lean

Lean applies everywhere, regardless of your particular position in the organization. We first touched on this in Chapter 3 when reviewing the Lean principles, such as the *customer* principle, where the *internal customer* concept was introduced, and the *everyone* principle means exactly that – Lean applies to everyone. However, due to the lagging engagement of office personnel in the Lean deployment strategy in a number of organizations, I thought a few more specific comments would be appropriate.

First of all, obviously, at the detail level, office processes and personnel have some different needs as compared with production operations. This starts sounding like the *"But we're different!"* argument that we recently debunked. A job shop has differences from a high-volume, low-mix environment, which is also different from a project-based company, which is different from a service or office environment. Yes, we *are* different. I won't repeat the whole *"But we're different!"* discussion here, other than repeating that none of these differences have anything to do with the applicability of Lean and your obligations within a Lean organization, whether you are a production assembler, design engineer, accounting clerk, HR manager, or vice president of sales.

Most administrative or non-production functions actually have a dual Lean role within the organization. These roles are not distinct and unrelated, but rather are interrelated within the overall value stream. One role is to provide support to the primary value-adding people and processes of the organization. The other role involves improving support processes.

Support Departments such as Engineering, Sales, and Human Resources

Let's use a typical engineering department of a manufacturing company as an example. They provide technical expertise and support for the production operations. Therefore, they have a responsibility to participate in the waste reduction efforts with operations personnel and they must be responsive to any requests for assistance. This support role to the value-adding production operations of the organization should be a primary component of their performance evaluation.

They also have a responsibility to help improve the support processes, whether they are the primary driver or a participant. The *product design* process and the *engineering change* process are just a couple examples where engineering is a primary driver. These processes are often full of waste which needs to be eradicated to improve performance. In information flows you may not see piles of inventory (though you might), but you will notice excessive delays. You'll find overprocessing in the form of multiple reviews and signatures, and rework due to missing and wrong information. These are just a few of the typical opportunities. This process improvement role should also be a key performance evaluation criterion. Most business processing is a team sport and not confined solely within a single function, so it is critical that all organizational functions are committed to continuous process improvement.

This dual Lean role exists in a number of other functions as well, such as the sales department. They need to integrate with their internal customers in the factory and they also need to continually analyze and conduct experiments focused on sales processes. Standardizing current sales processes is a good starting point.

The human resources (HR) department could very well have been listed in the *Key Roles and Responsibilities* chapter due to their critical role in staffing for Lean. They too have a dual Lean role. HR takes the lead in improving processes such as hiring and onboarding. Their other Lean role, which is tied to these primary processes, is the support role of staffing the organization to align with and build the Lean culture. I believe this latter role becomes more of a coordinator or facilitator role than in the past. The extreme anti-Lean hiring approach would be when a new team member shows up for their first day of work, and the supervisor and team members are seeing the new hire for the first time. This "drop a body" into the work team is not an effective Lean hiring process. In a Lean environment, HR works more closely not just with the area supervisor, but also involves at least some of the work team members, the new hire's peers, in the hiring process. Everyone's role is altered to some extent due to Lean, and the HR department is definitely no exception.

The value stream integrates administrative and production processes into an interrelated system which provides the product or service to the final customer. Even with awareness of this administrative/production linkage, there still has been a lag in administrative or office Lean applications as compared with their production partners. Let's delve a little into *why* non-production personnel have often lagged in Lean engagement.

Why the Lag in Office Lean?

We've Allowed It

The first reason is that we have allowed it! We have allowed the violation of multiple Lean principles such as *teamwork* and the related *optimize the value stream* principle. We've allowed people to opt out of what should be primary responsibilities of their jobs, supporting their internal customers and improving "the job." As has been reviewed, vertical functional silo-building, at the expense of horizontal value-adding flow of materials and information, should not be tolerated. As to why many non-production personnel are reluctant to participate, it's not at all because they are all concrete heads. *(Though, you might find a few of them around.)* Rather, the reasons are exactly the same reasons why any person resists change, as reviewed in Chapter 6. We need to understand these root causes and provide training, coaching, and ongoing support. And most importantly, communicate and engage people in changes which directly affect them, and if at all feasible, engage them at the *design* stage of any change.

The Non-Competitive Environment

I believe the other reason for the lag in office engagement, and why office processes are slow to be analyzed and improved, is related to competition, or lack thereof. We don't feel the competitive pressure to have a better engineering change process or invoicing process or accounts receivables process than our competitors. But we should! We should experiment and eliminate waste from all of these processes to improve performance of the value stream for the benefit of our customers, both internal and final customers.

This does require a proactive mindset, since someone in the office may not naturally appreciate the performance pressure from the final customer, as compared with someone like the production manager or the person working on the shipping dock. The antidote to this is adherence to Lean principles and clarification of each function's customer-focused purpose, both the internal customer and the final paying customer.

Simply understanding why a lack of engagement occurs is of no value without subsequent corrective action. It's time for us to commit to the principles of Lean which serve as our foundation. The value stream consists of various functions, all of which have an obligation to work as a team and remove wastes from processes, both the primary value-adding processes and the connected support processes. Of course there is always prioritization as to where and when to commit limited resources; however, simply choosing to opt out from Lean cannot be accepted and will put the whole organization at competitive risk. The competition may not be opting out!

Fun

You probably are wondering how the topic of *fun* found its way into a discussion of Lean deployment. I am quite serious about the topic of fun. In Raj Sisodia's book, which is interestingly titled *Firms of Endearment: How World-Class Companies PROFIT from Passion and Purpose*, he highlights a *culture of fun* as one of the common characteristics of these firms.[2] Sisodia describes a firm of endearment (FoE):

Quite simply, an FoE is a company that *endears* itself to
stakeholders by bringing the interests of all stakeholders groups
into strategic alignment. No stakeholder group benefits at the
expense of any other stakeholder group, and each prospers as
others do.[3]

He includes society, partners, investors, customers, and employees as the
stakeholder groups. As for the FoE firms, Toyota, Honda, Harley-Davidson,
and Southwest are a few of the organizations with which you may be
familiar. Fun has a place within these organizations.

I believe that fun should be a tactic of a Lean transformation for three
main reasons. First of all, well, the obvious reason. There's no explanation
needed. It's fun! So, no need to elaborate any further on this reason. The
other two reasons, which are a little less obvious, are:

1. To build camaraderie and teamwork
2. To highlight Lean behaviors

Let's take a closer look at these two purposes of fun in the workplace.

To Build Camaraderie and Teamwork

As you've heard before, Lean is a team sport. People Principle #3 reviewed
in Chapter 3 is *teamwork*, and Process Principle #2, *Optimize the Value
Stream*, requires teamwork across departments and work areas. Fun
gatherings such as company picnics, employee birthday and milestone
celebrations, and participation in athletic events are just a few examples
where employees can develop relationships and become more comfortable
with each other, and the developed camaraderie builds trust. Consider
a mixture of company-wide gatherings along with small, fun work team
activities. This mix can build rapport within the work teams and also
across departmental boundaries to internal suppliers and customers. In
the workplace, the developed comfort and trust can present itself in more
openness to discuss problems and improvement ideas. A team where trust
is high is more apt to challenge each other to improve performance of the
team and individuals.

To Highlight Lean Behaviors

Gatherings such as monthly or quarterly *all-hands* meetings and company picnics are great opportunities to keep the spotlight on Lean. Get Lean onto the agenda of every type of get-together like this and make it fun, such as having a raffle for a small prize for all employees who have contributed improvement ideas. Use these events for recognizing a team for their improvement progress this past month. Have them share their stories so others can learn and apply similar concepts in their own areas. This also feeds into earlier discussions of *social influence*. Heighten impact by getting Lean-minded *opinion leaders* up on the stage.

Also consider using these company gatherings to highlight a specific Lean behavior, such as the need for experimentation and to not fear failure. Recognize a team for an effort which didn't produce the results as expected, but have them elaborate on what they learned, and what's the next step. Make it as much fun as you can handle. How about handing out the "best try" award to a team to emphasize this experimental mindset?

Another Lean behavior which you could highlight is the implementation of small incremental improvements by everyone. Recognize someone who made an improvement which most would consider low-impact, at least from a financial perspective, but they took the initiative to think deeply about an issue and made a change. Put a spotlight on this desired kaizen behavior.

I'm sure you can come up with many more ideas for using company gatherings to promote Lean behaviors by having a little fun with awards and recognition, and don't some of these gatherings really need an injection of fun? I personally think some company communication meetings can become a little *dry*. Transparency of company performance and plans is critical in building a Lean culture. A *lack* of transparency can contribute to one of the root causes for resisting change, a lack of trust. However, sometimes the presentation of this information can be described as anything but *fun*.

Consider forming a fun committee to focus on this issue of building a culture where fun is an element. Also, consider providing each work area team with a small budget for a fun activity each month. One team may choose a movie night, but another may choose to attend a ball game. This brings in the motivational aspect of *autonomy*. Fun isn't only laughs and giggles; fun should be used as a strategic tactic throughout the Lean deployment process.

Lean Transformation Guidelines

This section gathers together and summarizes many of the Lean transformation topics reviewed in this chapter and some topics from previous chapters. Additional Lean considerations are also provided. I'd also suggest that you refer to the book, *The BASICS Lean Implementation Model: Lean Tools to Drive Daily Innovation and Increased Profitability*, by Charles Protzman, Dan Protzman, and William Keen, which provides details to many of the general concepts and ideas presented in this chapter.[4]

Lean Leadership

Stumbling Block

A typical stumbling block with respect to who should lead the Lean transformation is relying on the Lean facilitator or Lean team to do all of the heavy lifting, while allowing company leaders to provide passive support, or worse, opting out. Leaders, at all levels of the organization, must lead the transformation. Lean expert resources serve as subject matter experts, facilitators, and coaches. Immediately engage the leadership team/Lean steering committee to *steer* the transformation.

Lean Steering Committee

Establish the Lean steering committee to guide and monitor the Lean strategy and to initiate course adjustments when needed. This committee may be the current company leadership team along with key Lean support resources. The primary responsibilities of this group are to:

- Plan the Lean deployment strategy
- Establish measurement/KPI system
- Develop an improvement status/review process
- Establish workforce idea-generation processes
- Provide support
- Assure system and business alignment with Lean

Consider setting challenging goals to expedite the development of a new way of thinking and operating. For example, a lead time reduction of 50 percent, from raw material receipt to customer delivery of the finished product, cannot be accomplished by tweaking around the edges of the status quo. A rigorous Lean methodology is required. Consider stretch goals for non-production processes as well. What would be the business ramifications of a 50 percent reduction in quotation lead time? Again, this won't happen by dwelling in the comfort zone of today.

Front-Line Leaders

One of the most challenging leadership role adjustments involves the front-line leader. To engage this critical leader level, consider holding regular front-line leader meetings to share progress and obstacles. The purpose of these meetings is for the front-line leaders to:

- Participate in their role redesign
- Support each other
- Hold each other accountable
- Obtain uniform training and coaching

Lean Training

Following is a list of training considerations. Each organization must develop a training plan which works effectively for their organization, but the following is provided to initiate some internal discussion as to the most appropriate methods. Many of these items have been addressed throughout this book:

- Initial training should develop an understanding of Lean principles and an overview of Lean tools and techniques (the "what" of Lean), but more importantly, it must focus on the need for developing a Lean culture of continuous improvement (the "why" of Lean).
- If internal Lean expertise is not yet available, utilize external Lean resources for training, facilitating projects, transformation guidance, and developing internal Lean capability.
- Consider having managers and supervisors conduct or participate in the initial awareness-level training, and use expert support for guidance as needed. This will demonstrate Lean importance and leader commitment.

- Utilize application exercises and hands-on simulation exercises to enhance formal training sessions where feasible.
- Attempt to provide training at the point of need, *just in time*, so that application can follow training with minimal delay. This is the *train-do* approach.
- Consider short Lean training topics every day as a component of a broad organization-wide training and deployment plan.
- Incorporate a training component into Lean steering committee meetings and other standard meetings. Even a 15-minute daily huddle can include a short educational segment.
- Training should be a component of any improvement project or event.
- Consider short "lunch and learn" sessions.
- Build a physical and/or online Lean library which is accessible to all employees.
- Provide Lean training for new hires as a component of the onboarding process.
- Attend networking events and join organizations such as multi-company Lean peer groups to learn and grow with peers from other organizations.
- Develop leaders into teachers and coaches to transform the training process to a *continuous learning process*, an ongoing growth process for not only company leaders, but for every single employee.
- Both one-on-one mentoring and group/peer learning approaches should be utilized.

Lean Application Approaches

The following deployment information has previously been covered in depth in this chapter, but is provided here in summary form:

1. Model value stream – this enables a deep dive into a target value stream for extensive learning and application of Lean tools and practices. This approach provides a showcase of "how Lean applies here."
2. Broad engagement – this is more of a kaizen/incremental improvement approach. Though learning initially is not deep, this approach can build broad engagement and develop improvement

into a daily habit. Focus on workforce frustrations, which almost always have some sort of waste at their root.

3. Pilot area approach – a limited area is selected as the model. Reasons could include building a key capability or addressing a performance problem. These are often referred to as "point solutions." However, maintain a systems perspective and evaluate results based on value stream ramifications.

4. Hybrid – begin with the habit-forming #2 approach for broader workforce engagement and support for the Lean strategy, then #1 or #3 to develop deeper application of the Lean tools and techniques.

Basic Structural Elements

Following are structural elements of Lean which should be considered during early phase deployment planning since these provide a foundation for subsequent progress:

■ Establish a visual KPI system which will set the direction for improvement and help develop a data-driven/fact-based organization. (You have to keep score. How are we doing today? Are we improving over time?)

■ Build communication and improvement systems into the workplace, such as a daily huddle system and dedicated improvement time. (Designing-in Lean, rather than trying to "fit it in.")

■ Develop simple idea-generation and documentation mechanisms (e.g., whiteboard or flipchart methods.)

Process Improvement Guidelines

The following general guidelines are provided to highlight priority aspects of the process improvement challenge:

■ Basic stability – begin by establishing standardized and stable processes. Define the work content, sequence, timing, and outcome. This will establish the baseline condition for subsequent improvement. This also includes basic stability systems such as the 5S system of workplace organization.

■ The value stream – develop value stream understanding where improving the linkages to internal suppliers and customers is a priority. This "horizontal" or "systems thinking" is absolutely critical to effectively flow value to the ultimate customer. These linkages will only be tightened with proactive improvement steps; this won't happen naturally or automatically.

■ Lean tools – utilize the appropriate Lean tools and techniques to support your improvement efforts and align the organization with Lean principles. Tool usage in itself is not the goal, but you need the right tools to get the job done.

■ Everybody – Lean must be applied throughout the whole organization. Engagement of the workforce to maximize the brainpower of the organization must be an ongoing priority.

■ Lean is a never-ending journey! And have fun!

Ten Lean Transformation Questions to Consider

As you embark on your Lean journey, or when reflecting back on your current Lean strategy, consider the following ten questions. (One or more elaborating questions or comments accompany each of the ten questions.) Internal discussions based on these questions will help unify understanding of where you are now, where you want to go, and what you need to get there. The questions will encourage and facilitate planning as you move forward on your never-ending journey. The previous pages of this book have provided background information and insights regarding each of the questions:

1. What is Lean and why is it important? *(Lean principles and purpose – where are we going on this journey and why?)*
2. What is our current condition and how is Lean different? *(Where are we now? This defines the gap from current reality to desired future vision.)*
3. Are we committed to going on this journey? *(Commitment to the Lean principles is required and is an unarguable starting point. Lean is not simply a "tweaking" of the* status quo*!)*
4. Who is steering the transformation? *(Lean leadership cannot be delegated away.)*
5. What are the other key roles and how does everyone's "job" change? *(Roles and responsibilities change due to Lean.)*

6. What new skills and behaviors are needed and how will we develop those skills and behaviors? *(With new roles and responsibilities come the need for new capabilities and behaviors.)*
7. How will we prepare the workforce for the journey? *(How will we explain and train on the "what and why" of Lean and set expectations for the future? Failure to do so will heighten fear of the unknown and stifle progress.)*
8. What are our goals, objectives, and deployment approach? *(What is our deployment strategy to enable Lean learning and build momentum? How do we develop quick wins to get the ball rolling and engage people and make improvement habit-forming?)*
9. How will we spread the learning and improvement? *(Initial Lean efforts must be utilized as catalysts to expand Lean learning and build momentum throughout the enterprise.)*
10. How will we embed Lean into our culture? *(How do we put the "continuous" in continuous improvement?)*

Action Item – *Reflection*

Besides introducing some new discussion items, this chapter captured and summarized a number of this book's key topics and points. At the next Lean steering committee meeting, reflect upon your organization's Lean journey. Discuss whether any of the reviewed Lean deployment alternatives or transformation guidelines surfaced any items which need further discussion and analysis to enable strengthening of your Lean strategy. Review the *ten Lean Transformation Questions* to assure that there is clarity in your plan. Consider completing the *Quick and Dirty Lean Culture Assessment*, Figure A.1 in the Appendix, to deepen your reflection of your Lean journey, and your progress in *making it happen*.

Notes

1. "Vince Lombardi Quotes." BrainyQuote. Accessed January 9, 2019. www.brainyquote.com/quotes/vince_lombardi_115468.
2. Sisodia, R.S., D.B. Wolfe, and J.N. Sheth. *Firms of Endearment: How World-Class, Companies Profit from Passion and Purpose.* Upper Saddle River, NJ: Wharton School Publishing, 2007.

3. Ibid., 6.

4. Protzman, C., D. Protzman, and W. Keen. *The BASICS Lean Implementation Model: Lean Tools to Drive Daily Innovation and Increased Profitability.* New York, NY: Routledge, 2018.

Chapter 8

Final Thoughts

We've come to a milestone along our journey, the conclusion of this book. I don't consider it an endpoint, since our personal and company Lean journeys are never-ending, so it's simply a milestone along our pathway.

Review

We began in Chapter 1 by developing a working or baseline definition of Lean. The purpose was to create a uniform vision of our objective, to have clarity so that we were all heading in the same direction as we began our journey. This Lean definition was elaborated on in Chapter 3, where we reviewed the Lean principles. I compared the set of Lean principles to a country's constitution that captures the fundamental principles by which the government was formed and continues to be administered. I believe that the Lean principles should be viewed in a similar manner, as the governing foundation of your Lean organization. At the very start of the Lean journey, or at any point if not previously done, I believe that if the leadership team would agree and commit to a set of Lean principles to serve as the framework for their Lean strategy, many of the destructive landmines, stumbles, and missteps of a Lean transformation would be averted.

The Lean landmines, or what I refer to as "Lean failure mechanisms," were reviewed in Chapter 2. This chapter may seem misplaced, since a case could be made that the Lean principles of Chapter 3 should have followed the Lean definition-building topic of Chapter 1. I chose to insert the failure mechanisms into Chapter 2 since I felt that, along our travels, the sooner we become aware of the pitfalls ahead, the better to enable timely planning of alternative routes. I mentioned that these failure mechanisms, if properly addressed, can be flipped 180 degrees and be transformed into Lean success factors. This section could have simply been titled, "Key Lean Topics." If you address these topics poorly, they become failure mechanisms; if addressed effectively, they are Lean success factors. However, unfortunately, too many organizations have not provided sufficient focus on these topics; thus, I chose the "Lean failure mechanism" moniker.

Chapter 4 reviewed some Lean systems, practices, and tools. My intent was to highlight a few vital topics, such as key performance indicators; you need to keep score! KPIs are critical not only for improvement focus and tracking purposes, but the motivational aspect of meeting short-term objectives along with seeing progress towards longer-term goals should not be underestimated. This book was not meant to be an exhaustive review of all the tools and techniques in our Lean toolboxes. There are numerous excellent resources available for more information on application details of the powerful Lean tools.

Chapter 5 focused on key roles and responsibilities within a Lean organization. This chapter directly addressed Failure Mechanism #4, *Everyone's "Job" Isn't Being Changed*. The chapter emphasis was on what's different as a result of the organizational commitment to developing a Lean culture of continuous improvement. Besides reflecting on roles and responsibilities from an organization-wide perspective, my hope is that everyone, regardless of position, will look in the mirror and reflect upon whether their actions are aligned with Lean principles and the content of Chapter 5.

Chapter 6 focused on people topics, such as resistance to change, motivation, and engagement. This can be considered a discussion of the psychology of change. You can't even begin to alter a culture without accepting the fact that we humans are complicated, and we must view Lean as a *people process*. We must believe in the innate creativity and growth potential in every single person. Too many leaders and Lean practitioners still view this as "soft" stuff that is of secondary importance, if at all ... something that the HR folks deal with. Leaders need to quit viewing this as "soft" stuff and acknowledging this as "leadership" and "culture" stuff and arguably the most important part of their job. No wonder so many Lean transformations have failed to meet expectations; in many cases, leaders have not even concentrated on a primary obligation of their role within a Lean organization.

The Chapter 6 theme of how to engage a massive amount of people in the Lean strategy is one of the most challenging issues of Lean, but also the most rewarding. As discussed in the "Introduction," this book was written to help you develop a Lean culture to not only transform your company and gain a competitive advantage, but simultaneously to help you change the lives of your employees for the better. In fact, the improvement in company performance can be viewed as a result or outcome of the workforce transformation that enables everyone to participate, to be challenged, fulfilled, and to even have some fun during the workday where most of us spend at least half of our waking hours.

Chapter 7 is probably one which some readers wish was Chapter 1 due to its focus on a structure for application. Chapter 7 is about "making it happen." An underlying, and at times not so underlying, message throughout this book has been that each organization must experiment and determine their own Lean roadmap. There's no Lean cookbook or failsafe recipe. If so, I would have titled this book *The Lean Transformational Cookbook.* This chapter was purposely placed at the end of the book, since without the foundation of the previous chapters, any developed roadmap would be worthless. I believe I adhered to my commitment to not imply any specific roadmap or step-by-step approach; however, I did provide some guidance and suggestions as to components of a Lean deployment strategy, as well as various paths which have been taken in the past.

I Need Time!

This brings us to our current summary chapter. There's one more key topic or Lean challenge which I'd like to touch on before closing out this chapter and book, and this has to do with personal time management. I can hear some of you saying, *"Dave, the information in this book all sounds great and makes sense, but on a personal level, how the heck do I find the time to do this stuff? I don't have enough time now to do my job, let alone all of this improvement, teaching, coaching stuff!"*

This reminds me of a cartoon I once saw where a caveman with a couple of round wheels is offering these wheels to the other cavemen who are struggling with their cart which has square wheels. The cavemen with the ineffective square wheels state, *"No thanks! We're too busy!"* Well, as we discussed, as a leader, all of this improvement, teaching, coaching stuff must become a primary part of the job. Since I don't have a time-creation magic wand, nor do I have a resource to provide where this wand can be obtained, I suggest that we address this problem as we address any other problem along our Lean journey: analyze and experiment, PDCA. Break down the problem.

We do this all the time in other situations where we use tools such as process or value stream maps or various breakdown forms when reducing changeover times or designing work cells. This helps us identify processing steps and prioritize the wastes and improvement opportunities which we need to address. Do the same with your time. Break it down and identify the waste. You'll find things that maybe shouldn't even be done. We often make "to do" lists, but trying to make a "stop doing list" might be of even greater value. You'll also find some things that definitely need to be done, but should be done by someone else, or with guidance and training can be easily done by someone other than you.

You might discover some things which can be done at a less busy time, and some things which, if effectively addressed, would eliminate the need for them to be done at all. A quick example would be the fire-fighting which repeats itself due to a failure to address the root causes. Rather than only slapping on a temporary bandage, work with the team to dig in and ask the *5, or more, whys* and get to the root cause(s), and then experiment to develop countermeasures to address the root cause. When we do this we free up time. By addressing root causes to eliminate problems, the time dedicated to fire-fighting disappears, or at least declines significantly.

As for a breakdown structure, I'd consider a time management matrix which was created before we commonly used the term *Lean*. In Stephen Covey's 1989 book, *The Seven Habits of Highly Effective People*, he describes his Covey Time Management Matrix.[1] Of course, since this was published in the 1980s, you should update some items shown in the matrix to more current technology, e.g., mail to email or texts. However, surprisingly, many of the items, such as crises, pressing problems, and meetings, are as relevant today as in 1989, and I suspect will remain relevant for many years to come. Even though there is no *Lean* reference, I've always felt that this matrix was a Lean tool or technique since it doesn't just focus on prioritizing and rearranging all of the items which need to be completed, some of which can be considered waste. Rather, it provides a structure for analysis, reflection, and improvement by taking action to eliminate, streamline, or relocate some of the time elements in our day. That always sounded Lean to me. A detailed dive into his matrix is a discussion for another time. However, whether you use Covey's matrix or break down your "time problem" utilizing a different format, get to work addressing your time constraint issues as a problem to be analyzed and improved. Then document your improved process into a standard work format to define what should be done, to enable highlighting of abnormalities for investigation, and to facilitate continuous improvement. Exclamations of *"I have no time!"* are of no value.

Good Luck and Thanks!

I'll just end by saying good luck on your Lean journey, and thank you for allowing me to share a few experiences and observations from my own never-ending Lean journey! I hope you've found our discussions to be of value!

Note

1. Covey, Stephen R. "Principles of Personal Management." In *The Seven Habits of Highly Effective People: Restoring the Character Ethic*, 146–82. New York, NY: Simon & Schuster, 1989. The Time Management Matrix is shown on page 151 of Covey's book.

Appendix

Quick and Dirty Lean Culture Assessment

This assessment is meant to be a rough snapshot of your status regarding some key aspects of a Lean/continuous improvement culture. Further scoring criteria detail and categories would be needed to enable it to be any more than a rough snapshot; however, even this broad review can initiate discussion and be beneficial in identifying strengths, weaknesses, and opportunities.

How to Score the Assessment

On the ten assessment categories, indicate what you feel is your level of maturity for each category. In general, you can envision the rating scale divided into three levels of low, medium, and high levels of maturity. A rating of 0–1 would indicate a level where there is a severe deficiency. A 2–3 rating would indicate that some progress has been made, but there is still a significant improvement opportunity. A 4–5 rating would indicate advanced maturity in a particular category, but of course, there are always continuous improvement opportunities. It is encouraged that you elaborate on your score in the "comments" section to provide supporting evidence or data for your rating.

Who Should Complete?

If you have a Lean steering committee, or a management or leadership team which serves in this capacity, it is recommended that you meet as a group and complete the assessment. Prior to the scoring meeting, consider distributing the assessment to the Lean steering committee members to enable individual scoring. Then schedule a meeting to discuss and score as a group. Due to the lack of definition detail of scoring criteria, differences are expected; however, variances by two or more points would clearly indicate a difference in perception. A follow-up action item may be to gather more information or data to eliminate *perceptions* or *opinions* and replace with data and facts. Refer to Figure A.1 for the ten-category "Quick and Dirty Lean Culture Assessment."

Quick & Dirty Lean Culture Assessment

1. Leadership - Lean Understanding & Commitment

Leaders aren't leading Lean. "Opting Out" is allowed

0   1   2   3   4   5

Leaders as teachers and coaches, Visible and Active Lean Leadership throughout the organization

Comments:

2. Workforce - Lean Understanding & Commitment

No knowledge of Lean, its purpose, and expectations

0   1   2   3   4   5

Total workforce understanding and commitment to Lean and Continuous Improvement as part of the "job"

Comments:

3. Key Performance Indicators

Either don't exist or conflict with Lean Principles

0   1   2   3   4   5

Aligned with Lean Principles and monitored to support ongoing improvement

Comments:

4. Other Systems Alignment
(Not Including KPIs)

Existing Systems are not aligned with Lean Principles

0   1   2   3   4   5

All Systems and Policies are in alignment with Lean Principles

Comments:

5. Standardization

No activities are standardized resulting in excessive variation and ongoing chaos

0   1   2   3   4   5

Emphasis on standardized work, which is recognized as a key component of the improvement process

Comments:

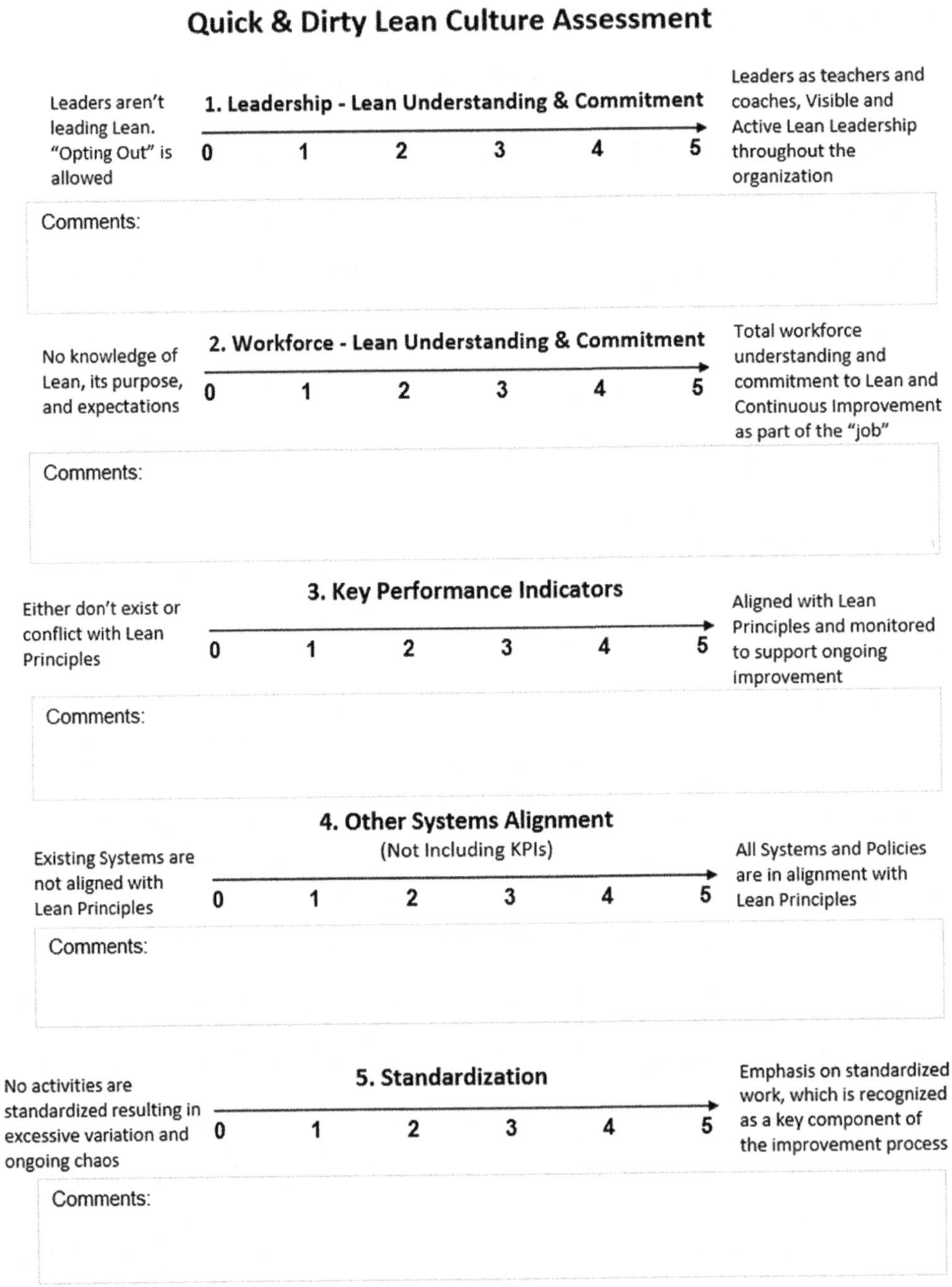

Figure A.1   Quick and Dirty Lean Culture Assessment

Quick & Dirty Lean Culture Assessment

6. Visual Systems & Workplace Organization

Disorganized workplace and no utilization of visual methods

0   1   2   3   4   5

Visuals used to communicate and provide process control

Comments:

7. Improvement Involvement

No one

0   1   2   3   4   5

Total Workforce (Everyone)

Comments:

8. Improvement Frequency

Status Quo, No Changes, No Experimentation

0   1   2   3   4   5

Continuous Improvement at all levels and areas of the organization (Every Day)

Comments:

9. "One Piece" Continuous Flow

Large batch (batch-and-queue) processing

0   1   2   3   4   5

"One Piece" Continuous flow matched to customer (internal & external) usage

Comments:

10. Empowerment

Autocratic, all activities directed from management above the front-line

0   1   2   3   4   5

Self-Directed Work Teams

Comments:

Figure A.1   Continued

Index

Page numbers in *italic type* indicate figures or illustrations

Printed in the United States
by Baker & Taylor Publisher Services